The Life of Prayer in a World of Science

Recent Titles in
RELIGION IN AMERICA SERIES
Harry S. Stout, General Editor

THE LIFE OF

PRAYER

IN A WORLD OF SCIENCE

Protestants, Prayer, and American Culture
1870–1930

RICK OSTRANDER

UNIVERSITY PRESS

2000

OXFORD
UNIVERSITY PRESS

Oxford New York
Athens Auckland Bangkok Bogotá Buenos Aires Calcutta
Cape Town Chennai Dar es Salaam Delhi Florence Hong Kong Istanbul
Karachi Kuala Lumpur Madrid Melbourne Mexico City Mumbai
Nairobi Paris São Paulo Shanghai Singapore Taipei Tokyo Toronto Warsaw

and associated companies in
Berlin Ibadan

Library of Congress Cataloging-in-Publication Data
Ostrander, Richard, 1965–
The life of prayer in a world of science : Protestants, prayer,
and American culture, 1870–1930 / Rick Ostrander.
p. cm.
Includes bibliographical references.
ISBN 0-19-513610-1
1. Prayer—Christianity—History—19th century. 2. Protestant
churches—United States—Doctrines—History—19th century.
3. United States—Church history—19th century. 4. Prayer—
Christianity—History—20th century. 5. Protestant churches—
United States—Doctrines—History—20th century. 6. United States—
Church history—20th century. I. Title.
BV210.2.O83 2000
248.3'2'097309034—dc21   99-39992

1 3 5 7 9 8 6 4 2

Printed in the United States of America
on acid-free paper

Acknowledgments

Financial support for this project came from a number of sources. This book began as a doctoral dissertation at the University of Notre Dame, and I am grateful to the history department there for a number of grants and assistantships. In addition, I am grateful to the Louisville Institute for the Study of American Protestantism for its generous support during the 1995–1996 academic year, and to the Pew Faculty Summer Scholarship Program for a research grant in the summer of 1998. Thanks also to the librarians at the University of Notre Dame, the University of Chicago, and the Moody Bible Institute for their help in tracking down obscure sources.

A number of scholars at the University of Notre Dame played key roles in improving the quality of this book. Mike Hamilton in particular provided helpful insights and criticism, while Jim Lanpher, Lee Camp, and Jay Case provided the diversions necessary to preserve my sanity during the research and writing stages. Most of all, George Marsden offered penetrating criticism and patient advice all along the way. He has modeled in his words, his books, and his golfing the high standards of a Christian historian. After years of practice I have finally equalled him in golf, but I doubt that I will ever attain to the quality of his scholarship.

Most importantly, I owe the completion of this book to the years of support and encouragement—not to mention the careful proofreading—from my wife, Lonnie. If this book's prose makes sense to the ordinary human being, it is largely due to her influence. She deserves better than to have a history book dedicated to her, but since this book represents years of my time and energy, it's the best that I can do. Perhaps dinner at the Ozark Brewing Company will adequately supplement this meager dedication.

John Brown University   R. O.
Siloam Springs, Arkansas
November 1999

Contents

The Life of Prayer in a World of Science

Introduction

On July 2, 1881, President James A. Garfield was shot. As he lay on his bed for weeks struggling for life, Americans united in prayer. Sunday, August 28, was named specifically as a day for earnest prayer. On that day, few pulpits of any denomination failed to make reference to President Garfield's condition, and worshipping assemblies across the land offered prayers for his recovery. The next week, Garfield's condition improved, and the nation's hopes rose that its prayers had been answered. However, the president soon took a turn for the worse and died a few weeks later.[1]

What had become of the nation's prayers for his recovery? That question apparently troubled many minds. The Methodist clergyman William Reddy observed: "no parallel is known in history of so many earnest prayers having been offered for any given object." Christians not only in America but across the Christian world had prayed for Garfield's recovery. "Why, then," asked Reddy, "was not the health of the ruler of our people recovered? Why did he die? Is prayer of no avail? . . . These are the questionings alike of the skeptic and the saint." Upon hearing of Garfield's death, one devout churchgoer exclaimed, "I am fearfully tempted to infidelity." American Christians, it seemed, had prayed for bread and received a stone.[2]

Twenty years later, another American president, William McKinley, was shot by an assassin. Once again, the nation was overcome with shock and outrage, and prayers rang out for the president's recovery. In the days following, doctors confidently predicted that McKinley would survive, but he died a week later. *The Independent*, a mainline Protestant news magazine, undoubtedly spoke for many American Christians when it asked in its editorial, "But What Became of the Prayers?"[3]

In 1914, the opportunity arose again for Americans to question the value of petitionary prayer. The onset of war in Europe set off a wave of national prayer in America for a resolution of the conflict. President Woodrow Wilson named Sunday, October 4, as a national day of prayer and supplication for peace in Europe. He instructed citizens to pray that God would "vouchsafe His children healing peace again and restore once more concord among men and nations." American Christians received Wilson's declaration with enthusiasm. Religious publications of all theological stripes endorsed it, and forms of prayer for peace appeared in daily newspapers across the land.[4]

Of course, not only did the carnage in Europe continue unabated, but eventually America was dragged into it as well. A contributor to the New York *Evening Sun* observed with perplexity, "our day of prayer for peace was unavailing." The *Evening Sun* editors gave prominence to the letter because, they said, "it expresses with evident sincerity a doubt that has clouded the minds of honest people in these days of battle." Four years later, the prominent New York minister Charles Jefferson observed:

> Have not millions of Christian hearts all over the world besought God in secret chambers, day and night, to have compassion on our poor bleeding mangled race, and to curb the wild passions of fighting men? Through nearly four long drawn years these prayers have continuously ascended, but the heavens have remained as brass and the earth still runs blood! It is not to be wondered at that the skeptics of the twentieth century repeat the questions of the Book of Job: "What is the Almighty that we should serve him? And what profit should we have, if we pray unto him?"

Once again, the prayers of millions of Americans had apparently gone unanswered.[5]

Turn-of-the century Americans undoubtedly had many opportunities to claim answers to prayer during these years as well, and every generation of Christians has had to face the problem of unanswered prayer. However, these modern episodes of unanswered prayer on a national scale came at a particularly inopportune time for American Protestants wishing to maintain belief in the efficacy of prayer. That is because the doctrine of prayer itself in the decades surrounding the turn of the century was, in the words of Princeton Seminary professor J. Ritchie Smith, "beset with difficulties on every side." Mainline Protestants across the denominational and theological spectrum realized that the ideological revolutions of the late nineteenth and early twentieth centuries affected the Christian idea of prayer just as they did other doctrines. Petitionary prayer was, for the first time in American mainline Protestantism, a contested concept.[6]

Historically, American Protestants had not doubted the doctrine of petitionary prayer. Individual Christians may have wondered at times why particular petitions were not granted, but from the Reformation on, the belief that God could and might, in answer to the believer's prayers, step into the natural order of the universe and change things for the better was common among Protestants. John Calvin, for example, was a firm believer in petitionary prayer. Prayer was for him a design "to make God conscious of our necessities and as it were to pour out our hearts before him." Through prayer, he believed, the Christian invoked God's providence, power, and goodness on his or her behalf. The Bible promised that God would answer prayer, and it was the duty and the privilege of the Christian to pray based on these promises. Prayer brought God's intervention and rescue from both spiritual and physical danger.[7]

Of course, Protestants valued aspects of prayer other than simply asking God for particular blessings; nevertheless the belief that God answered petitionary prayer loomed large in historic Protestantism. Calvin's Protestant counterparts in England believed that prayer brought about God's intervention on behalf of the Christian. Faye Kelly surveyed writings on prayer in sixteenth-century England and found that two aspects of prayer, petition for benefits and protection against danger, were the most frequently cited attributes of prayer. She concluded: "petition to God by man is the most common definition of prayer in the sixteenth century. . . . Even people not particularly fervid about religion seem to have taken for granted the necessity for and the effectiveness of prayer."[8]

The English Puritans brought this faith in the power and efficacy of prayer with them to America. Charles Hambrick-Stowe has observed, concerning the seventeenth century Puritans, "New Englanders believed in the efficacy of prayer. Their faith included belief in its almost magical effects noted by John Brock—'the worms annoy us; but prayer chases them away'—as well as to provide assurance and direction in life." Puritans prayed for spiritual graces, of course, but they also prayed for daily and earthly needs, and often claimed answers to their prayers. For instance, the minister Peter Thacher related a time that he prayed fervently for his wife in danger from childbirth. "Within a quarter of an hour after I had done," he claimed, "God answered by giveing me a liveing daughter and makeing my wife a liveing mother."[9]

Prayer brought about changes in the meteorological world as well, Puritans believed. Increase Mather testified in 1684:

> God hath answered our prayers in sending rain, and sometimes so speedily and so plentifully, after our seeking the Lord by fasting and prayer, that the heathen, now for more than twenty years upon occasion of want of rain, will speak to us to call upon the name of the Lord our God.

Roger Clap counseled: "Think with yourself, assuredly God is present, though none else; I will confess my Sins, and I will beg God's favour and grace, I will wrestle with God by faith and prayer. And you may every one of you prevail, if you pray sincerely, and persevere in it." As a seventeenth-century didactic couplet put it, "[o]ur prayers do pierce the starrie skie, / And fetch down blessings from on high."[10]

Of course, as sufferers of deaths and calamities that were common to New World colonists, the Puritans were not so naive as to consider petitionary prayer an Aladdin's Lamp bringing whatever blessings one desired. Like Christians through the ages, Puritans recognized certain conditions on prayer that had to be met, such as having faith, praying from a godly motive and with God's glory in mind, and praying in submission to God's will. However, if certain conditions were right, the Puritans believed, petitionary prayer might bring about tangible effects in the physical world.

Protestants in eighteenth-century America also maintained belief in the efficacy of prayer. Cotton Mather, like his father Increase, was a firm believer in petitionary prayer. Prayer brought real answers, he claimed, not just spiritual blessings but "temporal blessings" as well. "Secret prayers do an incredible deal," he said, "towards jogging the high wheels of Providence." Later he passed along to his congregation an account of the city of Bern, Switzerland, that was completely destroyed by an earthquake except for one house, where a family was praying.[11]

The eighteenth century in America witnessed the dawn of the Enlightenment, and with it a new view, among some Christians, of God's relationship to the universe. Enlightenment thought tended to push God further away from his creation, making him, in historian James Turner's words, "an abstract Supreme Being Who dealt with His cosmos and His creatures through impersonal secondary causes." In Europe, and among American deists, some writers (David Hume, for one) expressed doubts concerning petitionary prayer. Among rank-and-file American Protestants, however, faith in prayer's efficacy was generally left unscathed by these intellectual trends. Though Reformed Protestants relegated miracles to the biblical era, God still answered prayer, they believed, through what were called special providences. Elements of Enlightenment thought and a cosmology filled with supernatural events thus went hand in hand in eighteenth-century Protestantism. Cotton Mather, for instance, was an enthusiastic proponent of the natural sciences, and even a relative "liberal" such as the early Arminian Charles Chauncy gleaned divine messages from earthquakes.[12]

That the Enlightenment proved no obstacle to belief in prayer for most American Protestants was demonstrated in the person of Samuel Johnson. A graduate of Yale and a Congregational minister, Johnson scandalized the New Haven community when he left the Congregational Church to become an Anglican minister. He became president of King's College in 1754, and his *Elementa Philosophica*, published by Benjamin Franklin, was the first philosophy textbook published in America. An embodiment of Enlightenment sensibilities, Johnson engaged in numerous public controversies in his criticisms of strict Calvinism and the Great Awakening. Yet Johnson, no less than his Calvinist opponents, was a firm believer in the efficacy of petitionary prayer.[13]

In 1760, an anonymous manuscript reached Johnson's desk that argued that petitionary prayer was "an utterly impertinent and insignificant thing, and but a mere useless ceremony." Johnson, indignant at such an idea, whisked off a tract entitled "A Demonstration of the Reasonableness, Usefulness, and Great Duty of Prayer." His pamphlet displayed clear marks of Enlightenment sentiments. In addition to the "Reasonableness" in the title, prayer in Johnson's tract was seen as an important element in the attainment of virtue, which would in turn produce happiness. Prayer, said Johnson, helped to "promote universal benevolence, brotherly love, the love of the public weal, and all social virtues." However, Johnson did not stop there in his defense of prayer. God may answer prayer, he believed, "in varying the course of winds and weather, preventing or healing sicknesses, and the like." For Johnson, Enlightenment rationality did not nullify belief in petitionary prayer.[14]

The evangelical awakening that arose concurrently with the Enlightenment in the eighteenth century resulted in, if anything, an increased faith in prayer. In 1744, extra-ecclesiastical groups known as concerts of prayer for revival were organized in America for the first time, under the direction of Jonathan Edwards. Although leaders espoused petitionary prayer primarily for revival purposes, they never thought to make a distinction between spiritual and material possibilities in prayer. For instance, during an epidemic near Boston, Edwards was invited to preach a sermon on the appointed fast day. He took as the title for his address "The Most High a Prayer-Hearing God." God most definitely hears prayer, Edwards proclaimed, not only by giving a sense of his presence, acceptance, and mercy, "but outwardly in his providence ... by causing an agreeableness between his providence and their prayers." Edwards's colleague, the Great Awakening revivalist Solomon Williams, preached a sermon entitled "The Power and Efficacy of the Prayers of the People of God." Prayer, when rightly offered, Williams proclaimed, is always efficacious. The evangelical spirit concerning prayer was reflected in a stanza by the eighteenth-century British hymnist John Newton (of "Amazing Grace" fame), "Come My Soul, Thy Suit Prepare":

> Thou art coming to a King:
> Large petitions with thee bring;
> For his grace and power are such
> None can ever ask too much.[15]

Not surprisingly, one finds this confidence in petitionary prayer continued in leading voices of nineteenth-century Protestantism such as the American Tract Society. Formed by the merger of the tract societies in New York and Massachusetts in 1825, the American Tract Society was a leading promoter of traditional mainstream Protestantism in the Calvinist tradition throughout the nineteenth century.[16] One of the frequent writers for the American Tract Society was Archibald Alexander, the first professor of Princeton Seminary and a founder of the Princeton Theology, a bulwark of "Old School" Presbyterianism in the nineteenth century. In one of his numerous tracts, Alexander acknowledged that "the moral effect of prayer is important. ... Yet it would be a grand mistake to confine the efficacy of prayer to their moral effects." Prayer, Alexander maintained, "actually obtains for the petitioner the blessings which he needs," including "deliverance from a thousand evils." The prayer of faith, Alexander concluded, "is the mightiest engine upon earth."[17]

Alexander's Old School Presbyterianism may not have been riding the wave of the future, but his strong belief in petitionary prayer was perpetuated by nineteenth-century Protestants who left other parts of America's Calvinist heritage behind. The golden day of democratic evangelicalism, as historian Sidney Ahlstrom has called the antebellum era in America, contained a strong interest in petitionary prayer, as a look at Charles Finney shows. Finney was antebellum America's foremost revivalist and most famous Christian. As William McLoughlin has observed, "Finney stood for the evangelical outlook that became the prevailing one among middle-class churchgoers in mid–nineteenth century America."[18]

One of the more noteworthy aspects of Finney's life and impact was his strong belief in and reliance on prayer, as indicated in his *Memoirs*. Before his conversion as a young man, Finney attended services at the local Presbyterian church in upstate New York. "I was particularly struck," he recounted, "with the fact that the prayers that I had listened to, from week to week, were not, that I could see, answered." The Presbyterians asked Finney if he would like them to pray for him, to which Finney responded with characteristic bluntness: "I told them no; because I did not see that God answered their prayers." Finney searched the Bible on the topic of prayer and, he claimed, discovered that God promised to answer prayer if offered in faith and according to conditions laid out in Scripture. Finney's revivals were therefore characterized by prayer, typically in the form of daily prayer meetings. Describing one such revival, Finney wrote: "Christians would take the alarm, and give themselves to prayer that God would direct and control all things; and it was surprising to see, to what extent, and by what means, God would remove obstacles out of the way, in answer to prayer." He continued: "In regard to my own experience, I will say that unless I had the spirit of prayer I could do nothing."[19]

Finney is best known for his *Lectures on Revivals of Religion*, which shifted the focus in revivals from divine to human agency. Revivals, Finney argued, were not miracles but simply resulted from the application of appropriate human techniques. However, Finney also adamantly maintained that part of preparation for revivals was a heavy dose of prayer: "Prayer is an essential link in the chain of causes that lead to a revival." Thus, three of Finney's lectures on revival were devoted to explaining his doctrine of prayer. "The very idea of effectual prayer," Finney exclaimed, "is that it effects its object." Prayers were meant to be answered, Finney believed. The key to prayer, Finney taught, was to search the Bible to determine what God's will was in a certain matter, then pray with perseverance that God would bring it about.[20]

Because Finney was a professional evangelist, his teachings on prayer typically concerned religious revivals—prayers of parents for the salvation of their children, wives for their wayward husbands, Christians for revivals in their local churches, and so forth. However, Finney also combined revival prayer with requests for more miraculous occurrences. For instance, Finney was once informed that a female unbeliever was at death's door, upon which he received "an intense desire to pray for that woman." Finney prayed not only that the woman would be healed, but that she would become converted. He recounts: "At this time the Lord gave me power to prevail. I was enabled to roll the burden upon him; and I obtained the assurance in my own mind that the woman would not die, and indeed that she would never die in her sins. . . . She did recover, and soon after obtained a hope in Christ." Finney was even known to pray for rain on occasion, with reportedly successful results. His biographer George Frederick Wright described two such events when Finney was a professor at Oberlin College in the 1850s. America's premier revivalist of the antebellum era clearly believed in and practiced petitionary prayer on all levels.[21]

If Charles Finney highlighted the use of prayer as a spark for revival, prayer's existence was even more prominent during the Revival of 1857–58, often referred to as the Prayer-Meeting Revival. The revival began in New York City in the fall of 1857 when a city missionary named Jeremiah Lanphier began holding noon prayer meetings at the Dutch Reformed Church on Fulton Street. By February of 1858, prayer meetings were spreading to other churches in New York City and receiving extensive coverage in the secular press. Soon overflow crowds were filling churches and auditoriums in cities across America for noon prayer meetings. In Chicago, for example, the Metropolitan Theater was crowded with two thousand daily attendants. The prayer meetings led to an unprecedented level of cooperation among American Christians. Christians of all denominations joined together in prayer for revival, and the meetings even received support from Universalists, Unitarians, Episcopalians, and Old School Presbyterians. D. L. Moody's evangelistic career in Chicago was launched during the Prayer-Meeting Revivals, and according to historian Timothy Smith the religious excitement paved the way for revivals among Union and Confederate soldiers during the Civil War.[22]

The most thorough contemporary chronicler of the Prayer-Meeting Revival was Samuel Prime, a Princeton-educated Presbyterian clergyman, popular lecturer, and editor of *Harper's* magazine. In 1859, Prime published the robustly titled *The Power of Prayer Illustrated in the Wonderful Displays of Divine Grace at the Fulton Street and Other Meetings in New York and Elsewhere, in 1857 and 1858*. Prime's anthology devoted over four hundred pages to chronicling specific instances of answered prayer during the revival. Here "the connection between prayer and its answer," Prime asserted in his preface, "is confirmed by scores of facts and examples, not in history, sacred or secular; . . . but facts of present occurrence, in the midst of this noisy, busy, restless, wordly city; facts beyond all doubt or cavil, that the Lord will give his praying people whatsoever they ask in faith!" Prime concluded: "God is now, as in days of old, showing himself to be a God that hears prayer."[23]

Like Finney, who was himself involved in the Revival of 1857–58, Prime typically gave examples of answered prayers for conversions—drunken husbands reclaimed through the prayers of their wives, parents praying for children, children for parents, and so on. However, also like Finney, Prime never bothered to distinguish between such prayers and prayer for more miraculous effects. *The Power of Prayer*, for instance, gives an account of a leaking ship whose crew members are saved as a result of their prayers.[24] Over one hundred thousand copies of *The Power of Prayer* were issued in the first five years after its printing, and the book apparently sold quite well in Great Britain as well.[25] In subsequent years, Prime released two sequels chronicling many more answers to prayer, *Fifteen Years of Prayer in the Fulton Street Meeting* (1872), and *Prayer and Its Answer* (1882). If the Prayer-Meeting Revival and the success of Prime's books are any indication, prayer played a prominent role in nineteenth-century American revivalistic evangelicalism.

As the Prayer-Meeting Revival indicated, the efficacy of prayer was something that nineteenth-century Christians across the theological spectrum could agree on. Methodist and Reformed Protestants bickered about many things in antebellum America, but prayer was not one of them. In 1819, the *Methodist* used the words of Saint Chrysostom to express its belief in the power of prayer:

> The potency of prayer hath subdued the strength of fire; it hath bridled the rage of lions; hushed anarchy to rest; extinguished wars; appeased the elements; expelled demons; burst the chains of death; expanded the gates of heaven; assuaged diseases; repelled frauds; rescued cities from destruction; it hath stayed the sun in its course, and arrested the progress of the thunderbolt.... Assuredly, there is nothing more potent than prayer: yea, there is nothing comparable to it.

Such faith in prayer was shared by Reformed Protestants such as Amherst College professor W. S. Tyler. Prayer, like gravity and electricity, was, Tyler claimed, a physical force that brought about changes in the universe:

> It is, if we may so speak, one of the elementary principles, or forces, in the original constitution of things—not less so than light, or heat, or gravitation, or electricity.... When the sun sheds its quickening beams, or the rain descends in fertilizing showers, or drought, or famine, or pestilence is averted in accordance with the united and believing prayers of a prostrate church and nation, there is every reason to believe that the prayers are as efficacious and as essential to the results, as the natural causes.

Even the liberal Unitarian James Freeman Clarke affirmed his orthodox counterparts on this issue. "We may reasonably believe," he declared, "the power of prayer will accomplish what otherwise would not come to pass."[26]

The emblematic Protestant statement on prayer was expressed by Austin Phelps, a stalwart of nineteenth-century mainstream Protestantism. A Presbyterian minister educated at Yale and Union Theological Seminary, Phelps taught at Andover Seminary from 1848 until 1890. His book *The Still Hour*, published in 1859, was a popular devotional treatment of the doctrine of prayer that maintained a solid following over the decades. Petitionary prayer, Phelps concluded, was "a *power* in the universe, as distinct, as real, as natural, and as uniform, as the power of gravitation, or of light, or of electricity. A man may *use* it, as trustingly and as soberly as he would use either of these." Clearly, American Protestants possessed a heritage of unquestioning belief that God answered prayer.[27]

By the turn of the twentieth century, however, Protestant writers perceived that the question of prayer had become problematic in the modern world. Northwestern University professor George Coe trenchantly observed in 1902:

> Nothing more clearly shows the drift of religion in our days than the differences between the way we pray and the way our fathers prayed. The contrast is not a slight one. They agonized in prayer. They wrestled with God. They stormed the gates of heaven, and by sheer violence of desire seized upon the promises and made them a personal possession. We pray with far less assertiveness, with far less confidence in the power of prayer to work specific, tangible effects in the world about us. We question and hesitate where they simply believed. . . . There is something in our modern modes of thought, our modern attitudes toward religious problems, that involves hesitancy and confusion with respect to prayer.

Echoing Coe, Wheaton College president Charles Blanchard testified in 1915: "When I was a boy, I think it is safe to say that almost everyone, even people who were not Christians at all, believed that God did answer prayer and I question whether even infidels would have asked whether or not He did so." Now, however, times were different. The religious and popular literature of the period was peppered with remarks similar to one found in the denominational journal the *Baptist*: "A chill has fallen on the hearts of many. Doubts concerning the efficacy of prayer are far more common than some of us imagine."[28]

The problem, as perceived by Protestants of the day, was that science, in the broadest sense of the word, had made asking God for things seem both superfluous and unreasonable in their day. That was the conclusion of Union Theological Seminary theologian William Adams Brown in his book *The Life of Prayer in a World of Science.* The wonderful new technologies of applied science made much of the prayers of the ancients seem unnecessary. Brown observed:

> Where our fathers went into their closets to pray, we go into our lab-
> oratories to experiment and into our factories to create. When the
> drought came they prayed for rain. We replant the denuded moun-
> tain slopes, and the rain comes. When pestilence threatened, they
> cried to God for healing. We diagnose the cause of the disease and
> apply the appropriate remedy. Thus slowly but surely man's control
> over nature is increasing, and his need for prayer, in the older sense
> of that term, has grown correspondingly less.

More important, it was the "critical temper," in Brown's words, that science promoted that made petitionary prayer as traditionally conceived problem-atic. Petitionary prayer, with its vision of a God rushing to the rescue of his children, did not seem very reasonable in a culture in which science had seemingly ruled out supernatural intervention. The German scholar Friedrich Heiler claimed: "Natural science in our own time has strengthened belief in the immutability of natural law and has borne this belief far and wide. Tra-ditional prayer, therefore, has been to a great extent abandoned both in intellectual circles and among the masses of our great cities." In America, the Quaker spiritual writer Rufus Jones noted that to earlier Christians prayer was "an operative power. It accomplished results." But, he asked, "[i]s this two-sided and objective view of prayer, as real intercourse and as effective power, still tenable? Can men who accept the conclusions of science still pray in living faith and with real expectation of results?" It was a question on many minds. "The two great problems which to-day engage the interest of thoughtful minds," claimed the Episcopalian Samuel McComb in 1914, "are the problems of prayer and immortality."[29]

How widespread were doubts concerning prayer? That question is difficult to answer, for undoubtedly skeptics and believers have coexisted in every generation. A survey of Protestantism in general, as later chapters indicate, would yield mixed results. Nevertheless, there are signs, in addition to con-temporary observations, that belief in petitionary prayer was problematic for many in the decades surrounding the turn of the century. Two of the more prominent books on prayer around the turn of the twentieth century, Henry Clay Trumbull's *Prayer: Its Nature and Scope* and Leander Chamberlain's *The True Doctrine of Prayer*, were written, as Trumbull put it, "primarily for the meeting of difficulties which trouble many minds with reference to the true basis of prayer, its scope, and its limitations." Yet both Trumbull and Chamberlain based their support of petitionary prayer largely on the com-mands and examples of Scripture. Apparently these authors assumed that despite the rise of higher criticism, Scripture was still an unquestioned authority in the culture by which they could justify the doctrine of prayer to their readers. Trumbull and Chamberlain perceived that doubts concerning prayer had made inroads into American culture where questions about the veracity of the Bible had not.[30]

On a broader social level, the "world of science" posed a problem for prayer in another way for modern Americans. The intellectual difficulties surrounding petitionary prayer were accompanied by a more practical problem—simply put, many modern Christians saw themselves as too busy to pray. The bustling, middle-class urban culture that science had helped create seemed to leave little room for traditional Protestant devotional rigors. The Presbyterian Arthur T. Pierson exclaimed: "[T]he restless spirit invades all departments of life, and the modern motto seems to be 'push and rush.'" Observed Rufus Jones, "hush, waiting, meditation, concentration of spirit, are just the reverse of our busy, driving, modern temper." Thus, claimed the Methodist E. M. Bounds, "in these days of hurry and bustle, men will not take the time to pray." The Congregationalist Harris Hale apparently expressed the concerns of many church leaders when he exclaimed:

> There is no time to pray. The morning is so hurried. The evening is
> so crowded. It is impossible to get the family together for five
> minutes for the great act of worship. And so an institution which was
> the buttress of society is going to pieces: *there is no time to pray.*

Modern lifestyles as well as modern thought, therefore, posed a problem for traditional Protestant notions of prayer.[31]

The life of prayer in a world of science was indeed a difficult and important issue for turn-of-the-century Protestants. "Prove that prayer is of no avail," declared Charles Jefferson, "and you shatter the Christian religion." The Methodist writer E. S. Smith agreed with Jefferson: "At no point in the line of defense is the Christian faith more persistently assailed than at this; no doctrine is more vital to Christianity than that which this point covers." American Protestants of the early twentieth century may or may not have been interested in how many authors wrote Genesis, whether humans were descended from monkeys, or in the Social Gospel; but the serious Christian certainly prayed. This issue struck at the heart of the Protestant attempt to come to grips with modernity, not just among those in seminaries but among the rank and file as well. Yet while historians have devoted ample attention to the Protestant attempts to meet the intellectual challenges of biblical criticism and Darwinian evolution, not to mention the cultural challenges of a modern industrial society, the history of prayer in this era remains an untold story. This book, therefore, explores the attempts by American Protestants to articulate a convincing and satisfying ethic of prayer in the modern world, both intellectually and culturally.[32]

Introductory chapters are typically employed, among other things, to lower readers' expectations, and this one is no exception. I begin, therefore, by spelling out a few limitations on my subject. First, this book does not attempt to construct a history of all aspects of Christian prayer. Rather, it focuses on those two elements of prayer most affected by the "world of science" broadly defined: petitionary prayer and devotional disciplines. Prayer certainly involves much more than petition. A full-orbed history of prayer would include elements such as confession, thanksgiving, and adoration. Needless to say, most writers on prayer saw communion with God as one of the most important parts of prayer and believed that prayer's most important result was its "internal efficacy," that is, the spiritually rejuvenating effect it had on the person praying. However, traditional Protestant writers on prayer also adamantly maintained that, as the nineteenth-century cleric J. H. Jellett said, "if we arrive at the conclusion that prayer has no external efficacy, it is plain that its internal efficacy must speedily disappear." Moreover, it was petition (including intercessory prayer for the needs of others) that was most vitally affected by modern thought and that therefore received the most attention from turn-of-the-century Protestants. That emphasis is reflected in this book, most of which concerns petitionary prayer. Chapter 7, however, deals with the second problem in modern prayer, that of maintaining traditional Protestant devotional disciplines in the modern world.[33]

A second limitation in this book concerns the Protestant groups that receive attention. While chapters 1 and 2 analyze the attempts by traditional evangelical Protestants to justify prayer in the modern world, the majority of this book focuses on liberal Protestants. The liberals dealt with here are for the most part those early-twentieth-century Protestants studied by historians such as Kenneth Cauthen and William Hutchison (essentially those liberal Protestants who, as Martin Marty has observed, "are read only by dissertation writers"). Largely reared in evangelical Protestant homes, many of them came to be heavily influenced by philosophical idealism and its religious corollary, divine immanence. Believing that God was revealed in human cultural development, they sought, in varying degrees, to adapt Christian orthodoxy to modern thought. Though never synonymous with mainstream Protestantism, liberalism did achieve a large measure of influence in the northern mainline denominations and came to dominate most northern Protestant educational institutions. Union Theological Seminary in New York and the University of Chicago Divinity School were particularly well-known bastions of the movement. Liberal views were promulgated in journals such as Lyman Abbott's *Outlook*, the University of Chicago's *Biblical World*, and most notably the *Christian Century*.[34]

The focus on liberal Protestantism is not arbitrary, for prayer was vital to the liberals' concerns. As I argue in chapter 3, liberal Protestants perceived themselves as religious reformers; their mission was to promote a practical, meaningful Christian spirituality for Americans obsessed with material achievement on one hand and repelled by dry religious orthodoxy on the other. Harry Emerson Fosdick, the embodiment of classic liberalism, claimed that liberals were motivated primarily by spiritual concerns, not social or political ones. The liberal, he asserted, "has come into his new attitudes and ways of thinking . . . through the deepening of his spiritual life. He is a liberal because he is more religious, not because he is less." In his article "The New Religious Reformation," Fosdick trumpeted liberalism as "a vital spiritual reformation" inspired by "the emergence of an inward, conquering life." Liberal Social Gospel concerns included the need for Christian piety. "The remedy for the hatred, the greed and the materialism of the age," declared *Christian Century* editor Charles Clayton Morrison, "is in a conscious walk with God realized through the practice of prayer." Though historians have correctly noted the liberal Protestant emphasis on ethics, the liberals themselves maintained that, as Morrison exclaimed, "moral achievement must have its dynamic in spiritual experience." Liberals were vitally concerned with retaining spiritual experience in the modern world.[35]

However, liberal Protestantism also was a movement dedicated to adapting Christianity to modern culture, to staying up to date with whatever modern "experts" in the scientific world came to assert. Thus, unlike conservatives, who generally resisted all modern attacks on prayer, the liberals struggled to adapt traditional teachings on prayer to the modern worldview, to reconceptualize the life of prayer in a world of science. Since historians—myself included—are most interested in how and why things change, most of this book explores why it was that liberal Protestants felt it necessary to alter traditional Christian doctrines of prayer, and how they did so.

One final qualification. This study of prayer in American Protestantism focuses on speakers and writers, not listeners and readers. Though I occasionally take soundings of attitudes in American culture as a whole, my main subject of study concerns what certain religious leaders wrote and said about prayer. This approach has a weakness similar to that of watching flamboyant preachers on television with the surrounding sanctuary darkened so that one cannot tell if the service is attended by five thousand or by fifty people. Nevertheless, this method gains in accuracy what it sacrifices in scope, for an attempt to assess rank-and-file Protestant attitudes toward prayer would by necessity be impressionistic and tenuous. Moreover, indications are that the major writers who appear here have influenced American religion in significant ways. For instance, among Fosdick's voluminous works are four daily devotional guides written between 1913 and 1920 that Reinhold Niebuhr claimed, "probably exercised more influence in their generation than any other religious volumes. Their sale ran into millions." Fosdick himself called *The Meaning of Prayer* his most influential book. Furthermore, some of the conservative devotional writers discussed here have greatly affected popular American Protestantism, as the continued appeal of works by Reuben Torrey, Hannah Whitall Smith, E. M. Bounds, and Andrew Murray, among others, attests.[36]

In writing this book, I have had the privilege of striking out on relatively uncharted historical waters. Aside from numerous studies of mysticism and Catholic spirituality, secondary works on petitionary prayer from a historical perspective are quite rare.[37] Historians have generally ignored what has been to me, at least, a complex and fascinating aspect of American religion. This is not to decry a historical injustice, as individual historians are wont to do in their particular areas of interest; it is merely to note that the field is open.[38]

In this study of Protestants and prayer around the turn of the twentieth century, I have tried to keep my own theological views in the background. As an evangelical Christian whom liberal Protestants would have considered hopelessly unmodern, I do not share their desire to "save" Christianity in the modern world by stripping away traditional supernaturalism. Nor do I sense the inherent difficulty in petitionary prayer that the liberal Protestants did, for the idea of God working directly in the physical world seems reasonable enough to me (though I cannot personally testify to having experienced such an event). While I can sympathize with the liberals' struggle with traditional Christian devotional disciplines, I do not conclude from it, as they did, that traditional devotions are unworkable in the modern world. Instead, I attribute this difficulty to my own personal weakness as a modern Christian who usually prefers a good book to the rigors of individual silent prayer. Nonetheless, I have sought to portray the views and teachings of liberal—and conservative—Christians in a fair and accurate light.

At any rate, my purpose in this book is not to advise modern believers how to pray but to explore how some earlier Christians dealt with prayer in the modern world. If some readers happen to gain insights of their own into the life of prayer in a world of science, so much the better.

ONE

⟐

A Final Act of Purification
The Modern Scientific Attack on Prayer

It was an unusually wet summer in Britain in 1860, so wet that the nation's harvest was threatened. Church officials, responding in the customary way, had special prayers for fair weather read across the nation. However, an uncustomary thing happened. Some clergymen, most notably Charles Kingsley, the broad churchman, social reformer, and novelist, turned down requests to read such prayers. Praying for fair weather was presumptuous, Kingsley told his parishioners, for it supposed that we know what the order of nature should be better than God does. Praying for fair weather meant asking God "to alter the tides of the ocean, the form of the continents, the pace at which the earth spins round, the force, and light, and speed of sun and moon." The weather was based on the regularity of laws that God has instituted for our benefit, Kingsley said, and prayer should be directed at more productive ends than asking God to abrogate his laws.[1]

Kingsley and his counterparts were severely censured by other Christians but found support from the emerging scientific establishment in Victorian England. Most vocal in his support of the abstaining clerics was a young physicist by the name of John Tyndall. Born to relative poverty in an obscure Irish village and denied access to an elite education, Tyndall was a self-made intellectual. He read voraciously in mathematics, surveying, and theology and eventually made his way into the group of elite scientists who formed the X Club in London, including T. H. Huxley, Herbert Spencer, and Joseph Hooker. Though respected in his own right for work in glaciology, Tyndall was better known as the popular spokesperson for scientific naturalism, the belief that the boundaries of scientific knowledge could not be limited or superseded by religious convictions.[2]

In 1861, Tyndall wrote a short essay commending Kingsley and others for their stand against traditional prayer. Before the idea of scientific laws emerged, Tyndall said, "otherwise inexplicable effects were referred to personal agency. In the fall of a cataract the savage saw the leap of a spirit, and the echoed thunder-peal was to him the hammer-clang of an exasperated god." In such a world, petitioning the deity to bring about a change in the natural world made perfect sense. However, claimed Tyndall, we have come to be aware of a general law of nature that modern scientists call the Conservation of Energy. Though matter is constantly assuming new forms, no new agency or energy is created; nature is regular and uniform, and supernatural forces do not interfere with its workings. Thus, Tyndall maintained, "without a disturbance of natural law, quite as serious as the stoppage of an eclipse, or the rolling of the river Niagara up the Falls, no act of humiliation, individual or national, could call one shower from heaven or deflect toward us a single beam of the sun." Tyndall concluded by commending Kingsley and the others who abstained from prayer for fair weather—men who, claimed Tyndall, "prepare the public mind for changes which, though inevitable, could hardly, without such preparation, be wrought without violence."[3]

The religious establishment was undaunted by such criticism. Five years later, when a cattle plague threatened to wipe out English livestock, the archbishop of Canterbury issued a special prayer for use in schools and households, petitioning God to lift the plague. In 1871, a more prominent life was threatened than those of livestock. The Prince of Wales, heir to the throne, contracted typhoid and was feared to be at death's door in December. A committee including William Gladstone and the archbishop of Canterbury ordered that special prayers for the restoration of health to the heir be read in all parishes on Sunday, December 10. The next week the Prince's condition improved dramatically, and the crisis passed. Many clergymen attributed the recovery to prayer, and they used the event as an opportunity to thumb their noses at critics of prayer. In the words of one: "The wonderful change in the condition of the Prince of Wales will surely impress many hitherto doubtful minds with the efficacy of prayer."[4]

Tyndall, of course, was not impressed. In June 1872 he sent a proposal entitled "Prayer for the Sick: Hints towards a Serious Attempt to Estimate Its Value" to the *London Contemporary Review* intended to settle the matter once and for all. Tyndall's proposal sparked what has been dubbed the prayer-gauge debate, an event that took the English-speaking world by storm in the early 1870s. John O. Means, an American Congregationalist who compiled the documents of the debate and published them in book form for American readers, recounted:

> For weeks the great newspapers of London were loaded with editorials upon the Prayer-Gauge, and with communications prepared by all classes and conditions of men, from a bookseller's clerk to the highest dignitaries of the English Church and peers of the realm. The Prayer-Gauge debate was the sensation of the season.

The controversy surrounding prayer was not confined to Britain; Means's American volume indicates that it caused quite a stir in the United States as well. Tyndall's proposal, as well as his subsequent reply to critics, was reprinted for American audiences in the *Popular Science Monthly*, and his prayer-gauge proposal sparked comment by the major secular American magazines.[5]

Tyndall fanned the flames of controversy in America further when he embarked on a lecture tour of Boston, Philadelphia, and New York City in the fall of 1872. "You cannot imagine the stir this prayer question has excited in America," Tyndall wrote to a British friend in the midst of his trip. Tyndall's attack on prayer obviously earned him notoriety among American Christians. The bishop of New York boycotted a banquet held in Tyndall's honor, Methodist and Presbyterian presses attacked him, and wherever he traveled prayer meetings were held for his salvation. This attention, however, also ensured that Tyndall's lectures would be packed with interested observers. His lectures in Boston generated a thriving market for ticket scalpers, and his New York lectures made front-page news in the *New York Times*.[6]

The prayer-gauge debate was by no means the first time in Christian history that the efficacy of prayer had been called into question. As far back as the third century, one finds the church father Origen defending the efficacy of prayer against skeptics of his day. During the Enlightenment, moreover, a number of European intellectuals had ruled out petitionary prayer in a world of natural law. However, the widely publicized prayer-gauge debate of the 1870s did serve notice to large numbers of American Protestants that scientific skepticism, which heretofore had confined itself to issues of geology, biology, and biblical interpretation, also undermined the heart of Christian piety—prayer. Thus, observed the American Baptist Noah Davis, Tyndall's proposition "has stirred up afresh difficult questions about prayer. Some of us are talking, some thinking, some writing."[7]

For the next generation of Americans, therefore, John Tyndall's name would become synonymous with modern scientific attacks on prayer, and his prayer-gauge would continue to haunt American Protestants. It became almost obligatory for Americans writing on prayer in the late nineteenth century to devote at least a small part of their discussion to refuting the arguments of Tyndall and his skeptical cohort. In fact, well into the twentieth century, Christian writers were still referring to Tyndall when discussing the modern "problem" of prayer. For instance, in 1906, Evangelical Alliance president Leander Chamberlain felt obliged to address the prayer-gauge in his treatise *The True Doctrine of Prayer*, as did the prominent liberal Henry Churchill King in 1915. Even in 1930, nearly sixty years after the prayer-gauge debate, the Oberlin professor Walter Horton referred to Tyndall when discounting prayer for the weather. "Until Tyndall's 'prayer-gauge' challenge is answered more convincingly than it ever has been so far," Horton concluded, "one should not expect prayer to affect the weather." To understand the issue of prayer in late-nineteenth- and early-twentieth-century American Protestantism, then, the prayer-gauge debate is a fitting place to begin.[8]

The Prayer-Gauge Challenge

Tyndall's stated proposal was quite simple; as a scientist, he wished to set up an experiment to measure prayer's effectiveness. Since many of the requests Christians offered up to God were difficult to evaluate (prayers for moral virtues, for spiritual blessings, for national well-being, etc.), Tyndall suggested using prayers for the sick as a testable class of prayers. Such prayers were classified by the Book of Common Prayer as "*special* forms for occasional use" and were obviously employed by modern Christians. Tyndall thus submitted a letter purportedly sent to him by an eminent London surgeon, Henry Thompson, that proposed the following test. A special hospital ward should be set up, like all others in type of patients, quality of doctors and care, and so on, with only one difference: this ward should be made the object of special prayer for its patients. After a period of three to five years, the mortality rates in this "praying ward" would be compared to those in other wards. Such a test, observed Thompson tongue-in-cheek, might furnish believers with "an occasion of demonstrating to the faithless an imperishable record of the real power of prayer."[9]

Tyndall's proposal sparked an immediate and spirited response. If he expected support from the broad churchmen whom he had praised a few years earlier, Tyndall was clearly mistaken. The editors of the *Spectator*, the voice of broad church Anglicanism, called themselves "severely disgusted" with Tyndall's "unworthy piece of literary irony." While "simple religious people" might mistake Tyndall's proposal as sincere, the *Spectator's* editors recognized it as "a covert sneer, and not the frank challenge of a cultivated inquirer." The moment believers pray in order to see its effects on God, they exclaimed, it is no longer prayer but "an expression of their anxieties." Prayer is a true power in the external world, but in the same way that "the passionate desires of individuals so often realize themselves, and the hopes of multitudes create the great historic changes for which they cry." This takes place "through the providence of God" rather than "through the magic influence of human passion."[10]

In August, James McCosh, president of Princeton College in America, was one of the first to write a vigorous reply to Tyndall.[11] A "prayer-gauge," argued McCosh, was not consistent with the method and laws of God's spiritual kingdom. For one thing, "Christians would shrink from the idea of praying for the sick on one side of the hospital and not praying for those on the other." Furthermore, in answering prayer, God weighed many factors, including the motive and spirit of the pray-er and the millions of repercussions an answer to prayer would have. McCosh gave as an example the tragedy of Prince Albert, who, ten years before the illness of the Prince of Wales, had died of a fever despite the prayers of the nation for his recovery. In this instance, claimed McCosh, God knew the greater goods; perhaps the death of Prince Albert, who had been adamantly opposed to slavery, per-

suaded the queen to ignore pleas from her advisors to intervene in the American Civil War. Thus the death brought about a greater good that we did not
know of at the time. This was only a conjecture, said McCosh, but his point
was that there were other factors in prayer of which humans were unaware.[12]

Furthermore, argued McCosh, we do not pray to test God but because we
are commanded to and cannot help doing so, and we leave to God the best
means to answer our prayers. The Christian knows in *faith* that his prayers
are answered.

> In the course of years, and as he looks back upon his life, he can
> discover case upon case in which, unobserved by the world, his peti-
> tions have been granted; or, rather, he perceives, that, as he prays in
> duty and in faith, his whole life is ordered by the Lord. It is espe-
> cially so, when his requests are for progress in spiritual excellence.

According to McCosh, Tyndall's prayer-gauge merely showed "an utter ignorance, on the part of certain scientific men, of the kind of evidence by
which moral and religious truths are sustained." Scientists such as Tyndall,
McCosh concluded, should stick to physical experiments and leave "philosophical and religious questions" to more qualified thinkers.[13]

Tyndall did not wait long to respond. It seems that this was just the sort
of response he had expected, and he was ready with a devastating counter-
attack published on the eve of his American tour in the October issue of the
Contemporary Review. Christian critics had failed to address Tyndall's
charge, as he pointed out in his article, "On Prayer as a Physical Force."
Tyndall was concerned not with moral and religious truths but with scientific
ones. He claimed to harbor no personal antipathy toward prayer. "It is not
my habit of mind to think otherwise than solemnly of the feeling which
prompts prayer," Tyndall avowed. "It may, as alleged, be necessary to man's
highest culture." However, he continued, when religious men propose that
prayer invokes a *physical* power that "produces the precise effects caused by
physical energy in the ordinary course of things," then science has a right
to test such a theory. By claiming prayer's effect on physical phenomena
such as a cattle plague and the health of the Prince of Wales, religious men
had ventured into science's domain; as such, they should be prepared to play
by the rules of science.[14]

Though in his famous "Niagara Falls" remark Tyndall had argued a priori
against petitionary prayer, he now claimed to harbor no philosophical problem with prayer. "The theory that the system of nature is under the control
of a Being who changes phenomena in compliance with the prayers of men,
is, in my opinion, a perfectly legitimate one," he claimed. "I therefore urge
no impossibilities." But, he continued, "without verification, a theoretic conception is a mere figment of the intellect. . . . To check the theory, we have
simply to compare the deductions from it with the facts of observation."

While science cheerfully submitted to this ordeal, religious men seemed to fear it. By claiming that prayer could change the external world but refusing to submit to a test, religious men were attempting to have their cake and eat it too, and scientists would have none of it. As Tyndall's colleague Henry Thompson, the original formulator of the prayer-gauge, exclaimed in the same issue of the *Contemporary Review:*

> Do these people believe in the efficacy of petition? . . . Do they think that, without such prayers, there would be more deaths and smaller crops? It either is or is not so; and no discussion about direct and indirect influence will avail one jot to obscure the question. Is the world to go on forever with such a problem unsolved?

By proclaiming prayer's efficacy as a physical force and then refusing to submit such a force to a test, Tyndall concluded, religious men were showing their beliefs to be "a residue of that mysticism of the middle ages."[15]

Another scientist had already added fuel to the fire two months earlier; in August, Francis Galton's "Statistical Inquiries into the Efficacy of Prayer" had appeared in the British *Fortnightly Review.* Galton, a cousin of Charles Darwin and like Tyndall a champion of modern science, claimed that Tyndall's hospital test was unnecessary, since he had already acquired data from the past that demonstrated that prayer had no effect on the physical world. His study was essentially the age-old problem of unanswered prayer buttressed by the aura of modern scientific methodology.

Galton's contribution did seem to pose a serious challenge to prayer for a number of reasons. First, Galton dealt with past phenomena rather than a proposed test, so his work was free from the charge that it distorted the motive of prayer, a common rebuttal to Tyndall's test. Galton also eschewed ideology.[16] He studiously avoided the philosophical question of *how* God could answer prayer in the physical realm. Galton simply proposed to observe, through statistical comparison of similar phenomena, whether or not prayer worked. "We have no regard, in this inquiry," he claimed, "to the course by which the answer to prayers may be supposed to operate. . . . We simply look to the main issue,—do sick persons who pray, or are prayed for, recover, on the average, more rapidly than others?" Results, not reasons, were all that mattered. Finally, by using general averages rather than individual cases, Galton's study allowed for specific instances of unanswered prayer, such as McCosh's example of the death of Prince Albert, due to God's infinite knowledge of greater goods. God may know best, but if prayer had any physical efficacy at all, surely this fact would percolate up through a mass of data even if it were not manifested in each individual case. It is no wonder, then, that Henry Thompson praised Galton's work: "It is impossible to overrate Mr. Galton's laborious and scientific record relating to the subject, nor to overlook its importance. Had I done nothing more than elicit the production of this last work of his, I should have been amply content."[17]

Galton first tested a prayer that came directly out of the Book of Common Prayer, petition for the long life of the sovereign. Since at that time all nations of Europe said such prayers, Galton compared the life spans of members of royal houses to that of other groups of society and found the former to be the shortest lived of all groups. Next, he compared life spans of the clergy—assumed to be a prayerful group—with those of other professional classes, such as lawyers and medical men, and found no appreciable difference. "Hence," Galton concluded, "the prayers of the clergy for protection against the perils and dangers of the night, for protection during the day, and for recovery from sickness, appear to be futile in result." Galton also noted the tragic deaths of countless missionaries due to disease and hardship overseas, though they were probably the most prayed for of any group of people. Here Galton challenged those defenders of prayer who would suggest that God only answered prayer in nonmiraculous ways. "Immunity from disease," Galton pointed out, "compels the suspension of no purely material law." If God simply disinclined missionaries from eating certain foods or traveling on certain days, exposure to disease could be avoided. "Even if God acted only on the minds of the missionaries, his action might be as much to advantage of their health as if he wrought a physical miracle." No evidence existed, however, that such was the case.[18]

Galton performed his statistical inquiries in a number of areas, all of which gave, he asserted, no evidence that prayer had any effect. One particularly clever inquiry concerned the safety of ships bearing missionaries to their destinations—always a highly prayed-for thing—relative to other vessels. Once again, maintained Galton, no direct interference with nature was necessary to effect such an end. "It might have been put into the captain's heart to navigate in that course, and to perform those acts of seamanship which proved links in a chain that led to an eventual success." In the absence of readily available statistics comparing such ships to other vessels, Galton drew on insurance records. If any such difference existed, believed Galton, surely insurance companies that make it their business to monitor risk would notice. But are insurance premiums lowered for ships bearing missionaries? Of course not. "The notion that a missionary or other pious enterprise carries any immunity from danger has never been entertained by insurance companies."[19]

Implicit in Galton's article was a threefold scheme of prayer. Drawing this scheme out will help clarify the nature of Galton's attack as well as the tangled responses to Galton and Tyndall of the defenders of prayer. Prayer may be said to function on three levels. There is first an internal, or what is often called a subjective, function of prayer—it affects the inner life of the person praying. On the second level, it may be claimed that prayer functions externally by affecting other persons. In other words, God may answer prayer by influencing the mind or spirit of the person being prayed for. On a third level, it may be believed that prayer affects the physical, nonpersonal world as well. Such a belief would inspire prayer for rain or healing.[20] Tyndall, in "On the Physical Value of Prayer," voiced doubts about level three prayer. By acknowledging that prayer may be "necessary to man's highest culture," however, he left room for level one prayer as an act that benefited the individual praying. He was silent on level two prayer functioning as a real force in the interpersonal realm. In his conclusions concerning missionary deaths and missionary ships, Galton more forcefully than Tyndall undermined level two prayer as well. God could preserve missionary ships without resorting to level three interventions in nature, simply by influencing the minds of missionaries or ship captains. But Galton found no indications that God did.

Like Tyndall, Galton left room for level one interpretations of prayer, though perhaps not in a sense that would have satisfied many Christians.[21] "Nothing that I have said," he concluded, "negatives the fact that the mind may be relieved by the utterance of prayer. . . . Neither does any thing I have said profess to throw light on the question of how far it is possible for man to commune in his heart with God." But as to prayer as a real force in the physical world, Galton's answer was an emphatic no.[22]

The American Protestant Response

As mentioned earlier, Tyndall and Galton provoked a flurry of responses from British and American writers. Answering the famous scientists became part of the cost of doing business for writers on prayer in the late nineteenth century. The popular Protestant response is discussed in the next chapter; here I analyze the typical responses to Tyndall produced in American Protestant intellectual circles. One way to answer the prayer-gauge challenge was to deny that prayer entailed specific requests. Rather, some said, petition in prayer simply meant articulating one's desire to see God's will done. This did not specifically deny the external efficacy of prayer but instead made the nature of prayer such that no observable results could be expected from it. The best spokesperson for this response in America was Noah Davis, a prominent Baptist and president of Bethel College in Russellville, Kentucky. In 1873, Davis weighed in on the prayer-gauge debate with an article in the *Baptist Quarterly*.

After noting the widespread consternation that the prayer-gauge had produced, Davis proposed to set out "a touchstone principle" of prayer that, he believed, would "solve many of our difficulties." "The essence of all prayer is in these words: 'Thy will be done.' . . . Whatever will not bear this test, is not prayer." This fact, Davis believed, negated Tyndall's prayer test. The prayer-gauge was based on an erroneous notion of prayer as asking for things, when in fact petition can be no more than assent to God's unchangeable will. Davis declared not the scientific determinism of Tyndall but rather a theological determinism. Concerning natural events such as rain, storms, earthquakes, and the like, argued Davis, "no prayer can possibly induce their coming, arrest, or change, independently of natural order. We do not say the Almighty cannot, but that the Immutable will not." In other words, Davis was saying, God has sovereignly ordered natural events and does not change his plans; prayer works in the sphere of spiritual and mental forces but not in natural events. Davis thus posited two spheres, the natural and the spiritual, and restricted real petition to the latter sphere. When praying about matters in the physical world, said Davis, Christians did not bring requests for changes but rather asked that God's unchangeable will be done. Concerning the prayer-gauge, therefore, Davis concluded, "if Christians were unitedly to pray for the health of the patients in a hospital test ward, their petition must fundamentally be: God's will be done, that his name may be glorified; and this might be most perfectly answered by no difference between that ward and others." Davis thus denied Tyndall's prayer-gauge by claiming that prayer was untestable, "the essence of every prayer being answered by what comes to pass."[23]

Davis's response closely paralleled the beliefs of some Christians on Britain's liberal extreme. For instance, during the 1865 cattle plague, Arthur Stanley, dean of Westminster Abbey, broad churchman, and a conscientious objector to the prescribed special prayers, consulted his friend John Tyndall for advice on how to pray. "I hope and think," Tyndall replied, "that you will *not* pray as others will for the staying of this plague, but will ask on the contrary for strength of heart and clearness of mind to meet it manfully and fight against it intelligently." Heeding his friend's advice, Stanley, on the day appointed for prayer preached on the text "Thy will be done," saying that he considered it the only intelligent prayer for Christians.[24] Prayer as a desire for God's will to be done made no pretension to be an observable physical force and thus was compatible with the claims of modern science.

While Davis's understanding of petitionary prayer avoided conflict with modern science, it did not square well with the doctrine of prayer in traditional Protestantism. In fact, a similar explanation of prayer written by a Scottish Presbyterian minister, William Knight, earned him a censure by his church, the Free Presbyterian Church of Scotland.[25] Davis's "Thy will be done" prayer was close to but not quite the same thing as traditional Protestant prayer. As explained earlier, mainstream American Protestants had maintained that petitionary prayer entailed more than mere stated acquiescence to God's will; it also included the utterance of tangible requests to God over what his will would be in a particular spiritual or material case. Noah Davis's separation of physical and spiritual spheres and confinement of petition to the latter was a harbinger of things to come in liberal Protestantism. In the nineteenth century, however, his response was clearly the road less traveled, since it seemed to be giving away too much to the skeptics. American Protestants were not prepared to relinquish prayer for material objects.[26]

The traditional American Protestant mainstream maintained in the face of Tyndall's attack that prayer was a spiritual force with possible physical consequences whose realm was the weather as well as the spirit. Yet many did so while declaring that their ideas did no violence to modern scientific notions concerning the "reign of law." Tyndall and the scientists, these writers argued, misunderstood what Christians meant when they asserted that God answers prayer. Protestant writers used two ways to explain how God answered prayer without violating modern science. First, defenders of prayer asserted that God did not suspend natural law but rather that God, like humans, combined various forces to produce effects in nature that would not otherwise occur. When the Old School Presbyterian Charles Hodge discussed prayer in his *Systematic Theology* of 1872, he rebutted Tyndall using this rationale.[27] The Christian, Hodge began, believes that God can answer prayer for material as well as spiritual needs. But "this does not suppose that the laws of nature are mutable, or that they are set aside." Humans produce real effects by combining various natural forces. In like manner, "God accomplishes his purpose by a similar intelligent and voluntary combination of natural causes. When He wills that it should rain, He wills that all the secondary causes, productive of that effect, should be brought into operation." The Christian doctrine of prayer, then, "only supposes that God does, on the scale of the universe, what we do within the limited sphere of our efficiency." Thus, concerning Tyndall's "Niagara Falls" statement, Hodge sarcastically remarked, "man may deflect the beams of the sun at pleasure, but God cannot."[28]

Mark Hopkins, president of Williams College, president of the American Board of Commissioners for Foreign Missions, and nineteenth-century America's educator par excellence, explained all this in his discussion of the prayer-gauge in 1874. Nature, Hopkins said, is the region of necessity, while "supernature" is the region of will. Changes in nature "are produced by will. The will of man comes between these laws and their results as they would be without will." For example, humans build dams and so thwart the law of gravity that would otherwise assert itself over rivers. May not God do the same by introducing a new force into the equation? An act of God, Hopkins concluded, was simply "a variable combination of invariable forces," something that human beings did everyday.[29]

This argument from analogy with human action was repeated almost without exception by American Protestants who responded to Tyndall. For example, W. R. Atkinson, an American Presbyterian minister, in his article "Tyndall on the Physical Value of Prayer," noted that human beings knew how to make it rain; all it would take was a large, cold metal surface raised to the sky. All they lacked was the means of doing so. Surely, though, an omnipotent God could do such a thing. When Herbert Morris took up the prayer-gauge challenge for the American Tract Society in 1887, he repeated virtually verbatim Hopkins's remarks about God subtly combining natural forces to bring about new physical conditions. He concluded:

> If the divine will saw fit to effect certain meteorological combinations
> in order to bring on rain or to ward off disease, in answer to the
> prayers of a prostrate nation, no experiment of man, no application
> of his doctrine of the conservation of energy, would ever discover
> that his volition had been concerned in bringing about the result.

As a final example, the author and lecturer William Kinsley, in *Science and Prayer*, claimed that since humans impinged on nature every time they hold up their hands, so could God by his will make an axe-head float. A world of natural laws, concluded the nineteenth-century mainline Protestant establishment, did not negate the external efficacy of prayer.[30]

American Protestant defenders of prayer also deployed a second line of reasoning to argue that petitionary prayer was in keeping with modern science. They argued that God took into account the preordained prayers of Christians when he ordered the events of the universe. In other words, prayer was written into the fabric of a predetermined universe by God. This "foreknowledge argument," common in Reformed Protestantism throughout the centuries, was often employed in response to Tyndall.[31] As James McCosh stated it, "God commonly answers prayer by natural means, appointed for this purpose from the very beginning.... The God who created the need, and prompted the prayer, has provided the means of granting what he needs." The Congregational minister William Patton even used the theory of evolution to support this contention. Divinely directed evolution, Patton argued, implied that God prearranged the forces of nature to produce the natural and human world we see around us today. Evolutionists, Patton argued, "ought then to find it easy to believe that prayers and their answers formed part of this very system of pre-arrangement." Patton concluded:

> When, therefore, a man addresses to God a prayer worthy to be
> heard, that prayer was already heard from all eternity; and the Father
> of mercies arranged the world expressly in favour of that prayer, so
> that the accomplishment should be a consequence of the natural
> course of events. It is thus that God answers the prayers of men
> without working a miracle.

Through the analogy of human action or through the foreknowledge argument (they were usually employed in tandem), leading Protestants in America expressed confidence that the world of science posed no insuperable obstacle to the life of prayer.[32]

This seemingly effective (to them) response to science on the part of leading American Protestants brings up a puzzling question: Why would some leading Protestants in the early twentieth century claim that Tyndall's prayer-gauge had not been answered adequately? Nineteenth-century Protestant writers on prayer clearly believed they had dispensed with Tyndall and Galton, so why did Harry Emerson Fosdick and Walter Horton, to name a couple of prominent examples, claim that the scientific naturalists had gotten the better of the debate? Two factors may have been at work undermining late-nineteenth-century American Protestants' position in relation to Tyndall and Galton. The first concerns the scientific climate of the nineteenth century; the second concerns actual weaknesses in the Protestant response to science.

The prayer-gauge debate's significance was not so much it persuaded many Protestants to disbelieve in prayer; that is doubtful. As we have seen, traditional Protestants had on hand a number of responses to scientific naturalism, and Galton's prayer-gauge consisting of insurance records and life spans of kings amounted to little more than scientific gimmickry, as his critics pointed out. However, regardless of any particular conclusions he reached, Galton's statistical method, carrying with it the aura of dispassionate science, reflected an important underlying component of the prayer-gauge debate. Indeed, the scientific attack on prayer cannot be understood apart from the surrounding nineteenth-century context of scientific progress seemingly at religion's expense. Scientists throughout the century had been at work pushing God's activity further from the realm of daily experience. From the eighteenth century on, geologists had pushed the date of God's creation of the world further and further back, thereby creating troublesome questions for literal interpreters of Genesis. Many Christians accepted the findings of geology but retained divine intervention to account for the "gaps" in the fossil record. In 1830, however, Charles Lyell's *Principles of Geology* explained the earth's geological history in terms of gradual natural change, thereby precluding divine intervention.[33]

Darwin's epochal 1859 work *The Origin of Species*, which applied Lyell's principle of uniformitarianism to the biological world, not only pushed God's creative activity even further away; it signaled a new understanding of the task of science. While many scientists in the first half of the nineteenth century had pursued their endeavors in a theological context, scientists after Darwin increasingly saw their discipline as ruling out a priori any nonnaturalistic explanation of the data. Charles Lyell, even after he accepted biological evolution, maintained that divine intervention was responsible for the human species. In the post-Darwinian science rooted in naturalistic assumptions, Lyell's position came to be considered by many "real" scientists to be untenable. This was made clear when Darwin's *Descent of Man*, a more radical statement of evolution that argued for the inclusion of humanity in the sphere of natural evolution, appeared, only a year before the prayer-gauge controversy.[34]

The prayer-gauge debate thus took place in an era in which, as historian James Turner writes, "the mana of science glowed more brightly with each passing year." Science seemed to hold the keys for understanding all the secrets of the universe, either in hand or in the near future. Turner explains: "[W]hat really mattered was not that an agnostic had ready at hand a scientific explanation for the origin of life, the formation of the solar system, or any other specific problem; rather, it was that he had the impression that science could provide one—if not right away, then eventually."[35]

This sense of scientific momentum was for naturalistic scientists an important part of the attack on prayer. Tyndall began "On Prayer" with a brief overview of the rise of science from Galileo to Darwin, a story of constant advance by science and retreat by religion, he claimed. "Men still living remember the indignation excited by the first revelations of geology regarding the age of the earth." Yet today the "best-informed theologians" readily accept the findings of scientists concerning an old earth. "Look, finally, at the excitement caused by the publication of the *Origin of Species*; and compare it with the calm attendant on the appearance of the far more outspoken, and from the old point of view, more impious, *Descent of Man*." Religion, concluded Tyndall, has for centuries been undergoing a "slow process of purification, freeing itself slowly and painfully from the physical errors which the active but uninformed intellect mingled with the aspirations of the soul." What was now needed, he said, was "a final act of purification" that would push that most immediate of religious activities, prayer, out of the physical realm.[36]

Henry Thompson used much the same reasoning when he responded to critics in October of 1872. Though claiming only to be trying to ascertain the real value of prayer, Thompson admitted that he personally doubted petitionary prayer. There are two classes of things, he explained: things that no one prays about, such as the rising and setting of the sun, the tides, and the inevitability of death; and those things that may be prayed about. Yet the only basis for classification, Thompson argued, has been our declining ignorance. In earlier times savages prayed for everything, but as the human race has progressed, he maintained, "advance in knowledge has enlarged the class of objects not to be prayed for." Thus, asserted Thompson, "Class I must inevitably grow larger and larger; Class II, inevitably smaller." Many believe this analogy to be so strong, Thompson concluded, "that it is not improbable that there really are no events which are not equally determined by natural order." Thus, Thompson believed that the progress of science would bring about the ultimate extinction of petitionary prayer.[37]

As much as any specific test or argument, it was this imagery of an ever-expanding sphere of science producing an ever-shrinking sphere of things to pray for that would pose a challenge for those Protestants seeking to harmonize Christianity and modern science. Scientists could not yet fully explain things such as the weather or illnesses, but the trend of the past made it seem merely a matter of time until all natural phenomena would be adequately explained by science and thus lie outside the realm of prayer. That is why, for example, J. E. Wells, a respondent to Tyndall, writing in the theological journal *Bibliotheca Sacra*, missed the point when he asserted that science "utterly fails to account for a very large and important part of the phenomena of the physical world." Such was undoubtedly the case, but to place prayer in that sphere that had not yet been deciphered by science seemed a dangerous strategy, since this territory seemed to be shrinking year by year.[38]

One writer to the *Spectator*, Charles Stubbs, consciously linked the prayer question to the advance of science. Most Christians, he wrote, see prayer as affecting "external circumstances," while some see it as only affecting the person's relationship to circumstances. If as a result of the prayer-gauge debate the second view comes to prevail, Stubbs wrote, "it will not be the first time that theology has gone to school to science to be taught the true meaning of its books." The growing prestige of nineteenth-century science provided a powerful impetus for progressive Christians to curtail notions of petitionary prayer, one that would become an important factor for American Protestants who wished to adapt traditional theology to modern ways of thought. One of them, Walter Horton, spoke for many when he referred a generation later to the prayer-gauge debate as a victory for Tyndall.[39]

A second factor working against traditional American Protestants in their reaction to science was the nature of their response itself. Many writers seemed to avoid the real challenge that Tyndall and the scientists were posing. Tyndall's attack came on two fronts—a fact that was not always considered in the aftermath of the proposed hospital test. The earlier one of 1860 was an attack on the *possibility* of prayer as a physical force, based on the law of conservation of energy. The challenge of 1872 posed by Tyndall and Galton came on an entirely different front, that of *experience*. Whereas in 1860 Tyndall advanced theoretical reasons for denying level three prayer, the scientific attack of 1872 was couched in empirical terms. In the face of traditionalist rebuttals, the scientists, exuding (or, it may be said, feigning) an air of benign objectivity, claimed simply to be looking for evidence. Huxley, the most formidable of the scientific naturalists, remarked: "[I]t is not upon any *a priori* considerations that objections to the supposed efficacy of prayer in modifying the course of events . . . can be scientifically based. The real objection is the inadequacy of the evidence." Though Tyndall initiated the latter attack, his prayer-gauge was never tried—Galton's statistics, not Tyndall's philosophy, lay at the heart of the issue. However, most responses to the prayer-gauge in the respectable journals focused on the philosophical rather than the empirical objection to prayer. It seemed as if defenders of prayer were so alarmed by the naturalistic sword in Tyndall's left hand, they overlooked the empirical rifle in his right.[40]

The American Tract Society's Herbert Morris, for instance, devoted a lengthy section of his response to the prayer-gauge challenge to showing the vast amount of prayers that could be answered simply by God influencing human minds (level two prayer), not by altering the forces of nature. God could provide for material needs simply by prompting others to donate funds to that individual, Morris noted. God could provide physical healing by leading doctors to the correct cure for an ailment. God could even provide safety in travel, Morris explained, simply by influencing a traveler's own mind to choose particular routes, modes of travel, and departure times. Thus, Morris explained, "the field where answer may be given, independently of all natural laws, is very broad and large. . . . And when all such prayers are thus answered how little more is left for the Christian to desire!"[41]

Explaining the vast scope of level two prayer, however, did not solve the problem of evidence. Tyndall and Galton did not care whether God answered prayer miraculously or not. Galton, in fact, had expressly stated that any aspect of prayer that he was testing could have been accomplished through nonmiraculous means, as in his example of a ship bearing missionaries to their destination arriving safely by God's influencing the mind of the ship captain to take a particular course that avoided storms and other hazards. Galton was willing to accept the possibility of God working in the non-supernatural ways prescribed by Morris, but he supposedly found no evidence that prayer on the whole brought results. Traditional Christians who maintained that prayer had physical results claimed that there was a correlation between the specific requests of believers and resulting events, even if not every individual request was answered. Of course, God may not always answer prayer in the exact manner prescribed by the individual's petition.[42] However, if prayer was "a power in the universe, as distinct, as real, as natural, and as uniform, as the power of gravitation," as Austin Phelps had maintained, than one would expect *some* semblance of a measurable result from it.[43]

It is this grappling with tangible proof of answered prayer that one often finds missing from many of the defenses of prayer in the learned journals just discussed. The *Bibliotheca Sacra's* Wells, for one, did marshall a limited sort of evidentialist rebuttal. The lives of thousands of regenerated men, he asserted, "are *facts*, as patent and as worthy of study and explanation as any revealed by microscope or spectroscope." Of course, this did not exactly fly in the face of scientific naturalism. Tyndall had shown himself quite willing to grant that prayer could regenerate the life of the one who prayed when he praised prayer as perhaps "necessary to man's highest culture."[44]

Another type of "evidentialist" response—one intended to support level two and level three prayer—was offered by the Presbyterian Atkinson. Drawing on the biblical record of Jesus' miracles, Atkinson asserted:

Such proofs, however, as would satisfy even Professor Tyndall, have been given, and the testimony to the same is such as can never be gainsayed. In the evidences of the truth of miracles of healing and the like, performed by the Author of our religion, we have abundant testimony to the fact of the *physical value* of prayer."

For devout Christians, such as the readers of the *Southern Presbyterian Review*, in which Atkinson's article was published, this argument undoubtedly carried great weight. However, in the larger cultural arena of the nineteenth century, such "proofs" amounted to a kind of begging of the question. As historian Robert Bruce Mullin has shown, in late-nineteenth-century intellectual circles the miracles of Jesus were themselves a part of the Protestant inheritance that was being called into question by Christians and non-Christians alike. Using the miracles of Jesus to undergird the efficacy of prayer, therefore, would seem to the scientific establishment like jumping from a sinking ship onto a leaky raft. James Turner has observed, concerning the late nineteenth century, that "for thoughtful men and women, the Bible was no longer an unquestioned source of religious authority; it had become a form of evidence for Christianity that itself needed defending." Thus, claimed the Cambridge University theologian J. H. Jellett during the prayer-gauge debate, "the evidence of Scripture has been altogether banished from the discussion." Neither Wells's nor Atkinson's evidence was the type that the skeptics claimed to be looking for.[45]

In this context, the book *Prayer and Its Remarkable Answers* by William Patton becomes significant. Patton was a paragon of the Protestant establishment in the nineteenth century. Educated at Union Theological Seminary in New York and ordained a Congregational minister, Patton served as a pastor to large churches in Boston, Hartford, and Chicago. Throughout his long career as a Christian statesman, he also served as editor of the Protestant periodical the *Advance*, a lecturer at Oberlin College, a member of the American Board of Commissioners for Foreign Missions, and president of Howard University in Washington, D.C. Patton also found time in the 1870s to pen one of the longest books on prayer in late-nineteenth-century America, much of it written as a response to modern attacks on prayer.

Patton wrote his book on prayer, he said, to combat "a pervading unbelief on the subject outside the church, and a paralyzing uncertainty inside of it." His target was not only Tyndall and the skeptics but also those Christians (such as Noah Davis) who asserted that prayer was "only a submission of the human to the divine will." "There is a disposition at present," Patton lamented, "to concede too much to the objection of the philosophic skeptics, and to render prayer unobjectionable by making it almost objectless." After surveying the subject of prayer in the Bible, Patton maintained that prayer was "not merely submitting in ignorance to whatever God may choose to send; but it is asking Him, reverently and in a childlike way, to send specific things felt to be pressingly needed." True prayer entails petition, Patton avowed, a request to God to actually do something.[46]

Patton went on to devote a lengthy defense of petitionary prayer against "skeptical assaults" from Tyndall and the like. He employed the typical strategies such as the analogy of human action and the foreknowledge argument to explain how God could answer prayer without violating natural laws. In all, Patton devoted over a hundred pages to such theological and philosophical issues, but this was just a prelude to his real defense of prayer. Patton's main strategy, as the title indicated, was to *demonstrate* prayer's efficacy by documenting "remarkable answers" to prayer. As stated in his preface, "the chief aim of the book is to furnish authentic facts, so grouped and explained, in the light of the principles set forth in the early chapters, as to dispel doubt, and encourage a rational and Scriptural faith." In other words, Patton moved from arguments to evidence—just the sort of thing Tyndall and Galton claimed to be looking for. Moreover, Patton's instances of answered prayer would not be primarily based on Biblical events, as Atkinson's had been. Instead, he wrote, "preference has been given to those of a later date."[47]

Patton was well connected in American Protestantism, and he had sent a circular note to Christians around the nation before writing his book, asking them to send him testimony of answered prayer to include in his book. *Prayer and Its Remarkable Answers* was the result. So although Patton devoted thirty pages to examples of answered prayer in the Bible, the majority of the book (two hundred pages) was devoted to classifying and relating various modern evidences of answered prayer. In a section entitled "Prayer for Supply of Temporal Wants," Patton related accounts of God supplying money for Christians, a Christian escaping from a bear, a few answered prayers for rain (one related by Charles Finney), and many other examples of God answering prayer. Patton also related countless examples of answered prayer for physical healing. In all, Patton saw his book as a complete response to the skeptical spirit of the age, not only establishing a philosophical basis for prayer but providing plenty of the evidence that the scientific naturalists claimed to be looking for.

Patton's book, in fact, represents a transition to an entirely different kind of religious response to scientific naturalism. His book straddled the world of learned Protestant theologians and popular, revivalistic Protestantism— written by a scholarly Christian but employing the evidentialist apologetic of grassroots Christianity. While Protestant elites such as Charles Hodge and Mark Hopkins may have considered it vulgar or misguided to put prayer to a test, grassroots Christians claimed to be doing just that in the late nineteenth century. Patton's work thus represents the tip of an iceberg of "evidences" of answered prayer that was emerging in American religious culture concurrently with scientific naturalism. Outside the pages of the learned journals, such a strategy would be employed repeatedly in the decades to come to answer modern skeptics. The next chapter explains an increased emphasis on answered prayer concurrent with the rise of scientific naturalism, as well as the ironic similarities between the John Tyndalls and evangelical Protestants of the nineteenth century.

Two

✠

Proving the Living God

*Answered Prayer as a Modern
Evangelical Apologetic*

Four years before John Tyndall proclaimed the inalterability of the meteorological world through spiritual forces, another Englishman faced the issue of prayer and the weather. In November 1857, George Mueller of Bristol had a problem on his hands. This man cared for hundreds of orphans, and a dangerous leak had been detected in the boiler that heated the orphanage's buildings. Mueller had to shut down the boiler in order to repair it. The shutdown and repair were scheduled to take place on Wednesday, and all the preceding week a frigid north wind had been blowing. What was to be done with the children if on the day of the shutdown the weather remained so intemperate? George Mueller solved this predicament in his customary way: He prayed, asking God to shift the direction of the wind from the north to the south. "The evening before," recounted Mueller in his journal, "the bleak north wind still blew; but, on the Wednesday, the south wind blew: exactly as I had prayed. . . . Here, then, is one of our difficulties which was overcome by prayer and faith." The American editor of Mueller's 1873 autobiography remarked: "[I]f Mr. Galton and Prof. Tyndall ask for proofs of the value of prayer in common life, they may be directed to the Bristol Orphan Houses, for the facts of which they are in search."[1]

Mueller's account indicates that a frank supernaturalism could coexist with the emerging scientific ethos of the nineteenth-century world. Indeed, supernaturalism had by no means died out with the Enlightenment. John Wesley, the eighteenth-century founder of Methodism, retained, in the words of his biographer, a "strong sense of the supernatural intervention of God" despite his affinity for Lockean thought. Wesley claimed to have witnessed or experienced supernatural healing and answered prayer for rain, and once he even prayed—successfully, he claimed—for his lame horse. Wesley's Methodist offspring in postrevolutionary America capitalized on the latent supernaturalism of American folk religion, according to historian John Wigger. Prophetic dreams, visions, ghost sightings, reports of divine healing, and other such manifestations of religious "enthusiasm" were common in the early days of American Methodism.[2]

Methodist supernaturalism waned in the 1820s and 1830s as the movement became more socially respectable, but one may question to what extent supernaturalism ever really declined in American Protestantism. To be sure, Reformed Protestant elites had long since reached a compromise with Enlightenment rationalism through the doctrine of cessationism. Miracles, they said, had been confined to the biblical epoch for the purpose of confirming divine revelation. Thus, they were not appropriate for modern times. Rather, "special providences," in which God acted directly through but not against natural laws, were all that could be expected in present times.[3]

Horace Bushnell upset this orthodox apple cart rooted in Reformed theology. Bushnell's *Nature and the Supernatural* (1859) broke down the distinction between biblical miracles and God's present "providential" action in the world. In place of the classic Reformed system that relegated God's miraculous activity to the biblical era, Bushnell proposed a model of "oscillation" throughout Christian history between the extremes of cold rationality and unchecked supernaturalism. When orthodoxy became cold and lifeless, a miraculous age would ensue to enliven the church and remind Christians that they served a living God. When such miracles reached excess, as they inevitably would, a period of rationalism would follow to provide stability. Bushnell saw dawning in the nineteenth century a new age of miraculous acts of God and closed his book with accounts of modern "miracles" that he had either witnessed or been told of.[4]

Whether Bushnell helped spawn interest in the supernatural or, as is more likely, his book was itself a product of an emerging ethos, nineteenth-century Protestantism clearly witnessed widespread interest in supernatural, experientialist forms of religion. Indeed, whether one views the nineteenth century as an age of rising skepticism or as one of widespread supernaturalism largely depends on what segment of society one observes. American revivalism had always shown an affinity for the supernatural. As noted earlier, Charles Finney, despite his application of rational methods to revivalism, maintained what William McLoughlin has called a "mystical element" to his makeup. He claimed visions and believed that the Devil sometimes tried to kill him by frightening his normally tame horse.[5]

Across the Atlantic, what historian David Bebbington has called a "heightened supernaturalism," stemming from the influence of Romanticism, affected British evangelicalism in the 1820s and 1830s. The renewal of premillennialism, with its belief in the impending supernatural return of Christ at any moment, arose at this time, as did more robust views of biblical inspiration and, among a few, the practice of speaking in tongues.[6]

Another example of the supernatural, experientialist impulse in nineteenth-century religion was the rise of interest in the Holy Spirit and "holiness." In the mid–nineteenth century, holiness teachings began to spring up across a wide range of denominations in American Protestantism. The essence of the holiness idea was a second experience after conversion in which the struggling, defeated Christian surrendered to Christ and received supernatural power to live a sinless life. A life of victory over sin—even perfection, some believers taught—was possible for the Christian. All one had to do was cease striving, surrender completely to Christ, and let the Holy Spirit supernaturally empower one to lead a life of holiness and effective service.

Among Methodists, Phoebe Palmer revived the perfectionist teachings that had languished among Wesley's followers. She promoted a "second blessing" through an act of total consecration that purified the Christian from all known sin. Charles Finney promoted a similar holiness theology, known as Oberlin Perfectionism, among Reformed Protestants. The revival of 1858 was largely a result of the spread of these holiness networks throughout the American Protestant landscape. Two influential books emerged from these revivals, the Presbyterian William Boardman's *Higher Christian Life* (1859) and Hannah Whitall Smith's *Christian's Secret to the Happy Life* (1875), both of which would inspire the "Keswick" version of holiness that became popular among Reformed Protestant conservatives by the end of the century and that heavily influenced American fundamentalism.[7]

Keswick holiness owed its name to a series of conferences that were established at the English Lake District site of Keswick in 1875 by Hannah, her husband Robert Pearsall Smith, and William Boardman. Under the influence of Anglican clergymen such as H. W. Webb-Peploe, American holiness teachings were modified at Keswick in two ways. First, the notion of the "eradication" of the sin nature popular among Methodist holiness proponents was firmly squelched, replaced by that of sin's "suppression" by the constant influence of the Holy Spirit. Second, the idea of the baptism of the Holy Spirit as an instantaneous experience was downplayed and subsumed under the broader idea of a "filling" of the Spirit that needed to be done daily. It was this version of holiness spirituality that was brought back to America by Dwight L. Moody and others in the 1890s and that permeated conservative Bible conferences, missionary organizations, and Bible institutes. By the late nineteenth century, both Keswick and perfectionist holiness teachings, promising a deeper experience of the Christian life, were widespread in American Protestantism.[8]

Another example of this supernatural, experientialist impulse was the rise in some religious circles of the practice of divine healing. As mentioned earlier, Wesley promoted physical health among Christians, both through natural remedies and through supernatural means, when necessary. After Wesley's death in 1791, interest in supernatural healing receded. Mainstream Methodists of the nineteenth century retained his concern for physical health, as evidenced by their numerous hospitals, but generally came to do so by predominantly natural means. However, the holiness revivals among

Methodists would produce a fertile seedbed for teachings on divine healing to be renewed.[9]

In the 1850s news spread to the English-speaking world of the healing ministries occurring in Europe under the German pietists Johann Christoph Blumhardt and Dorothea Trudel. Inspired by these examples, the Episcopal minister Charles Cullis opened the Home for Indigent and Incurable Consumptives in Boston in 1864. Initially devoted to providing Christian charity and comfort to those dying of disease, by the 1870s Cullis's institution was stressing divine healing and was growing in popularity among holiness advocates. Buoyed by these developments, as well as a growing interest in physical health as a whole throughout the culture, interest in divine healing spread through American Protestant circles, especially among holiness proponents, for whom divine healing fit well with an increased emphasis on the power and present working of God. Though Methodist holiness advocates were most heavily influenced, divine healing attracted the attention of Reformed Protestants in Keswick holiness circles such as the Baptist A. J. Gordon and the Presbyterian A. B. Simpson.[10]

All this meant that American religious culture in the second half of the nineteenth century witnessed an emphasis on experiential religion, often coupled with supernatural displays. As Stephen Gottschalk explains in his account of the rise of Christian Science in America, there existed a "longing, expressed in different ways, for religious experience which was vital, immediate, and comprehensible in practical terms, . . . a desire to seek religion in concrete experience rather than in abstract formulations." William James's *Varieties of Religious Experience*, published shortly after the turn of the century, epitomized this pragmatic mood in religion by locating the meaning of religion in terms of concrete experience rather than abstract theological formulations.[11]

Anyone familiar with Pentecostalism will undoubtedly recognize the movement's roots in this supernaturalist, experientialist seedbed of nineteenth-century popular religion. As Edith Blumhofer has shown, Pentecostalism emerged out of certain elements of what she calls the "radical evangelicalism" of the late nineteenth century, such as restorationism, premillennialism, belief in divine healing, and emphasis on the Holy Spirit. But the radical, pietistic evangelical ethos encompassed more than merely proto-Pentecostals. Moody, the evangelist who was to the Gilded Age what Finney had been to antebellum America, exhibited many of the same tendencies. In 1871 Moody himself underwent a "baptism of the Holy Spirit" that reportedly dropped him to the floor, where he "lay bathing his soul in the divine." As Grant Wacker has observed, the Keswick Higher Life spirituality characteristic of Moody and other evangelicals was itself a reaction against the perceived spiritual aridity of nineteenth-century Reformed orthodoxy. These pietistic Christians articulated an emphasis on religious experience and a God who was active in the world through the person of the Holy Spirit.[12]

Answered Prayer Narratives

Part of this radical evangelical spirit of the nineteenth century was an emphasis on, and for some an apparent fascination with, answered prayer. Just as Charles Finney had complained about the unanswered prayers in his home church, these late-nineteenth-century evangelicals described prayer not as an end in itself but as a means to an end, and that end was a specific request granted. Moody, for example, sounded Finney's theme when he exclaimed, "How often we go to prayer-meetings without really asking for anything! Let us remember that when we pray we ought to expect an answer. Let us be looking for it." Gordon, who in addition to his interest in healing was an associate of Moody and founder of the Boston Missionary Training School, wrote:

> There are multitudes of prayers in these days, written prayers and extemporaneous prayers, prayers in the Church, and prayers in the family; but how many Christians out of the great mass have any very extensive record of direct, definite and unmistakable answers to their petitions?

The turn-of-the-century evangelist William Biederwolf remarked: "[S]ome say that 'asking and getting things from God is a pitiably small conception of prayer.' . . . Nevertheless, the fundamental idea of prayer is just that."[13]

Prayer was, to Moody's protégé the Keswick holiness writer Reuben Torrey, "God's appointed way of getting things." Torrey's colleague, Wheaton College president Charles Blanchard, emphasized petition as *the* central element in prayer. In a chapter entitled "Asking Things from God," Blanchard wrote: "It is this which is the principal element in prayer. . . . If there is no request, there is no prayer, and meditation upon the character of God, upon our own characters and humble submission to God inclines us to ask things from him and enables us joyfully and perseveringly to do it." Blanchard's 1913 book on prayer was titled, appropriately enough, *Getting Things from God*.[14] As we have seen, Protestants have historically valued petition as an important part of prayer. In these evangelical circles, however, petitionary prayer with an expectation of tangible results was raised to a higher key. E. M. Bounds, a prolific devotional writer popular among turn-of-the-century evangelicals, summed up the ethic of prayer in his typical blunt style: "What a world of waste there is in praying. What myriads of prayers have been offered for which no answer is returned, no answer longed for, and no answer is expected. . . . Prayer looks directly to securing an answer. This is its design. It has no other end in view."[15]

The radical evangelical emphasis on prayer as a means to an object spawned a staple of turn-of-the-century devotional literature, the answered prayer narrative. Specifically, the origins of the modern evangelical answered prayer narrative lie in the orphanage of George Mueller. Mueller began his spiritual odyssey as a profligate college student in Halle, Germany; he converted to evangelical Protestantism at a home group sponsored by the London Missionary Society. For a short time, he stayed at an orphanage founded by A. H. Francke, a disciple of the pietist Philip Spener. Soon thereafter, Mueller migrated to England in order to become a missionary for the London Missionary Society with plans to spread the gospel in Palestine. However, he came to believe that God wanted him to stay in England, and in 1834 he founded the Scriptural Knowledge Institution for Home and Abroad to promote biblical education, circulate Scriptures, and support missionary work.[16]

Inspired partly by the atmosphere of radical faith in God surrounding him in England and partly by Francke, Mueller founded his orphanage at Bristol in 1835. Of course, starting an orphanage was not new. What was unusual about Mueller's enterprise—and what made him famous in Britain and America—was his strict policy of never soliciting funds. No workers at the orphanage were allowed to mention to any outside party any needs of the work, however pressing the emergency. The only means of raising money was prayer. Through such a method (or through the publicity it generated, skeptics would say), Mueller managed to keep his enterprise afloat for over half a century.

Mueller maintained a detailed record of how God answered his prayers at the orphanage that was periodically published in book form for both British and American readers. His memoirs chronicle an endless litany of close calls and seemingly providentially timed gifts. Time and again, the orphanage would be out of food and money, Mueller and his associates would pray, a person would feel strangely moved to give, and the specified gift would arrive. A typical example reads:

> Aug. 6, 1844. Without *one single penny* in my hands the day began. The post brought nothing, nor had I yet received anything, when ten minutes after ten this morning the letter-bag was brought from the Orphan-Houses, for the supplies of to-day. Now see the Lord's deliverance! In the bag I found a note from one of the laborers in the Orphan-Houses, enclosing two sovereigns, which she sent for the Orphans, stating that it was part of a present which she had just received unexpectedly, for herself. Thus we are supplied for to-day.

Though most of the answers to prayer claimed by Mueller were of this level two variety (God influencing the minds of other persons), he also reported physical healings and more overtly miraculous answers to prayer such as the incident with the north wind. In the process, Mueller claimed over fifty thousand specific answers to prayer.[17]

The success of Mueller's orphanage inspired a second Briton who would influence American evangelicals, Hudson Taylor. In the 1850s, the young

Taylor read of Mueller's exploits in prayer and was inspired to found the China Inland Mission, the first evangelical "faith-mission." Taylor adopted Mueller's no-tell principles for his own enterprise, resolving, in words that would become well known to American evangelicals, to "move man through God by prayer alone."

In the span of his lifetime, Taylor testified to many Muelleresque accounts of money arriving at the last possible instance in answer to prayer. In addition, like Mueller, Taylor also claimed to have received answers to level three prayers concerning natural phenomena. He claimed the miraculous recovery of his wife from illness in answer to prayer. Once the ship Taylor was sailing on was being driven by a relentless storm into a treacherous rock-filled bay so that its doom appeared certain. The only recourse was to pray, after which, Taylor claimed, "the wind most providentially veered two points in our favour, and we were able to beat out of the Bay."[18]

When holiness teachings spread from America to Britain in the 1870s, George Mueller and Hudson Taylor became early and enthusiastic converts and proponents, for the radical faith of the holiness ideal meshed perfectly with their own beliefs (one contemporary called Taylor "an embodiment of Keswick teaching").[19] In the late 1870s and early 1880s, Mueller, whose autobiography had preceded him, became a national figure in America through a series of four speaking tours that took him to prominent churches and pulpits across the nation.[20] Taylor visited America in 1888 at the invitation of Moody and spoke at Moody's Northfield Conference and the opening of the Niagara Conference. Soon thereafter, an American branch of the China Inland Mission was opened under the leadership of Henry Frost, and Taylor became an important figure in both the emerging Student Volunteer Movement and American premillennialist networks.[21]

These men also influenced American evangelicals through the printed word. George Mueller's exhaustive day-by-day account of the Bristol orphanage, *The Life of Trust*, was first published for American readers in 1860. It was periodically revised, updated and reprinted thereafter until 1885. A year after Mueller's death in 1898, he was the subject of a lengthy biography by the prominent premillennialist and Mueller disciple, Arthur T. Pierson. Taylor's spiritual exploits were enshrined for British and American evangelicals in a lengthy two-volume biography by his daughter-in-law, Geraldine Taylor.[22]

Mueller and Taylor set the pattern for a number of answered prayer narratives in American evangelicalism in the late nineteenth and early twentieth centuries, typically produced by missionaries. American Christians read personal accounts such as Louisa Vaughan's *Answered or Unanswered? Miracles of Faith in China*; Francis McGaw's *Praying Hyde: Glimpses of the Amazing Prayer-Life of a Missionary in India*; and Rosalind Goforth's *How I Know God Answers Prayer*. Goforth's was the most colorful—but by no means unrepresentative—example of the lengths to which the Muelleresque autobiography could go. Rosalind and her husband, Jonathan, were missionaries for the American branch of the China Inland Mission stationed in northern China in the late nineteenth and early twentieth centuries.[23] Goforth chronicled a lifetime of answers to prayer both large and small. Tables, chairs, and stoves came in for her family's mission and clothes for her children in the most remarkable ways. For example, once Rosalind needed new clothes for her baby but was too exhausted to sew. Instead, she uttered a prayer. A half hour later, a package arrived from another missionary. Her baby had recently died, so she was sending the clothes to Rosalind, having sensed that she needed them.[24]

God showed Goforth that she could pray for seemingly trivial things. Once she lost a key to her money drawer and searched frantically for hours. Then, realizing she had not prayed about it, she stopped and prayed that God would pity her and guide her to the key. "Then, without wasting a step," she recounted, "I walked through the dining room, hall, and women's guestroom into Mr. Goforth's study, to the bookcase, opened the door, slipped two books aside, and there was the key." God also allegedly altered the weather for Goforth's sake, just as he had for Mueller. In one such reported instance, when the family needed new clothes, God sent a storm to keep a Chinese seamstress at her house for a month to sew clothes. Recalled Goforth in retrospect, "I find it most difficult to record just what 'asking and getting things from God,' meant at that time, but it now seems to me to have been the very foundation of the whole life."[25]

In addition to individual narratives, compilations of answered prayer stories circulated throughout the evangelical world. As discussed in chapter 1, William Patton's *Prayer and Its Remarkable Answers* appeared in 1875, two years after the prayer-gauge debate, bristling with 260 pages of answered prayer anecdotes. Ten years later, D. W. Whittle, a member of Moody's revival team, outdid Patton with the 370-page *The Wonders of Prayer: A Record of Well Authenticated and Wonderful Answers to Prayer*, a collection of accounts of answers to prayer gleaned from Christian history and Christian magazines and denominational journals. A generation later, the Moody Bible Institute issued an updated compilation of answered prayer stories, *I Cried, He Answered*. In addition, stories of answered prayer were a mainstay in Keswick-oriented nondenominational evangelical journals such as Pierson's *Missionary Review of the World*, the Moody Bible Institute's *Christian Worker's Magazine*, and Charles Trumbull's *Sunday School Times*.[26]

Not only evangelical literature but evangelical institutions of the late nineteenth century reflected an emphasis on answered prayer. Charles Cullis, for example, founded his Boston health clinic in 1864 on Mueller's example. No funds were to be solicited; prayer was to be the only means of bringing in resources for the clinic. Over the years, Cullis issued annual reports that, like Mueller's, chronicled numerous stories of financial crises being averted at the last minute in answer to prayer. In addition, the evangelical "faith missions" inspired by Taylor's China Inland Mission that were founded in the late-nineteenth century, historian Joel Carpenter has observed, typically stressed that a string of "remarkable Providences" in answer to prayer underlay their founding. For example, Henry Frost, who established the American branch of the China Inland Mission, recorded instance after instance of remarkably answered prayer. At one time, Frost recalled checking his books and finding that the mission needed six hundred dollars, so he prayed specifically for that sum.

> The next morning's mail produced one letter, written by a friend in Cleveland, asking me to accept for the Mission the gift which it enclosed and telling me to use it for any purpose whatever. I looked at the check and found that it was for just six hundred dollars. Afterwards I traced the matter and discovered that our friend's letter had been written a few moments after I had spread my paper of figures before God and had asked him to supply the need which it represented.

Since then, Frost went on, "the China Inland Mission in North America, as elsewhere, has never known any other way from that day to this than that of asking the Father, in the name of Christ, for its temporal and spiritual supplies, and also that prayer in that name has always and abundantly been answered."[27]

Even Moody's Chicago Evangelization Society, later renamed the Moody Bible Institute, perceived itself as Taylor's prayer life in institutional form. The Institute did not charge tuition and like Taylor maintained a debt-free policy. Having no endowment, the Institute was completely dependent on donations from the faithful prompted by God. Moody Bible Institute's early history, therefore, was replete with answered prayer stories of how God provided funds for the Institute. In one oft-told anecdote of the early days of the Institute, Moody knelt down and led his colleagues as he prayed, "Heavenly Father, we need six thousand dollars right now to meet our honest obligations. Send us that six thousand dollars today." Soon thereafter a telegram arrived from A. J. Gordon. It read, "D. L. Moody: Your friends at Northfield had a feeling you needed some money for your work in Chicago; we have just passed the baskets and there are six thousand dollars in the baskets and more to follow." As Reuben Torrey, the Institute's dean in the early twentieth century, said at the twenty-fifth anniversary of the founding of the school, "Moody Bible Institute has stood for the tremendous efficacy and the immeasurable importance of prayer. . . . We believe in prayer as a means of getting funds for carrying on God's work."[28] Among Keswick-oriented, pietistic evangelicals in America, answered prayer was clearly supposed to be an important part of the Christian life.

Answered Prayer as a Modern Evangelical Apologetic

This fascination on the part of evangelical Christians with tangible and often remarkable answers to prayer was one manifestation of the renewed quest for spiritual experience of an intimate deity that fueled much of late-nineteenth-century religion. Answered prayer undoubtedly served similar purposes for these evangelicals that speaking in tongues did for Pentecostals and healing did for Christian Scientists. As one missionary put it, an instance of answered prayer conveyed "a vivid sense of the nearness and care of God." When recounting the incident of finding her lost key in answer to prayer, Rosalind Goforth recalled the intense religious experience that answered prayer produced: "So near did the Lord seem at that moment that I could almost feel His bodily presence."[29]

However, answered prayer had other purposes as well.[30] It would be going too far to say that the emphasis on answered prayer among late-nineteenth-century American evangelicals was a response to naturalistic science, since much of it emerged before Tyndall and Galton challenged prayer. But answered prayer narratives did come to serve a useful purpose in the late nineteenth-century as a response to doubters. In other words, the skepticism emerging in some parts of nineteenth century culture, of which the prayer-gauge challenge was one manifestation, gave the answered prayer narrative particular significance for some evangelicals as a grassroots apologetic enterprise. Late-nineteenth-century evangelicals sought to combat such skepticism with tangible proof not only that God existed but that he answered prayer. If the skeptics wanted evidence, answered prayer advocates were eager to provide it. Whatever else answered prayer meant for these Christians, for a number of them it was a way to directly combat the unbelief of the day with a sure-fire apologetics.[31]

Answered prayer offered a means of defending the faith that seemed more attuned to the pragmatic temper of the day. Keswick holiness pioneer Hannah Whitall Smith explained the new, empirical task of Christianity in her 1875 work *The Christian's Secret of the Happy Life*:

> As we all know, this is an age of facts, and inquiries are being increasingly turned from theories to realities. If our religion is to make any headway now, it must be proved to be more than a theory, and we must present to the investigation of the critical minds of our age, the grand facts of lives that have been actually and manifestly transformed by the mighty power of God.

Especially when it came to prayer, modern people needed evidence, not argumentation. The British evangelist Charles Mason remarked that "arguments are not of any great value, but examples of the power of prayer are of great weight." Answered prayer practitioners, then, perceived themselves as Elijahs before the modern-day prophets of Baal, demonstrating to an unbelieving world the existence of a living, powerful, prayer-hearing God. As E. M. Bounds wrote, "there is no proof so clear and demonstrative that God exists than prayer and its answer."[32]

Once again, the experience of George Mueller is illuminating, for it was apologetics, not charity, that motivated Mueller to found his orphanage. Even in the 1830s, forty years before the prayer-gauge debate, Mueller sensed a spirit of unbelief among Christians concerning God's activity in the world and the power of prayer. He recalled:

> So many believers with whom I became acquainted were harassed and distressed in mind [because] God was not looked upon as the *Living God*. My spirit was ofttimes bowed down by this. I longed to set something before the children of God, whereby they might see, that He does not forsake, even in our day, those who rely on Him.

Mueller intended to demonstrate God's power "by giving them not only instances from the word of God . . . but *to show them by proofs*, that He is the same in our day." The Word of God *ought* to be enough, but unfortunately for many it was not. Instead, the proof "needed to be something which could be seen, even by the natural eye." Mueller thus founded his orphanage as a City upon a Hill in a spiritual sense. The thousands of stomachs filled and millions of dollars raised were to be irrefutable evidence to an unbelieving world of the power of prayer. If Mueller's apologetic did not convince everyone, it was not for lack of exposure. In 1875 one exasperated American minister complained: "[W]herever I go, I find that the Christian world is always sticking that man, Mueller, in my face, as a proof that God does answer prayer."[33]

Mueller's testimony was primarily intended to convince other Christians. As the nineteenth century progressed, however, testimonies of answered prayer came to be addressed more directly to the John Tyndalls of the world. The transition can be illustrated in the works of Samuel Iraneous Prime, the chronicler of the 1857–58 Prayer-Meeting Revival and the compiler of three answered prayer books that spanned the years of the prayer-gauge debate.[34] As I noted in the introduction, Prime's first book, *The Power of Prayer* (1864), was a lengthy compilation of testimonies of answered prayers for spiritual conversions surrounding the revival in New York City. Prime issued another catalogue of answered prayers in the fall of 1872, a few months after Tyndall's prayer-gauge challenge. It was virtually identical to the first, except that Prime demonstrated a growing awareness of religious doubt in the culture. He did not suggest at this point, however, that the examples in his book could serve as a refutation to skeptics:

> Those who do not believe that God is, and that He rewards those
> who diligently seek Him, may smile incredulously at the simplicity of
> those who accept these statements as illustrations and proofs of the
> power of prayer. But to us who believe, these are the records of our
> own experience and observation. . . . Skepticism may reject the record.
> But Christianity finds its faith strengthened and its heart cheered by
> these great truths.

Essentially, then, his book was an encouragement to Christians to keep praying for their unsaved friends and relatives; it was not necessarily an answer
to skepticism.[35]

Prime's last book of answered prayer, published in 1882, also showed a
heightened awareness of challenges to prayer. "Let the Pagan philosophers
of the 19th century rage and call to naught the fanatics who believe and
pray," he wrote in reference to Tyndall and Galton. "God has them in de-
rision and so will we." However, Prime had apparently come to reappraise
the apologetic value of answered prayer. Thus, he concluded his final work
with the assertion, "the review of these twenty-five years of prayer, is a more
effective argument against the skepticism of the day than any essay which
the most learned theologian could construct." Prime thus signaled a more
overtly apologetic use of the answered prayer narrative, not only providing
evidence to renew the believer's faith but also serving to confound the skeptic.[36]

The use of answered prayer to refute doubters thus shows up repeatedly
in the popular devotional literature of the late nineteenth and early twentieth
centuries. An anecdote from the life of Hudson Taylor provides one of many
such examples. At one time, Taylor was seriously ill and was treated by a
"skeptical" doctor. As Taylor prayed during his illness, he began to feel a
burden for this doctor. Though he could barely stand up, he sensed God
guiding him to walk two miles to his place of employment to inquire about
a delayed paycheck. Under divine power, he staggered the two miles, received
his pay, then sensed God leading him to go pay his bill to the skeptical
doctor. He did so, and he found that the remaining amount was exactly
enough to pay for a bus fare home. "To my mind," Taylor said, "the whole
thing seemed a wonderful interposition of God on my behalf." When Taylor
relayed the whole story of his walking there and the money, the doctor
"completely broke down, and said with tears in his eyes, 'I would give all
the world for a faith like yours,' " upon which Taylor shared the gospel with
him. Answered prayer had broken down the resistance of the educated skeptic.[37]

The answered prayer as a kind of grassroots apologetics was epitomized
in an incident related by Major Malan, a missionary to South Africa:

> There had been a long drought in the Transkei and throughout the
> country. "I hope we shall soon have rain," a lady had remarked to

me some days previously. I replied that I believed the Lord was
holding off the rain until I had passed the Orange River. She
laughed and asked when that would be. I told her. My faith was verified. I crossed the Orange River at about 11 a.m. today. Another
hour and it began to rain, and by night it was impassable for the first
time this summer. Whatever infidels may write or think, I believe in
prayer, for I always find that my prayers are answered.[38]

As God's emissaries, missionaries especially could expect miraculous answers
to prayer on their behalf and could use them to upbraid those who mocked
their simple, childlike faith.

As the previous anecdotes indicate, answered prayer could function as a
kind of nonelitist apologetics for evangelicals whose piety outstripped their
theological learning. In a characteristic anecdote, Moody, who had only a
fifth-grade education and whose sermons were known for their simplicity,
used answered prayer to awaken his college-educated son to belief in a
prayer-hearing God. Moody and his son were on a ship in a severe storm,
so all those on board prayed. His son was a student at Yale at the time,
recalled Moody, "and the learned professors there have instilled in him some
doubts about God's direct interference in answer to prayer." Therefore, this
situation seemed to Moody to be "the grandest test of prayer I ever knew."
At daybreak, "the waves were stilled and the winds were hushed by Divine
command." His astounded son became a believer in prayer.[39] Answered
prayer apologetics of this sort was thus ideally suited for the world of revivalistic evangelicalism. Bible schools such as Moody's were intended to be
practical training academies for Christian workers who did not have the skills
or educational background for college or seminary. The curriculum focused
on a straightforward knowledge of the Bible and practical Christian ministry
skills. As Moody said, concerning his educational philosophy, "what we want
is men who go right into the shop and talk to men. Never mind the Greek
and Hebrew, give them plain English and good Scripture. It is the sword of
the Lord that cuts deep." In such a culture, the answered prayer apologetic,
with its supposed avoidance of theological pretensions, and emphasis on
observable facts, was quite at home.[40]

Since testimonies of answered prayer were not unique to the late nineteenth century, one may well question what was new about this use of answered prayer. In fact, the late-nineteenth-century evangelical approach to
answered prayer in this respect represents a variation on an old Protestant
theme. Traditionally, Protestants tended to cite the Bible for evidence of
answered prayer of the level three sort. For instance, Jonathan Edwards,
when supporting the assertion that prayer caused "an agreeableness between
His providence and their prayers," marshaled biblical events such as Elijah's
prayers for rain as evidence. Similarly, the colonial American Quaker John
Tomkins wrote a book that contained, as its title indicated, "many eminent

and select instances of God's answer to prayer collected out of the record of the Holy Scriptures." This tradition was perpetuated by late-nineteenth-century evangelicals, often to an astounding degree. William Campbell Scofield's *Bible History of Answered Prayer* (1899), for instance, detailed one hundred thirty-four specific incidents of answered prayer recorded in the Bible.[41]

Protestants had also typically buttressed the biblical evidence of answered prayer with Samuel Prime–style accounts of conversions in answer to prayer. W. S. Tyler of Amherst College, for example, claimed a correlation between the concerts of prayer for colleges, begun in 1820, and the rash of revivals that swept colleges in the 1820s and 1830s, especially since the revivals generally occurred in the winter term when the concert of prayer was observed. Charles Finney too cited numerous examples of such prayers for revival answered.[42]

Late-nineteenth-century evangelicals, of course, continued the tradition of chronicling conversions in answer to prayer. However, in order to convince the skeptic, the Christian needed better examples of answered prayer than mere spiritual conversions. Thus, while all answered prayer narratives included numerous conversion stories, other, more dramatic answers to prayer typically took prominence. As Arthur T. Pierson explained, "unbelief is always ready to suggest that it is not a strange thing if a prayer for the conversion of another is answered, when we have been bending every energy toward the winning of that soul." But if the defender of truth found him- or herself in a situation where a tangible, observable answer to prayer had to come, then answered prayer acquired real apologetic value. Continued Pierson, "when one can do nothing but cry to God, and yet He works mightily to save, unbelief is silenced, or compelled to confess, this is the finger of God." Since accounts of answered prayer were to be evidence to the modern scoffer of the living God, the more remarkable the incident, the better.[43]

This modern answered prayer apologetic also differed from the Puritan Increase Mather's famous *Remarkable Providences Illustrative of the Earlier Days of American Colonization*. Mather's method was similar to that of the answered prayer compilations such as William Patton's *Prayer and Its Remarkable Answers* and D. W. Whittle's *Wonders of Prayer*. Mather sent out a proposal in 1681 to the ministers of Massachusetts that they send him any "illustrative providences" that may have occurred in their districts. The result was a lengthy collection of floods, shipwrecks, earthquakes, strange apparitions, coincidences, and close calls in which prayer was sometimes involved but more often not. One typical "personal deliverance" concerned a man who became accidentally tied to a runaway horse. The horse stopped just long enough for him to slip his foot out of the rope. No prayer was involved, but this event seemed to Mather an example of the mercy of God. In all, Mather's purpose in *Remarkable Providences* was different from that of late-nineteenth-century evangelicals. Mather simply sought to show that God was active in New England, and prayer was tangential to his purpose. Late-nineteenth-century evangelicals, on the other hand, saw their task in different terms. Since prayer itself was the issue and apologetics the purpose of answered prayer literature, only those incidents with "proof value" could serve as evidences of a living God who answered the prayers of his children.[44]

Answered prayer apologetics thus shows the adaptation by American pietistic evangelicals of the Christian doctrine of prayer to a scientific age. The use of answered prayer as apologetics reflected a scientific, empirical impulse that coexisted in late-nineteenth century American evangelicalism with its supernaturalist impulse. James Turner has observed a trend in the nineteenth century toward what he calls "analytical-technical thinking," the belief that knowledge was reliable only when verified in experience. The analytical-technical mind displayed a thirst for precision in knowledge and valued statistics—"the distinctively modern species of fact," in Turner's words. Clearly, scientists such as Tyndall and Galton lived by such principles, as their empirical challenge to prayer demonstrated. Answered prayer advocates also showed their affinity with the scientific temper by accepting the empirical challenge and marshaling data to support the efficacy of prayer. They even used scientific terminology to describe their findings. *I Cried, He Answered* was like "a note-book of the results of laboratory experiments," according to Charles Trumbull, and Presbyterian minister Charles E. Bradt described each request as "a test case before God in the laboratory of faith and prayer." Answered prayer advocates thus displayed a mix of the experiential and analytic minds. They emphasized supernatural reality but verified it with physical data. Their highly experientialist religion emphasized the Holy Spirit and intuition in getting truth, but they sought observable phenomena—even statistics of answered prayer—in confirming that truth.[45]

This paradoxical combination of analytical and supernatural impulses among late-nineteenth-century evangelicals should not be surprising, for it had other parallels in American culture.[46] Nineteenth-century spiritualism exhibited the same traits. The second half of the nineteenth century witnessed a wave of interest in spiritualism in the Western world. One of its appeals, as R. Laurence Moore explains, was that spiritualism "offered Americans a 'reasonable' solution to the problem of how to accommodate religious and scientific interests." It offered people in an age that venerated science the opportunity to believe in spiritual values, but to do so based on empirical data gained from seances rather than from religious pronouncements. In other words, spiritualism was another manifestation of the analytical-technical mind flowing in religious channels in the nineteenth century. Spiritualists used shaking tables to prove life after death, while grassroots evangelicals used answered prayer to prove the living God.[47]

Not all observers, of course, were enamored of this evidentialist use of prayer, even within the Christian community. Critics could point to certain problems with this apologetic strategy. First, it was impossible to isolate any particular event to such an extent as to prove that *prayer* was the causative factor. Coincidence could not be ruled out in any particular case of answered prayer. The renowned psychologist Joseph Jastrow observed:

> It is only necessary to become deeply interested in coincidences, to look about with eyes open and eager to detect them, in order to discover them on all sides; resolve to record all that come to hand, and they seem to multiply until you can regard yourself and your friends as providentially favored in this direction.

In a world of complex phenomena the fact that the wind shifted from north to south after George Mueller's prayer, for example, proved nothing, since it was impossible to pinpoint his prayer as the real cause of this phenomenon.[48]

Answered prayer proponents did not consider this objection to be fatal. Each instance may have been only a remarkable coincidence, but, in a kind of reverse Galtonism, the cumulative force of the incidents was intended to overwhelm the reader. When so many of God's children testified that rain followed their prayers, it was believed, the circumstantial evidence gained in strength. Similarly, in the case of raising funds, one could perhaps explain away one instance of answered prayer, but when this happened over and over again, a convincing argument was thought to have been marshaled. As Mueller recounted, "it has been a rare case that there have been means in hand to meet the necessities of more than 100 persons *for three days* together." Yet the supplies always came in when needed. God, he concluded, worked this way to continually prove himself to be a prayer-hearing God. Thus, answered prayer testimonies were like King Lear's troubles: they marched in battalions rather than alone. The argument was to be cumulative rather than singular.[49]

Another criticism of the answered prayer enterprise concerned Francis Galton's challenge—the problem of unanswered prayer. As one minister exclaimed in the 1870s, "millions of saints are praying, all over the world, and when I ask, 'Are your prayers answered?' they say, 'There's Mueller, at Bristol, see how his prayers are answered.'" This objection was most forcefully stated by the liberal Methodist James Campbell, a noted writer on prayer in the early twentieth century. "Volumes have been written recounting marvelous answers to prayer," Campbell observed, "but many more volumes might be written telling of similar prayers that were not answered." Recounting a well-known incident told by Moody of a miraculous answer to prayer, Campbell said, "a ship is driven on the rocks and is fast sinking, when in answer to prayer the captain of a passing vessel, who has been strangely moved to change his course, comes to its relief. This is regarded as wonderful providence; and so it is." However, continued, Campbell, soon another ship is in danger. "No timely deliverance comes, and they are engulfed in the waves, at the very moment when they are upon their knees." Campbell believed that prayers to stay disaster were sometimes answered, but he criticized placing any evidential value on them. Testing the efficacy of prayer by whether tangible answers come as a result, Campbell warned, "has proved to many a rock on which they have made shipwreck of their faith."[50]

The problem of unanswered prayer on a general level, however, was not especially troubling for answered prayer apologists. This was because their notion of what was truly prayer and who could pray was so exclusive that they did not expect evidence of answered prayer to appear in Christendom as a whole. Answered prayer, these apologists believed, was a by-product of the completely surrendered life, something few Christians had really achieved. It was for the Christian soldier risking his or her life in the line of spiritual duty, as Henry Clay Trumbull, editor of the *Sunday School Times* (and Charles's father) made clear in his 1896 book on prayer. Suppose, wrote Trumbull, a commander sent a colonel and his regiment into battle and said, "Call on me for whatever you want, and you shall have it promptly."

> That promise had reference to you as a soldier, under authority, in
> time of warfare.... If you had asked for forty rounds of ammunition
> per man, or for three days' rations, or for a supply of shovels and
> picks, or for a covering party on either flank, or for an explanation of
> your orders on a doubtful point, you might have been as sure of an
> answer as of the sun in the heavens.... You had a right to make a
> requisition in the line of your designated service.

In the same way, claimed Trumbull, God's promises of answered prayer applied only to those Christians who were working on the front lines of spiritual battle. Most Christians lacked the commitment, concentration, and life of dedication required to truly offer prayer to God. William Patton remarked:

> Multitudes "say a prayer," who yet do no praying. Many Christians
> and churches also pray so defectively ... that they do not come
> within the scope of the Scriptural promises. What is their experience
> worth, then, in the matter before us? It should not be said that their
> prayers are not answered; but that they do not pray—in the Bible
> sense.[51]

Rosalind Goforth's life serves as a vivid example of the soldier's regimen that daily experiences of answered prayer required. Born in London and raised in the cream of Toronto society, she had turned her back on a promising career as an artist to dedicate herself to missions. Living in rural China, she depended on God for her family's subsistence, and thus had earned the right to claim answers to prayer. "Had I been living a life of ease or self-indulgence," she recalled, "I could not have been justified in expecting God to undertake for me in such matters as here recorded. It must be remembered that I had stepped out into a life which meant *trusting for everything*." Rosalind's life was not for the weakly committed. Four of her children died of illness in China. Goforth described her family's experiences during the Boxer Rebellion in which they expected death at any time. During an attack by an angry mob, she recounted, "one struck at the baby, but I parried the blow with a pillow, and the little fellow only received a slight scratch on the forehead." At another point, she recalled,

> Mr. Goforth had jumped off our cart to get fresh water for our head cloths, a crowd gathered round him and became very threatening, raising the cry, "Kill, kill." All the other carts were ahead, and the carter would not wait for Mr. Goforth, as he was afraid. During the few moments that elapsed before my husband was allowed to join us even the carter paled with suspense—and oh, how I prayed!

Not all surrendered lives were as difficult and dramatic as the Goforths', but they were nevertheless lived far above the plane of most everyday Christians. It was upon such lives that the apologetics of answered prayer was built.[52]

A good example of how the problem of unanswered prayer was met by this exclusivist prayer ethic is the case of Galton cited in chapter 1, "prayer for sovereigns." The assassinations of Garfield and McKinley, as mentioned earlier, sparked questions about prayer among some Americans. These apparently unanswered prayers became fodder for Campbell's warning against making too much of answered prayer: "A nation is upon its knees pleading for the life of its ruler; . . . the life of the honored and useful ruler is taken." Such instances, believed Campbell, posed a real difficulty for the doctrine of answered prayer. He concluded that "any theory of prayer that ignores any of these facts must utterly fail to yield satisfaction and to win acceptance."[53]

Answered prayer advocates simply denied that national prayers for dying Presidents were really prayer. A. J. Gordon addressed this issue in the case of President Garfield, an event that opponents of prayer evidently had sought to capitalize on.[54] "We must decline to have this event established as a prayer gauge, as many are insisting on making it," Gordon asserted. Prayer for physical things such as healing requires "the strongest and most enlightened faith" and "minute and obedient submission to every condition named in Scripture." However, the prayers for Garfield—"a call issued by the secular authorities; a day of prayer in which believers and formalists alike unite; the incense of the Romish mass ascending with the intercessions of the Protestant prayer meeting"—hardly measured up to true prayer. "God forbid that we should by the slightest criticism seem to mock the grief of a suffering nation," maintained Gordon, but the national prayer for Garfield "was simply a national fast day, concerning which we proffer no remark." Real prayer, the kind that effected the healing of the sick, "is a service which belongs to the Holy of Holies of the Christian Church, and which cannot be brought out into the court of the Gentiles." The kind of prayer that could be used to demonstrate the existence of a living God was limited to fully surrendered Christians; therefore, answered prayer apologists were not troubled by the kind of counterevidence put forth by Galton and Campbell. To them, the evidence of answered prayer gleaned from the writings of the champions of the faith was more than enough to silence the scoffers.[55]

Thus, criticisms of answered prayer apologetics had little effect on its advocates in turn-of-the-century America. In fact, the use of answered prayer apologetics continued well into the twentieth century, decades after John Tyndall's initial challenge. The answered prayer apologetic culminated in 1911 with Arthur T. Pierson's "Proof of the Living God, As Found in the Prayer Life of George Mueller, of Bristol." This article was Pierson's contribution to *The Fundamentals*, a collection of books distributed throughout the English-speaking Protestant world between 1910 and 1915. Subtitled "A Testimony to the Truth," their purpose was to defend traditional Christianity against the inroads of modern critical thought. Pierson sought to do just that by appealing to Mueller's life, which offered, Pierson asserted, "convincing proof that God hears prayer."[56]

Pierson used Mueller's life to challenge the skeptics with a new version of the prayer-gauge. In language reminiscent of Tyndall and Galton, he proposed to have an "experiment conducted" in "strictly scientific method," only this one was to make the John Tyndalls of the world, not the believers in prayer, look ridiculous. Let an institution be founded similar in every way to that of Mueller's, he suggested, including no direct appeals for funds. The only difference would be that in this test institution, no prayer would be used. When such an institution succeeded, vowed Pierson,

> we shall be ready to reconsider our present conviction that it was because the living God heard and helped George Mueller, that he who began with a capital of one shilling, took care of more than ten thousand orphans ... and in the course of his long life expended about $7,500,000 for God and humanity.[57]

Answered prayer had clearly come to have apologetic purposes for American evangelicals.

Prayer and Twentieth-Century Fundamentalism

The fact that Pierson's answered prayer apologetic appeared in *The Fundamentals* indicates that an important development was taking place in twentieth-century American religion: The emphasis on answered prayer characteristic of late-nineteenth-century evangelicals channeled itself into a large segment of the fundamentalist movement of the twentieth century.[58] Moody Bible Institute, for example, whose early history had been influenced by Mueller and Taylor's faith principles, became known in the twentieth century as "the West Point of Fundamentalism," and Bible conferences held at the school became one of the vehicles through which fundamentalists organized themselves and condemned modernism.[59] Rosalind and Jonathan Goforth, whose lives epitomized the answered prayer narrative, became ardent fundamentalists, even refusing to join the United Church of Canada in 1925 because of its toleration of liberals in the ranks.[60] The fact that Rosalind Goforth's answered prayer narrative was published by Moody Press demonstrates the interdenominational fundamentalist networks that were forming in the early twentieth century. Furthermore, Charles Blanchard, author of *Getting Things from God*, steered Wheaton College into fundamentalist networks in the 1910s and was the first vice-president of the National Fundamentalist Association.[61]

Concerns over modernism, while obviously the motivating factor in fundamentalism, did not push prayer and spirituality to the periphery for these conservatives. The pietistic evangelicalism, out of which answered prayer apologetics emerged, predated fundamentalism and was always larger, both geographically and institutionally, than the antimodernist movement that emerged in some parts of early-twentieth-century conservative Protestantism. Fundamentalism's foremost historian, George Marsden, who defined fundamentalism as "militantly anti-modernist Protestant evangelicalism," also noted that "militancy was not necessarily the *central* trait of fundamentalists. Missions, evangelism, prayer, personal holiness, or a variety of doctrinal concerns may often or usually have been their first interest." The interest in prayer among fundamentalists even during the modernist controversies of the 1920s bears Marsden's assertion out.[62]

Reuben Torrey's example is especially revealing in this context. Torrey, one of Moody's revivalist lieutenants and a popular writer on prayer, went on to become the president of the Bible Institute of Los Angeles in the 1910s and a leading fundamentalist. However, throughout the modernist controversies Torrey retained his pietistic focus. He announced in 1917: "I think if God has given me any special message it has been to call people to prayer." Even in 1924, at the height of the modernist controversies, Torrey published his second book on prayer, *The Power of Prayer*. Furthermore, Torrey's teaching on prayer represented no new fundamentalist innovation but rather rested squarely in the American revivalist tradition. His discussion of the so-called prayer of faith in *The Power of Prayer*, for example, was virtually identical to Charles Finney's teaching on the prayer of faith in his *Lectures on Revivals of Religion* nearly a hundred years earlier. For Torrey, opposition to modernism was never to outweigh a vibrant, experiential prayer life rooted in the American revivalist tradition.[63]

Other leading fundamentalists exhibited the same tendencies. J. Oliver Buswell, Blanchard's successor as president of Wheaton College, offered in 1928 his own book on prayer, *Problems in the Prayer Life*. In good answered prayer tradition, Buswell encouraged his readers to keep a "prayer list" in which to record daily examples of answers to prayer. Torrey's counterpart at the Moody Bible Institute, James Gray, articulated similar concerns. In a 1924 address, Gray proclaimed that "fundamentalism represents a revival of our holy religion." He went on to place fundamentalism in historic succession to seventeenth-century Pietism and eighteenth-century Methodism, movements that spiritually revived the dead orthodoxy of their day. Gray's school clearly backed him up in this claim. In 1922, the Institute's leaders reported that there were 1,324 "stated prayer meetings" being held at the school per month.[64]

One response to the life of prayer in the world of science, therefore, was to emphasize the personal experience of answered prayer, not just as a way to feel God's presence but as a rebuttal to modern skeptics. A strong belief in petitionary prayer survived into the twentieth century among a significant number of American Protestants. Indeed, books on prayer by prominent fundamentalists such as Torrey and Blanchard, one suspects, continue to fill church libraries, long after their condemnations of modernism have become historical artifacts. For these evangelicals, the proof of the living God was just an answered prayer away.

THREE

✜

The Spiritual Unrest

The Cultural Context of Liberal Protestant Devotionalism

By the end of the nineteenth century, the scientific attack on prayer and the conservative Protestant response had been clearly stated. American theologians and professors such as Charles Hodge and Mark Hopkins had written their reasoned defenses of petitionary prayer, while revivalism-oriented evangelicals such as Samuel Prime and William Patton had cited numerous answers to prayer to combat the skeptics. Early-twentieth-century evangelicals, as we have seen, inherited this fervent belief in petitionary prayer and perpetuated the tradition in their own writings.[1] However, by the early twentieth century, in another part of the American Protestant world, a very different understanding of prayer was just beginning to appear. What could be called a recognizably "liberal" Protestant ethic of prayer did not fully emerge until the 1910s.

In fact, if one were to plot on a time line the major classic liberal writings on prayer and devotion, a distinct cluster of writings would appear in the decade of the 1910s. Most notable were Harry Emerson Fosdick's four devotional books, *The Manhood of the Master* (1913), *The Meaning of Prayer* (1915), *The Meaning of Faith* (1918), and *The Meaning of Service* (1920). Along with these, the *Christian Century*'s "Daily Altar" devotional movement (the subject of chapter 7) was launched in 1918. In addition, Henry Churchill King's three-part series "Difficulties Concerning Prayer" appeared in the *Biblical World* in 1915, and Lyman Abbott frequently expounded on prayer during these years in his journal the *Outlook*. The liberal Methodist James M. Campbell published two books on prayer, *The Place of Prayer in the Christian Religion* and *Prayer in its Present Day Aspects*, in quick succession in 1915 and 1916. Other liberal books on prayer and spirituality in this decade included Charles Slattery's *Why Men Pray* (1918), Walter Fiske's *Finding the Comrade God* (1918), and the Quaker Rufus Jones's *World Within* (1916) and *The Inner Life* (1918). Although liberal books on prayer continued to appear in the 1920s—most notably William Adams Brown's *Life of Prayer in a World of Science*—by 1920 the classic liberal ethic of prayer had been fully elucidated.

What explains this interest on the part of liberal Protestants in prayer in the early twentieth century? The liberal ethic of prayer was largely a response by pious churchmen to the perceived cultural milieu of the day. Thus, this chapter explains the specific cultural setting that surrounded liberal Protestants, one that was extremely important to them. While cultural factors such as an analytic/scientific impulse and an emphasis on experience, it has been suggested, contributed to the understanding of prayer among late-nineteenth-century evangelicals, this may be said to have been accidental rather than intentional. Such evangelicals believed that they were simply articulating the ethic of prayer found in the Bible. They were not interested in consciously adapting their theological notions to modern culture; in fact, they specifically tried to resist it.

Liberal Protestants, however, were modernists in the truest sense of the word. At the heart of American Protestant liberalism lay what William Hutchison has called the modernist impulse, that is, "the conscious, intended adaptation of religious ideas to modern culture." Since God was believed to be immanent in the world, modern culture was one manifestation of what God was like. Indeed, it would not be too strong to say that the ideas and values of modern American culture were, for the liberal, part of God's revelation. American culture, however, is too broad a concept. Liberal Protestantism was the adaptation of Christianity to the worldview of respectable American middle-class culture, of which liberals were an influential part. While conservatives became increasingly out of step with American elite culture, the liberals remained firmly ensconced as part of the cultural establishment. They perceived themselves as guardians of American culture; hence what went on in mainstream society played a role in their spiritual writings just as did intellectual developments such as the rise of modern science and divine immanence. The liberal ethic of prayer, then, did not develop in a cultural vacuum.[2]

If one were to label the cultural mood concerning religion that existed in educated middle-class America in the early decades of the twentieth century, one could do no better than the title of a 1909 book, *The Spiritual Unrest*. Cultural observers perceived a yearning for spiritual values and hopes for a better society coupled with a disaffection with the church and traditional Christianity. This mood, which liberal Protestants in large measure shared and which the experience of World War I intensified, formed an important backdrop to the liberal concern for spirituality and helps to explain the flurry of liberal prayer writings during this period.

Harry Emerson Fosdick, in a 1911 article, "Heckling the Church," observed an important trend in the culture when he wrote, "the present vogue is, by any means, to drub the church." The prevailing sentiment, Fosdick noted, was that "Christ is all right, but damn the church." There had of course always existed Americans who generally assented to Christian teachings but exhibited, in historian Jon Butler's words, an "aloofness from churches," and church leaders had often complained about a lack of esteem given their institution by outsiders. Abraham Lincoln and Emily Dickinson are only two prominent examples of nineteenth-century figures who were deeply religious but tended to keep organized religion at a distance. Moreover, many nineteenth-century reformers—among them the abolitionists William Lloyd Garrison and Theodore Weld—had left the orthodox church when they perceived that it was slow to embrace their moral crusades. However, in the early twentieth century cultural observers perceived this disaffection with the church occurring on a broad level in what had been the traditional bastion of the Protestant church: educated, middle-class America. There appeared to be a growing sentiment that the truly spiritual people were not in the church or need not be in the church, and also that the church was late in taking up the chief moral cause of the day: social service. Indeed, some were questioning whether organized Christianity was worth retaining in modern times. In all, the church was being summoned to the bar of social utility and found wanting.[3]

This modern attack on the church appears in the bestselling fiction and middle-class magazines of the day, two excellent barometers of American middle-class opinion. Popular novels are one useful way of getting at this antichurchly attitude, for, as cultural historian James D. Hart has noted, "the popular author is always the one who expresses the people's minds and paraphrases what they consider their private feelings." Ernest Hemingway may have brilliantly expressed the despair of a Lost Generation, but sales figures would indicate that middle-class Americans identified more with the mediocre novels of Charles Sheldon and Harold Bell Wright.[4]

In 1896, Sheldon, a Congregationalist minister in Topeka, Kansas, published what became one of the best selling novels in American history. *In His Steps*, a precursor to the Social Gospel novel, was a mildly critical appraisal of the spiritual complacency of old-stock Protestant churches. In the book, Henry Maxwell, a small-town pastor, is awakened to active Christianity when a "dusty, worn, shabby-looking young man" interrupts his Sunday morning service to reprimand the congregation for failing to live out the religion they profess. The vagrant soon dies, and Reverend Maxwell is spurred on to a new life of Christian discipleship. He gathers a group of volunteers from his congregation, all pillars of the community, and together they pledge to ask in every situation, "What would Jesus do?"[5]

Since these people are prominent members of society, the application of Jesus's principles to everyday life requires significant sacrifices for them. A railroad superintendent decides he must resign his position rather than participate in corrupt business practices. A wealthy young woman with a talented voice gives up a career in the opera in order to sing for tent revivals in the town's saloon district. Also, this being the turn of the century, practical Christianity impels all of them to fight the liquor interests in town, the root of all evil. In the process, they gain a new vision of the Kingdom of God and of Christianity as a matter of conduct, not creeds.

In Sheldon's bestselling novel, all of this spiritual revival and social activism takes place within the confines of traditional organized religion; the pledge-takers remain active church members. Their practical Christianity only makes them more active in church. Reverend Maxwell initiates the pledge with a prayer meeting, "and almost with the first syllable he uttered there was a distinct sense of the Spirit felt by them all." The pledge-takers are constantly driven to prayer in coming days. Sheldon writes: "Within the two weeks since Henry Maxwell's church had faced that shabby figure with the faded hat more members of his parish had been driven to their knees in prayer than during all the previous term of his pastorate." Though Sheldon defines Christianity basically in terms of service, Christian spiritual experience fed by a life of prayer remains its source. Thus, the life of service, of true Christian piety, is open only to those in the Christian church, for, as Maxwell tells his fellow pledge-takers, "[w]e must know Jesus before we can imitate Him."[6]

Furthermore, Sheldon's idea of Christian service is ultimately traditional church work: getting souls. Maxwell's pledge leads him to the tent revivals, where he implores the drunken and lawless working-class people to come to Jesus. His reward is in seeing "the transformation of these coarse, brutal, sottish lives into praying, rapturous lovers of Christ." The church members involve themselves in social reform and fighting the liquor interests, but since in Sheldon's world true change can only come to a person by supernatural regeneration, their ultimate goal remains bringing people the message of the Gospel, however pared down that may be.[7]

In His Steps, then, was in many ways a transitional novel. As a forerunner to the Social Gospel, it urged Christians to take seriously the call to discipleship as it related to the social order, but the result was a mix of revivalism and social work. Moreover, while *In His Steps* criticized the spiritual and social complacency of American churchgoers, it ultimately affirmed the Protestant church as the vehicle of social transformation and Christian spirituality as the wellspring of social service.

A harsher criticism of the church can be seen emerging in the next decade in the works of the prince of early-twentieth-century popular novelists, Harold Bell Wright, a former Disciples of Christ minister from Missouri whose books sold in the millions. Concerning his most popular book, one reviewer wrote: "Best sellers run away and hide when the author of *The Shepherd of the Hills* comes into the running." The *Philadelphia Sunday Dispatch*, trying to probe the depths of Wright's genius, mused: "The secret of his power is the same God-given secret that inspired Shakespeare and upheld Dickens."[8] Historians have typically seen Wright's religious novels as statements of "muscular Christianity," social Christianity, or as an affirmation of country life and traditional values in a modernizing culture.[9] However, these books also serve as a vivid, somewhat autobiographical protest against the church as a beneficial institution in America.

That Printer of Udell's (1903), Wright's first book, was advertised as "A Story of Practical Christianity." Dick Falkner, the hero of the story, is an orphaned, drunken tramp who decides to turn his life around when he learns that his even more drunken father has died. He goes to Boyd City and finds work under George Udell, an unchurched, skeptical, but virtuous printer. There Dick reforms his life and falls in love with the beautiful daughter of the evil, wealthy church elder Adam Goodrich. Though he despises the church because when he needed help churchgoers had ignored him, Dick joins the progressive pastor Cameron and the young people's society at church, thereby becoming involved in their efforts to help the city's poor. This expression of practical Christianity overcomes Dick's antipathy toward Christian hypocrites; he undergoes a traditional walk-the-aisle conversion experience to get right with God and to set things straight in the church. He then leads a cooperative project between church and business leaders to help the poor that revolutionizes the church and city. George Udell and other skeptics become converted by seeing real Christianity lived out, and Boyd City thus achieves the highest church membership in the nation.

Like Sheldon's *In His Steps*, *That Printer of Udell's* expresses the author's frustration with a socially unconcerned church grown complacent with wealth. Reverend Cameron, the Social Gospel pastor, complains: "The world really believes in Christ, but has lost confidence in the church." A rustic character says of church people, "They've been tryin' fer 'bout two thousand years to fix this business, an' ain't done nothin' yet." Nevertheless, Wright does not give up on the church. One of his characters says: "The church with all its shortcomings and mistakes, is of divine origin." It just needs to get back "to the simplicity of Christ's life and teaching." Thus, as with *In His Steps*, the endeavor to change society goes on within the church. Dick Falkner and George Udell join the church, and at the end of the story churches are booming.[10]

While Wright thus affirms the value of the church as did Sheldon, one can detect a shift in the church's function in *That Printer of Udell's*. The spiritual and revivalistic elements found in the *In His Steps* church have largely disappeared in Wright's novel. Christianity is synonymous with service to others; hence the church's function is to actively work for social betterment, not win souls. Pastor Cameron laments when he thinks of "the secret societies and orders, doing the work that the church was meant to do," and concludes that the church must "talk less and do more." It must do "practical work," as the lodges do. Thus, when the church is galvanized into real "ministry," it sets up a settlement house and employment agency for the down-and-out and a reading room where young men can read books and magazines and socialize. Cameron's vision of the church is essentially that of a progressive Rotary Club.[11]

Wright, like Sheldon, collapses Christianity into a way of life, of doing as Jesus would do. His governing verse is "Inasmuch as ye have done it unto the least of these, my brethren, ye have done it unto Me." Yet while Sheldon would have Christians undergo a spiritual conversion as well as help the least of these, Wright leaves out the former. Social work is essentially divorced from any distinct spiritual experience. Thus, although Dick Falkner eventually joins the church, his question remains unanswered: "Where can a fellow go to live the [Christian] life, and why are you and I not living it as well as the people who have their names on the church books? Must I join a company of canting hypocrites in order to get to heaven?"[12]

By 1909, Wright had tired of trying to reform canting hypocrites and had completely left the pastorate to pursue a career in writing. His change in attitude was reflected in *The Calling of Dan Matthews*, a bestseller in 1909 and many years thereafter. Dan Matthews is a rugged, well-bred mountain boy from the Ozarks who, in true Christian fashion, wants to make his life "count for the greatest possible good." Seeing the church as "divinely given to serve the world," Dan decides to become a pastor, because, he says, "I feel that I can serve men better in the church than in any other way." He eagerly takes over his first small-town church, intent on preaching nothing "but the simple old Jerusalem gospel."[13]

Problems soon develop, however. Dan is troubled by the meanness and backbiting of his congregation, from the elders whose words "carried an accusation, a condemnation, a sneer" to those "heresy hunters, who sniffed with hound-like eagerness for the scent of doctrinal weakness in the speeches of their brothers." Moreover, he discovers that the truly virtuous people are outside of the church, people such as the good old Doctor with whom he lives, who dedicates himself to the "great stream of life, that is in the race for the race and finds expression in sympathy and service." Dan meets and falls in love with a beautiful nurse from Chicago, Hope Farwell, who happens to end up in small-town Arkansas and who demonstrates to him true spirituality. Hostile to the church, Hope nevertheless asserts: "I am a Christian if trying to follow faithfully the teachings of the Christ is Christianity."[14]

Under Hope's influence Dan's idea of "ministry" evolves from primarily preaching to that of social service. In his later sermons, writes Wright, there was much about widows and orphans but "not a word of the old Jerusalem gospel." When the parishioners, especially the deacons and elders, oppose Dan's attempts to help a Catholic boy and a woman of questionable character, he begins to lose faith in the church. He becomes impatient with the evangelist who declares "the awful, eternal disaster that would befall every soul that did not accept the particular brand of salvation which he and his church alone offered." He becomes embittered especially toward the "ruling class" of deacons and elders who sought "to prove to the world wherein it was all wrong and they were all right."[15]

Such criticism of the old guard in the church echoes that found in *That Printer of Udell's* and *In His Steps*. But whereas in these earlier books the hero took over and reformed the church, Wright gives up on such an idea in *The Calling of Dan Matthews*. The inertia is just too great; people's minds are not changing rapidly enough. Elder Jordan, paragon of the established church, sees Dan's new outlook as, in Wright's words, "a weakness of Christian character—to be overcome if possible, but on no ground to be tolerated, lest the very foundation of the church be sapped." Dan in turn, who once saw the church as a divinely established institution, now sees it as a "selfish, cruel, heartless thing that men have built up around their opinions, and whims, and ambitions." Eventually, the wise old Doctor explains to Dan that religion, that is, service to humanity, is like a garden, constantly growing, while the church, like the town monument, is simply the fossilized remnant of one group's version of religion.[16]

As a result, Dan Matthews quits the church and becomes a successful businessman, thus fulfilling his real "calling." He had learned that "wherever men toil with strength of body and strength of mind for that which makes for the best life of their kind—that ministry is sacred and holy." For Dan Matthews, and presumably for Wright, the idea of Christian ministry has become universal. Dick Falkner had equated Christianity with social service, but he did so within the sphere of the church. In Wright's ensuing novel, however, the church has nothing to offer society but narrow dogmatism. Far from being a vehicle for social progress, the church in *The Calling of Dan Matthews* is portrayed as a hindrance to it.[17]

Wright continued to crank out bestsellers through the 1920s, but he never again addressed the church or Christianity specifically. Wright's final, vivid farewell to the Christian church was an episode at the close of *Dan Matthews* in which the departing pastor gives the church elder Judge Strong a thrashing "until he lay half-senseless, moaning and groaning in pain, on the ground" and then leaves the town to become a businessman. One may expect American middle-class readers to be scandalized at such a portrayal of the church, and perhaps many were. However, some of Wright's reviewers described the novel as "strong and wholesome," "attractive," and "wholesome in the best sense."[18]

Similar antichurchly themes can be found in the works of another middle-class novelist of the early twentieth century, Winston Churchill. Though by some strange coincidence he came to share the name of a much more famous personage (by present-day standards), the American Winston Churchill earned great popularity and critical acclaim as a novelist in the first two decades of the twentieth century. In 1924, by a vote of 1,753 readers of the *Literary Digest*, he was named fourth in a list of the era's ten greatest writers.

Though usually given to secular themes, Churchill spent the years from 1910 to 1913 reading theology and pondering the social problems of the day. The result was *The Inside of the Cup*, the bestselling novel of 1913. This work was similar to those of Sheldon and Wright but added to the moral dilemma of a minister in a worldly church the intellectual crisis of historical criticism. The minister in Churchill's novel becomes more radical than Reverend Henry Maxwell both theologically and socially.[19]

The Inside of the Cup tells the story of Reverend John Hodder, an Episcopal priest at a large, wealthy, prestigious urban parish. He becomes frustrated with the social complacency and materialism of his congregation, and he grows discontent with charity work for the city's poor, which does little to transform their lives. Hodder's social concerns combine with intellectual doubts when he reads German theology and loses his religious faith. It is reconstructed, however, under the influence of the saintly Mr. Bentley, a former church member who singlehandedly runs a social service organization in the city's slum district. After his conversion to a new Christianity—essentially a blend of transcendental idealism and social Christianity—Hodder brings about a religious revival in his church. Many of the rich capitalists leave, but workers and intellectuals who had been alienated from the church fill the pews. And true to popular novel fashion, Hodder marries the beautiful, equally enlightened daughter of the villainous church elder, Eldon Parr.

For Hodder, even more than for Henry Maxwell, Christianity becomes "not a collection of doctrines, . . . but a mode of life." Devoid of any personal religious experience himself, Hodder concludes that "the whole meaning of life is service to others. . . . All is service." Moreover, as with Dan Matthews, this service is generalized to include just about anything. "Every work of the Spirit is a sacrament," says Hodder. "Not baptism and communion and marriage only, but every act of life." Yet the church is still the arena where Hodder's new ethic of service is worked out. It functions essentially as an organization for recruiting and training social workers. Concerning the evils of capitalism, Hodder tells his parishioners,

> [t]here is one force, and one force alone, able to overcome the power
> of which I speak,—the Spirit of Christ. And the mission of the
> Church is to disseminate that Spirit. The Church is the champion on
> which we have to rely, or give up all hope of victory. The Church
> must train the recruits.[20]

Churchill expressed in *The Inside of the Cup* the belief that a new religious upsurge was on the way. A wise old librarian exclaims to Hodder: "If my opinion's worth anything, I should not hesitate to declare that we're on the threshold of a greater religious era than the world has ever seen." This religion, however, would express itself not in traditional revivals but in social service. And even though Hodder's church succeeds, there remains in Churchill's novel a sense of doubt about whether institutional Christianity is the most efficient vehicle for bringing about social progress. Hodder's fiancee Allison Parr, formerly a religious skeptic, is caught up in his new vision of Christianity; she exclaims: "Oh, I *can* believe in that, making the world a better place to live in, making people happier." And yet, she admits later, "I am willing to work for such a Cause, but . . . I am still unable to identify that Cause with the Church."[21]

Such ambivalence over the church's worth and role in the new religious era was widely expressed in the middle-class journals of the early twentieth century. A spiritual revival was seen to be underway, one that replaced devotion to traditional creeds with a spirit of social service and was largely independent of the church. *Harper's* observed in 1924: "Many who have ceased to believe in traditional theology transferred their religious interest to the hope of social improvement." In this way, "certain values which had once found expression in traditional religious symbols may be preserved in new forms." As Hope Farwell, the icon of piety in *The Calling of Dan Matthews*, had said, "man serves God only by serving men. There can be no ministry but the ministry of man to man." If the Christian church did not minister to men effectively, its usefulness was in doubt.[22]

A short story in *Harper's* in 1916 encapsulated well the mood of many middle-class Americans for whom traditional Christianity had grown stale and who thought it needed reforming in a more service-oriented mode. Juliet Tompkins's "Missionary Blood" was the story of Marilou Truslow, a daughter of a long line of missionaries, who has rebelled and is running in New York City's swinging circles. The missionary zeal of her ancestors is unintelligible to her. Upon reading the story of her grandfather's immense sacrifices in order to bring the Gospel to a native tribe, she marvels, "All that trouble, just for that!" Yet she remains sensitive and deeply self-conscious about her background; "reference to her missionary inheritance was the only attack that roused Marilou. . . . Call her any other name, and she laughed and perhaps agreed with you; but the term 'missionary' was known to have a galvanic effect."[23]

Marilou meets her third cousin Jonathan (far enough removed to allow for romantic possibilities), whose orthodox zeal and petty legalism repulse her. Yet, unlike her nonreligious friends, Jonathan is strong, purposeful, and sincere. She is already dissatisfied with her aimless life, and he makes her aware of something larger than her own life to live for. In the end, Marilou comes to see that

> Jonathan with the bristling antagonisms laid down could change the
> course of history. What he was took on the aspect of a great, lost
> reservoir, needing only to be connected with the world to enrich it
> with its stored-up power and purity. And the woman who saw all this
> and loved him could lead him out.

So Marilou becomes a "missionary" after all, but of a kind very different from her ancestors. Her mission is to get Jonathan—the embodiment of the traditional Protestant church—over his narrowness and petty judgmental nature so that he can work for social betterment.[24]

In 1909, Ray Stannard Baker, a church layman, gave voice to this sentiment in a series of articles in the *American Magazine* that were subsequently published in book form under the title *The Spiritual Unrest*. Baker took stock of the Protestant churches of America and perceived them to be weak, complacent, and decaying despite their impressive buildings, activities, and wealth. However, Baker claimed that a spiritual revival was going on nonetheless:

> More religion is to be found in our life today than ever before, more
> hearts respond to its inspiration; it is found among common men
> and women everywhere. . . . In short, there is not less of moral enthu-
> siasm or spiritual activity in American, rather far more of it, but the
> church somehow has ceased to lead and inspire it as it did in former
> times.

Baker concluded: "Religion is not decaying; it is only the church."[25]

This new faith, as Baker saw it, was not a faith in a vague deity but rather a "faith in people, in the coming of the kingdom of heaven on earth"; thus, the modern settlement house served for Baker as the modern equivalent to medieval cathedrals. He believed he saw "the true spirit of religion" in a tuberculosis exhibit in New York City where he "seemed to feel a great surge of faith in the possibilities of a newer, finer, sweeter life in New York City, without creed, or doctrine, or church edifice." The problem with the institutional church, Baker asserted, was that it had failed to fully catch on to the new spirit of religion. "The church, even the institutional church, is still content with a religion that is a thing apart, that concerns only small, superficial things."[26]

Baker thus applied the test of service not just to individuals but to institutions: "The final test is service, and to that end institutions and professions must shape themselves." Every human institution has one supreme function: to serve the people in one way or another. "It is as proper to ask of a church as of a railroad company: Is it doing its work efficiently?" According to Baker, the work of the church was to "draw all men together in a more friendly and democratic relationship." It needed to be evaluated on the basis of how well it performed that function. We need to ask the church, he concluded, "what are you doing that you should be retained as the approved tool of civilization?"[27]

H. A. Overstreet, a professor of philosophy at City College of New York, echoed Ray Stannard Baker in outlining the new task of the church, as he saw it. In a 1914 article for *Forum*, Overstreet asserted that "God the Perfect

Person no longer lives to hear the old supplications." Thus, real prayer was not addressing words to a nonexistent deity; rather, "there is prayer wherever there is service, service of any kind that makes for self-betterment." What, then, was the role of organized Christianity? The church of the future, he said, "will primarily be a clearing house of service." If the church failed to generate efficient, effective social service, other institutions would have to replace it.[28]

Many felt that the church did not measure up. In response to claims that a decline in Sunday School attendance meant a decline in spirituality, a contributor to the *Atlantic* wrote: "It is doubtful whether at any past time so many of our ablest men have given themselves with anything like the devotion of our own age to the causes that make for truth and righteousness." The disinclination on the part of parents to send their children to church reflects, he avowed, "not an unwillingness to have them attend the 'house of God,' but a profound doubt whether the church may always fairly be described as the house of God." Another writer noted "vast and constantly increasing numbers" of what she called "unsocial Christians" who did not associate with the church. They "bring such intelligence as they have to bear on the relation of the various churches to Christ, and find that relation too frail, too disingenuous, too inconsistent, to become, or to remain, committed and militant members thereof."[29]

Titles in these middle class magazines such as "The Failure of the Church," "Ought I to Leave the Church?" "Shall I Remain in the Church?" and "Shall We Send Our Children to Church?" reflected the outlook of many middle-class Americans. One layperson lamenting the state of his local church remarked sadly: "If a man . . . should say to me, 'I want to put my life where it will count most. Ought I to come to your church?' I, to be conscientious, would have to reply, 'No; there are a thousand fields needing such ministrations as yours far more than we need them, and yielding to you a richer harvest.'" A minister who explained in *Harper's* why he wanted to become a pastor admitted: "[M]ost of my acquaintances seem to regard it as an exhibition of magnificent folly."[30]

In "The Failure of the Church," Edward Lewis, himself a former pastor, argued that while religion was reviving, the Christian church was decaying and bound to pass away. This was because, first, it was a "closed system" that "believes in its own potential finality, . . . that in essence it is the final word in Religion," and also because of "its despair of the world," its tendency to see the world as sinful and to look to another life to come: "For the robust, vigorous, vital self-reliant, venturesome man, . . . the Church has no message, no pride in him, no acclaim for him, no smiling 'bon voyage.'" Thus, because of its dogmatism and pessimism, concluded Lewis, "Christianity as we know it today, must ultimately be dissolved in a new religious synthesis. . . . The passage into this 'Beyond Christianity' is inevitable in the natural course of events." Concerning the prevalence of such a position, the

Atlantic's editor claimed that Lewis "typifies in large measure that spirit of religious revolt which is one of the most interesting phenomena of our time." A few years later, Herbert Parrish, in an article entitled "The Breakup of Protestantism," exclaimed: "It is my conviction that the sooner Protestantism disappears from American life the better."[31]

Such sentiments, regardless of how prevalent certain observers thought them to be, do not represent Americans as a whole. Church attendance rates for the early twentieth century reveal no widespread disaffection with organized religion. However, for mainline Protestant leaders, the *perception* of disaffection among a significant segment of American Protestantism's historic constituency—the white Anglo-Saxon educated middle-class—was a matter of some concern.

One way to react to such criticisms of the church, of course, was to reject the assumption that the purpose of the church was social betterment. This was the response of Protestant traditionalists. For instance, the Presbyterian minister John J. Munro exclaimed in the *Presbyterian*:

> Public opinion in our day has ceased to demand that a man should belong to a church to be pure, righteous and holy. Let men and women be charitably disposed, and the world will laud them to the skies. Within a quarter of a century, there has been a craze for settlements, parish houses, charities and benevolences, and these have almost destroyed personal piety and the real work of the Church of the Living God.

That "real work," conservatives believed, was to make known the offer of salvation from sin.[32]

Since sin and coming judging were the real facts of existence, orthodox Protestants believed, the church's central task was not social service but preaching the traditional gospel. "If men be not lost, and if the Bible be not a revelation from God to show them the only way of salvation, . . . then why insist upon Christianity as we do, and why seek to propagate it at so great a cost?" asked *Christian Worker's Magzine*. If the Protestant churches were moribund, conservatives believed, it was because they were not preaching the old doctrines, not because they had failed to join the social service crusade. "Churches would be revived and the cause of the Lord would prosper at home and abroad," they claimed, "if the truth were really taught and if men and women knew the eternal condemnation that is impending." The Baptist conservative William Bell Riley exclaimed: "We have got to preach the gospel message to have a future for the church. . . . It works, and nothing has been found as a possible or even passable substitute for the same." As for the disaffection of the young generation with the church, the fundamentalist pastor Hillyer Hawthorne Straton claimed: "[A]ll I do is to preach the word of God, and it holds the young people as well as the old." Traditionalists believed that preoccupation with social service and eschewing of doctrine was the *cause* of the decline of the church, not the solution to it.[33]

Other Protestants, however, too closely shared the assumptions of those disaffected with the church to propose these apparently outworn solutions. Indeed, the affinities between the secular writers discussed earlier and liberal Protestants are obvious. Like Marilou Truslow in "Missionary Blood," liberal Protestants found traditional Christianity untenable. Their choice, they claimed, lay between liberal Christianity or none at all.[34] The old dogmas propagated by conservatives they saw as a reproach to true religion. They shared Edward Lewis's criticism of traditional churches as dogmatic and pessimistic and they praised the spiritual mettle of the unchurched. The liberal Methodist Charles Fiske wrote: "God has many unattached followers, men of religious feelings and convictions who are not enrolled anywhere as Christian believers, . . . men who are doing Christ's work and yet have not the stimulus of fellowship in Christ's Church."[35]

Since they saw religion as primarily a matter of service, liberals shared the view of the church as an important vehicle for social betterment. Explaining his rationale for the church, Fosdick argued that those who are motivated to work for social progress "must combine in a fellowship of faith and of labor to seek common ends. . . . And to fall in with others to serve Christian ends means some kind of church." For the liberals as for the critics of the church, the essence of religion was a life of service to others. The true way to God, *Christian Century* editor Herbert Willett explained, was "the simple and homely way of loving service to our fellow men. God is among His people, and we shall find Him in the degree to which we enter into the struggles and needs of men and women in the work-a-day world." Such remarks closely resembled those found in *Harper's* and the *Atlantic*.[36]

However, an important distinction set liberals apart from many critics outside the church. While sharing secular America's enthusiasm for social service, liberal Protestants remained deeply spiritual men and sought to base social betterment in Christian spirituality. Unlike Dan Matthews, who had discarded piety as well as church dogma, liberal Protestants retained spiritual devotion. Their mindset was best expressed in a short devotional entitled "The Primary Thing Which Should Be Permanent" by the early-twentieth-century devotional writer George Matheson:

The first faith is not always the best; thy thought of the Father may be purified by the fire through which it passes, but thy first love, thy morning love, that ought not to die! . . . There may be starless nights to the eye of the intellect; the old tongues may cease in which faith once expressed itself. . . . But, if thy *love* remain, the eye of the *heart* will not be starless. . . . Never let out the fire of the heart!"

The first generation liberals, typically raised in devout Protestant homes, sought to maintain the heartfelt religious devotion of their parents even as the old thought forms of Christian orthodoxy died off.[37]

The practical, devotional spirit of early liberalism infused the first liberal textbook of theology, William Newton Clarke's *Outline of Christian Theology*. The theologian, said Clarke, needs to be a person in whom the life of Christianity exists in vigor and fullness. "The qualities of the Christian character and the habits of the Christian life need not only to be approved but to be possessed. Prayer and fellowship with God must be moulding influences in the personal life." Using his book to teach theology to students at Colgate University (among them Harry Emerson Fosdick), Clarke closed with the words: "[T]he work of our classroom will have accomplished its purpose if young men go out from it with the true secret of the Lord in their hearts, with a faith that cannot be perplexed, a love that burns in fellowship with him who gave himself for men, and a hope unquenchable."[38]

This pietistic bent led liberal Protestants to applaud the social temper of the day but also to insist that Christian spirituality had to undergird it for any lasting benefits to accrue. This spiritual underside to social service set liberal Protestants apart from their peers outside the church. True service, they believed, could only be generated from a renewed inward life. Said Fosdick: "The great need of the world is for spiritual quality in men, for depth and altitude of soul, for wealth of inward life, out of which special deeds shall come like a brook from the mountains, with power." Thus, while liberals commended the social spirit of the age, they warned that an overemphasis on service could lead to superficiality. Lyman Abbott wrote: "Savonarola said that, in his time, the saints were so busy talking to God that they had no time to listen to Him. In our time there is danger that the saints will be so busy serving that they have no time to listen." Fosdick feared that "in its splendid enthusiasm for work" his generation had "neglected that culture of prayer, on which the finest quality of spirit and deepest resources of power must depend."[39]

Liberals feared that without deep roots in spiritual experience, the exemplary social spirit being displayed in their generation would wither and die. William J. Dawson, a Methodist pastor and traveling speaker, wrote:

> God soon fades out of the life of the man who does not pray. And if
> our consciousness of God diminishes, we may also be sure that it
> will not be long before the spiritual energies, which are a source of
> all our pious activities, will diminish too; and with them the activities
> themselves will be atrophied or arrested.

For liberals, devotion to social service was not a substitute for spirituality but an outgrowth of it.[40]

The Social Gospel lay at the root of liberal Protestant concerns in the early twentieth century, yet for many liberals, the success of the Social Gospel depended on the retention of Christian piety in individuals' lives. The new social order based on Christian love was possible only if individuals were infused with spiritual power. A good society was founded on good individuals, yet, exclaimed Fosdick, "as well might a tree try to be sound without drawing on the physical energies that are around it, as a man might expect to be inwardly good without appropriating the help of the Spirit of God." Herbert Willett echoed: "[T]he new society cannot be solved by laws and devices of state, but only by the spiritual forces centering in men of moral high-mindedness and unselfish devotion to the public good." Personal piety, therefore, was essential to the creation of the kingdom of God on earth. The liberal Quaker Rufus Jones wrote: "[W]e cannot shuffle the cold, hard, love-less atoms of our social world into lovely forms of cooperative relationship. The atoms must be changed." Charles Slattery, an Episcopal minister in New York, summarized the liberal fusion of Social Gospel optimism and Christian spirituality when he wrote:

> There is a dazzling plan, shining before humanity, of a world where Christian nations exist as well as Christian individuals, where inter-national relationships are honestly Christian as well as the relation-ships between two people living on the same street. . . . To pray is to make oneself ready to receive such visions for the individual and for the world.

For these Christians, the Social Gospel and personal piety were inextricably linked.[41]

If the desire to provide spiritual underpinnings for the new society helps explain the liberal concern with spirituality in the early twentieth century, the experience of World War I was an important catalyst. The war intensified liberal Protestants' awareness of the need for vibrant spirituality and appar-ently convinced others of this as well. If prayer is common in foxholes, as many have claimed, it may be said that the Western world experienced a foxhole mentality in the late teens. As a result, observed *Current Opinion* magazine in 1914, "a widely prevalent state of mind produced by the great war is represented by the editorial exhortation: 'At least we can pray.'" Charles Jefferson wrote:

> The immediate effect of war is to drive men to their knees. Any sud-den catastrophe awakens the soul, and the soul, when facing imme-diate peril, throws itself back on God. It is as true today as it was when the Hebrew poet wrote the 107th Psalm, that when men are overtaken by disaster, they cry unto the Lord in their trouble.

The Presbyterian *Continent* noted what it believed was a "prayer revival" underway during the war years. One of the more prominent Presbyterians, the missionary statesman Robert Speer, claimed in retrospect that "there was more praying in America among all classes of people than ever before in our history."[42]

In Scotland, the University of Saint Andrews in 1916 issued a worldwide summons for essays on prayer with a one-hundred-pound prize to the essay deemed most useful because, trustees said, "at this time of world-tragedy the significance of prayer in daily life is everywhere becoming more widely recognized." The United States was second only to England in number of contributors, and an American clergyman, the Episcopalian Samuel McComb, won first prize. The essays as a whole revealed, according to their compiler, "the discontent of a section of Christians with commonplace Christianity, and their aspiration after the deeper or more ecstatic experiences."[43]

Many liberal Protestant devotional writings reflected this renewed emphasis on prayer and the spiritual life that the war sparked. Some of the connections were quite obvious, such as Walter Fiske's *Finding the Comrade God: The Essentials of a Soldierly Faith*, a 1918 liberal devotional that baptized the American war effort and appropriated martial terminology for the Christian life. On a more general level, however, liberal Protestants sought to provide spiritual underpinnings for the effort of war and rebuilding that would follow. As Fosdick observed in *The Challenge of the Present Crisis*, "we are challenged by this war . . . to a new experience and a more intelligent expression of vital fellowship with God." His four devotional books, the first of which (*The Manhood of the Master*) was distributed to American soldiers in Europe, along with other liberal writings in these years, sought to motivate modern readers to seek vital fellowship with God.[44]

Rufus Jones, who wrote two books on spirituality during the war, explained the spiritual task as seen by liberal Protestants:

> The struggle for a conquering inner faith has in these strenuous days
> been laid upon us all. The easy, inherited, second-hand faith will not
> do for any of us now. We cannot stand the stern issues of life and
> death with any feeble, formal creed. We demand something real
> enough and deep enough to answer the human cry of our soul to-
> day.

The war in Europe, Jones continued, will not be won with military brute strength. "Those impalpable things which we name *faith* and *vision* and *spirit* and *nerve* are greater elements in the determination even of outside victories than are miraculous long-distance guns." Even after the war, Jones said, "we cannot build this new world of ours out of material stuff alone. . . . The ultimate issue will turn upon the quality and character of the *soul* of those of us who are to do the building." Thus, Jones concluded, the war years were "a particularly opportune time to speak of the interior world where the issues of life are settled and the tissues of destiny are woven."[45]

Prayer and devotion, therefore, remained important to liberal Protestants, even as they left behind old dogmas and focused on social transformation. The liberal Episcopalian Joseph Fort Newton wrote that "spiritual sanity and balance demand that we take time to cultivate the deeper, quieter life, if our social service is not to be fretful and disappointing." "An immense amount of good work is done by all branches of the Christian church," observed the Congregational pastor George Gordon. However, Gordon believed that a religion of mere service was destined to come up short. "The pervasion of man's whole being by the Eternal is what we need." This interest in under-girding social reform with deep spiritual impulses explains in part the plethora of liberal writings on prayer in the early twentieth century.[46]

Liberal Protestants earnestly sought to give modern Americans convincing reasons why Christian prayer should not be left behind along with other traditional beliefs such as the virgin birth. However, expounding on prayer was not as simple a task for liberal Protestants as it had been for devotional writers of earlier eras or even for their modern conservative counterparts. Liberals could not simply tell Americans to pray more or pray harder. A variety of ideological factors, many of them unique to liberalism, made it necessary to reappraise the traditional understanding of prayer. The next chapter explores factors that made traditional prayer problematic for liberal Protestants.

FOUR

⊹

Divine Immanence

The Ideological Context of Liberal Protestant Devotionalism

To understand why prayer became problematic for liberal Protestants in the early twentieth century, an excursion into the intellectual universe of classic liberalism is necessary. The prayer-gauge debate of the late nineteenth century had proceeded on the basis of a traditional Christian cosmology, one that posited a personal God who created the universe and remained separate from it. This cosmology was expressed by Charles Hodge in his *Systematic Theology*, which appeared concurrently with the prayer-gauge debate. "Prayer," Hodge had said, "takes a great deal for granted." Among other things, it assumed a personal God "independent from the world" who listened to the prayers of his children and sometimes adjusted the natural order of the world in answer to prayer. This Christian God could operate "without second causes as well as with them, or against them." Conscientious theologians such as Hodge preferred the term "special providence" to miracle, since the latter term was reserved for the biblical epoch. But by whatever term, the effect was the same: God, Christians believed, supernaturally altered the state of the universe in answer to prayer. As the turn-of-the-century Chautaucqua lecturer William Kinsley explained, an answer to prayer required that God "interfere by stepping outside his general providence, in which the evil and the good are served alike, to confer especial favors."[1]

This cosmology underlay Britain's prayers for the Prince of Wales and America's prayers for President Garfield. In each case, Christians were praying that God would intervene with the natural order, either by giving doctors special knowledge and skill or by directly healing the leader. Similarly, when George Mueller prayed for a change in the direction of the wind, he was seeking a special providence of God. Even prayers for spiritual conversions such as those of Samuel Iraneous Prime were based on a traditional supernatural conception of the universe. Petitioners were asking God to break into the natural order to directly influence the soul of a friend or relative. Scientists such as Tyndall were in turn trying to close off nature to divine interference, to impose, in Robert Bruce Mullin's words, a "hermetic separation" of the spiritual and natural worlds.[2]

However, for some Protestants in the late nineteenth century, this traditional conception of the universe became increasingly difficult to defend. Liberal Protestantism was predicated on a fundamental revision of traditional supernaturalism. As William Hutchison has observed, the heart of the movement was an obliteration of the distinction between the religious and the secular, and by implication the natural and the supernatural. Henry Churchill King, a noted liberal, exclaimed: "our generation has witnessed the denial of the separation of the sacred and the secular." This redefinition of the relationship between God and the universe made petitionary prayer problematic to liberal Protestants.[3]

An explanation of how individual liberal Protestants came to understand and practice prayer would undoubtedly have to take into account each person's unique personality, background, and life experiences—a well-nigh impossible task. Nevertheless, a number of factors within the movement as a whole—each of them related to some degree or another to the idea of divine immanence—worked to push liberal Protestantism toward new understandings of petitionary prayer. For the sake of clarity, the various ways that divine immanence pushed liberals to redefine prayer can be divided into four categories—their understanding of the world, their understanding of God, their veneration of science, and their view of the Bible. These factors led American Protestant liberals to depart from the traditional understanding of prayer even while promoting Christian spirituality as an integral part of modern life.

A True Naturalism

At the heart of Protestant liberalism lay the doctrine of divine immanence. This was the belief that, as William Newton Clarke declared in his theological textbook, "God in the universe is like the Spirit of a man in his body." For too long, complained liberal forerunner A. V. G. Allen in 1884, Christian theology had been "built upon the ruling principle that God is outside the world and not within." However, Allen proclaimed that "the idea that God is transcendent . . . is yielding to the idea of Deity as immanent in His creation." A change so fundamental, he continued, "involves other changes of momentous importance in every department of human thought, and more especially in Christian theology." Protestant liberalism was in large part the corresponding revision of Christian theology to fit the concept of an immanent God.[4]

The most original and influential articulator of divine immanence in America was Borden Bowne, a professor of philosophy at Boston University.[5] His two main works on the subject, *The Immanence of God* (1905) and *Personalism* (1908), represented the liberal doctrine of divine immanence in its most complete form. Sensory objects, according to Bowne, have only a symbolic importance. Like words on a page, they are meaningless except as symbols of something deeper. An act such as a kiss, for example, is the manipulation of sense objects by persons for symbolic purposes. As human beings, said Bowne, "we impress ourselves upon the spatial system and manifest our thought and purpose in it and through it"; thus the face of the earth reflects our will. In the same way, concluded Bowne, "there is a great invisible power behind the space and time world as a whole, which is using it for expressing and communicating its purpose." Thus, believed Bowne and classic liberals, the universe was "a world of persons with a Supreme Person at the head" and the visible world was "only the flowing expression and means of communication of those personal beings." Visible objects were the means of discourse between humans and God.[6]

Through this doctrine of divine immanence, liberal Protestants claimed to offer an alternative to the naturalism of science and the supernaturalism of orthodoxy, which seemed to be at loggerheads. Bowne's book *The Immanence of God* sought to rescue readers from two equally erroneous ideas, "the undivineness of the natural and the unnaturalness of the divine." We are slowly outgrowing the crude anthropomorphism and "sense dogmatism" of an earlier day that made for deistic religion on one hand and skeptical naturalism on the other, began Bowne. Both orthodox Christianity and naturalistic science erred by separating God from the world and viewing the natural order as a self-sustaining mechanism. Instead, God was "the omnipresent ground of all finite existence and activity." The Congregationalist minister George A. Gordon concurred; just as the human body was the mechanism through which the human spirit expressed itself, so the universe was the mechanism through which the Eternal Spirit expressed itself.[7]

However, argued Bowne, the presence of God in nature meant not that he was here and there in the world performing miracles, but rather "that the whole cosmic movement depends constantly upon the divine will and is an expression of the divine purpose." A "false supernaturalism," Bowne said, looks for God in "melodramatic irruptions" such as storms and miraculous healings, but the "instructed theist" has learned not to fear naturalism, "for naturalism is now merely a tracing of the order in which the divine causality proceeds." Thus, the age-old distinction between general and special providences was obsolete, according to Bowne, for "all providences are special providences."[8]

All of this meant that there was no such thing as miracles, or rather, *all* was miracle. A miracle, Bowne explained, was "simply an event in which the divine purpose and causality which are in all things could be more clearly traced." As George Gordon explained in *Religion and Miracle*, "if there appears to be no longer any room left for miracle, it is that the whole creation may appear miraculous." Union Seminary professor William Adams Brown went so far as to label as miracles such items as "a sunrise, for example, or a birth, or the look in a woman's eyes." In other words, liberals such as Bowne believed that miracles were "interpretations rather than descriptions." When biblical writers described miracles, they were merely expressing in prescientific modes "a strong conviction of God's presence and activity," claimed Bowne, not that there were no natural causes for the event. Bowne thus advocated what he called a "true naturalism," one that saw the natural order as divine and the divine working in strictly natural ways.[9]

This new understanding of miracles had important implications for liberal prayer writings, for when it came to petitionary prayer, Bowne's "true naturalism" sounded strikingly similar to Tyndall's scientific naturalism. Wrote Bowne, "all is law; all is God. All is God; all is law. We read it either way. . . . For those who have not learned the lesson of law, who are seeking short cuts, . . . we say, All is law." Was not praying for the healing of a President a short cut? Was the drought-stricken farmer who prayed to God for rain instead of patiently waiting on the forces of nature seeking a short cut? Was not even praying for the dramatic spiritual conversion of a loved one seeking a short cut? The logical conclusion of Bowne's doctrine of divine immanence—of a God that worked exclusively through the natural order and did not allow short cuts—would seem to wipe out the traditional notion of petitionary prayer.[10]

Such, however, was not necessarily the case. In fact, in relation to prayer and the supernatural, divine immanence was a protean term, cited by liberals and traditionalists alike. While for some Protestants the doctrine of divine immanence necessitated Bowne's "true naturalism," others writing on prayer around the turn of the century used divine immanence in an opposite fashion: to justify supernatural intrusions of God into nature in answer to prayer. From Bowne's point of view, of course, these latter writers just didn't get it.

Even among Bowne's fellow Methodists, the doctrine of divine immanence was often cited in order to negate "true naturalism." The Reverend E. S. Smith, for example, writing in the *Methodist Review*, rested the doctrine of prayer on the distinction between special and general providence. Scientists, Smith recognized, opposed petitionary prayer because it stood in the way of an all-comprehensive philosophy of matter. "Many Christians feel the pressure of these assaults, and are disposed to yield the doctrine of a special providence, and rule prayer out of the material realm as an irrational performance." For Smith, the culprit behind scientific naturalism had been the emphasis on God's transcendence that Augustine brought into the church and whose logical outcome was naturalism. But with the idea that God was immanent in his creation, Smith believed, God was free to work in any way he saw fit, just as humans did. The blooming of the flowers and the raising of Lazarus from the dead were equally supernatural but *possible* ways that God worked in the natural world. While Borden Bowne—whom Smith ironically quoted—used divine immanence to wipe out the distinction between general and special providences (and by extension do away with the latter), Smith used immanence to make them both equally possible.[11]

In a similar fashion, the Methodist William Kelly decried the "decided tendency to deny specific answers and to eliminate the element of petition" that he detected among some Christians. Kelly maintained that petition was the heart of prayer and that "the now generally accepted doctrine of the immanence of a personal God implies the possibility of answer." Though God was immanent in the natural world (or rather *because* God was immanent), "if he should see fit to deviate from his usual course of action at the request of a human being there is nothing and no one to hinder him." On this basis, Kelly justified praying for rain, showing that the doctrine of divine immanence was a truly protean concept among Methodists.[12]

This linking of divine immanence and traditional supernaturalism was not unique to Methodists. The Presbyterian Leander Chamberlain justified prayer through divine immanence. In fact, nothing exemplified the divergent approaches to divine immanence better than the contrasting analogies of language used by Chamberlain and Borden Bowne. To Bowne, who discerned the revelation of God in the order of nature and the gradual unfolding of history, miracles in the traditional sense would be "irrational interjections, and not parts of articulate speech." However, according to Chamberlain, a miracle was analogous simply to raising one's voice: "At no time is it more a violation of the fundamental plan of nature, than a teacher's unusual tone of voice, in admonishing an inattentive pupil, is a violation of the laws of articulate utterance." These analogies illustrate the divergent understandings of divine immanence.[13]

One cannot simply conclude, then, that an understanding of the world as permeated by God's presence forced liberal Protestants to alter traditional notions of petitionary prayer. No inevitable line of causation between belief in divine immanence and lack of belief in petitionary prayer can be established. Rather, three additional factors—the liberal understandings of God, science, and the Bible—worked in conjunction with the doctrine of immanence to help push liberal Protestants away from traditional notions of prayer.

"How Shall We Think of God?"

In 1926, Harry Emerson Fosdick wrote an article for *Harper's* magazine entitled "How Shall We Think of God?" The question was an important one for liberals desiring to maintain and promote a vibrant spiritual life. "Unless there is a real God to whom to pray," explained William Adams Brown, "we shall soon stop praying." Yet liberals wanted to avoid what they considered to be the crude anthropomorphism of their predecessors. They sought to think of God in a more spiritual, intellectual, and abstract way, but doing so had important implications for the Christian doctrine of prayer. If the liberal understanding of the world made traditional modes of prayer seem unreasonable, the liberal understanding of God made prayer as commonly understood seem unspiritual.[14]

Liberal thinking about God reflected the change in epistemology effected by Immanuel Kant that had had far-reaching implications in the modern world. Kant forced philosophers to reconsider the possibility of gaining objective knowledge about the nature of reality. Since all perception was filtered through the human categories of space, time, and causation, Kant argued, humans did not have access to what was really "out there" but only their subjective apprehension of it. Kant thus led thinkers to concentrate on the observable realm, "phenomena," and give up pretensions of gaining any certain knowledge about "noumena," or spirit. Friedrich Schleiermacher applied Kant's ideas to religion, locating the source of religion in the human consciousness—in a feeling of dependence—rather than in objective revelation.[15]

Liberal Protestants inherited this epistemological tradition, and thus while God may have also been transcendent, since God was only known in his works, it was his immanence that was emphasized. Humans had two means of access to knowledge about God, liberals believed: the steady unfolding of history and the inner consciousness. In each case, it was the immanent side of God—the point at which he intersected with humanity—that was revealed. Whatever else God was like was beyond the capabilities of human knowledge. Traditionally, Christians had supplemented this "general revelation" of God with "special revelation" in the Bible—objective propositions that told humans about God apart from what could be gained from human experience. However, Fosdick wrote, "God can be experienced only within our own hearts. . . . If we are to think of the Eternal at all, we must think in terms of something drawn from our experience."[16]

The importance of this epistemological tradition to the liberal idea of God was that while traditional Protestants had unreservedly used anthropomorphic concepts of God drawn from the Bible (God's revelation) when explaining prayer, liberal Protestants sought to conceive of God in what they considered more spiritual and less vulgar terms. Central to the liberal thought of God was what William Hutchison has called a Germanizing trend that influenced American liberalism beginning in the 1890s. Many of the important liberal theologians of the early twentieth century, including Borden Bowne, William Adams Brown, George Coe, Henry Churchill King, and Shailer Mathews, received part of their training in Germany. The personal idealism of the German theologian Rudolf Hermann Lotze, his pupil Albrecht Ritschl, and Ritschl's disciple Adolf von Harnack dominated American liberalism into the 1920s.[17]

This Germanizing trend lay at the root of the doctrine of divine immanence as conceived by liberal Protestants. German idealism, even when modified by Bowne's personalism, put forth a less anthropomorphic deity than that of traditional Protestantism and one less likely to base the running of the universe on the personal decisions of humans whether or not to pray. While it may not have been the "oblong blur" that opponents of liberalism in the twenties called it, the immanent God founded in Kantian epistemology bore little resemblance to the anthropomorphic, willful, prayer-hearing God of the Bible.[18]

It was no accident, then, that the German idealist tradition had little room for petitionary prayer as American Protestants had conceived of it. Immanuel Kant, for one, castigated petitionary prayer. Along with his "Religion within the Bounds of Reason Alone" came an understanding of prayer within the bounds of reason alone. Kant viewed prayer as aspiration after higher things. Voicing petitions was merely "fetish faith." The end of religion, Kant believed, was ethics, and prayer served to establish the desired goodness in the one who prayed. It did not induce God to alter the order of the universe for one's personal advantage. Prayer, he concluded, "is a way of working on oneself. One is quickening one's disposition by means of the idea of God." The German religious historian Friedrich Heiler called Kant's understanding of prayer "philosophical prayer," a version of prayer with a long lineage from Stoicism to Voltaire.[19]

Kant's disciple Friedrich Schleiermacher, generally considered to be the father of modern religious liberalism, placed the locus of religion not in ethics but in feeling. Still, his idea of prayer was quite similar to that of Kant in that he thought petition played little part in prayer. Echoing Kant, Schleiermacher described prayer as the attempt to get oneself in agreement "with the order according to which Christ rules his church, so that the person who prays may as such be regarded as a true and acceptable representative of Christ." The results of such prayer were purely subjective. One should nevertheless present requests to God in prayer, Schleiermacher affirmed, as long as one realized that doing so was only "a means of allaying our disquietude." However, the idea that one should actually expect God to intervene in the world to answer one's requests was, he claimed, "a lapse into magic."[20]

The towering figure in nineteenth-century German liberal theology Albrecht Ritschl also conceived of prayer in a way quite different from American traditional Protestantism. For him, the essence of prayer was thanksgiving. Prayer was "thanksgiving, acclamation, praise, recognition, and worship of God." "Thanksgiving is not a kind of prayer beside petition," Ritschl maintained, "but is the universal form of prayer; and petition is only a modification of the prayer of thanksgiving to God." Ultimately, for Ritschl prayer was "the expression of humility and patience and the means of confirming oneself in these virtues."[21]

To the extent, then, that American liberals imbibed the view of God put forth by German idealists, their ethic of prayer would encounter the same difficulty that an abstract deity created. Asking for things simply did not seem to square with a "more spiritual, more intellectual, more comprehensive interpretation of the Christian faith," as A. V. G. Allen had called the doctrine of divine immanence. "The very act of spiritualizing our conception of God and of the world," the liberal Methodist George Coe warned, "involves danger of vagueness, and consequent lack of intensity in the sense of personal relationship to the divine."[22]

Liberals lampooned conservative notions of God as, in Fosdick's words, "an individual off somewhere, inhabiting a local heaven, tending to his favorites with affectionate indulgence." They argued that the idea of a "God as a king on high" was possible only under an outdated cosmology. Those who pictured Jesus's ascension as a physical levitation saw his return through the clouds "as easily imaginable as the return of a friend from San Francisco." The marvel, exclaimed Fosdick, was that now, when in the modern cosmology there was no longer any up or down, "men on this whirling planet in the sky should still be preserving in religious imagination what they have discarded everywhere else." The God of traditional Protestantism did, however, have one benefit; it was easy to visualize and pray to. With divine immanence, on the other hand, that was not always the case. Fosdick admitted that "there is indeed this danger in the approach to which we have been describing, that we may conceive God as so dispersed everywhere that we cannot find him anywhere."[23] And a dispersed deity was less likely to sustain a vibrant prayer and devotional life.

Henry Sloan Coffin, in a 1914 sermon to college students, encapsulated the liberal enterprise in thinking about God when he described three stages in religious experience that the thoughtful Christian should pass through. "God, as we conceive of Him in childhood," said Coffin, "is a mysterious and magical creature not unlike Ezekiel's compound of wind, cloud, flame, wings, wheels, lightning. . . . He is utterly different from us." In the second stage, Coffin maintained, we come to see our childish beliefs as ridiculous, hence come to doubt the existence of God altogether. However, if we are true to ourselves and to the universe, we will progress to a third stage, that of seeing all as divine due to divine immanence. "Of course we do not see in unusual occurrences past or present anything peculiarly Godlike, for the regular and ordinary are equally divine." This outlook was, for liberals, the culmination of the normal religious life.[24]

Yet even as he railed against the distant, childish God of Christian orthodoxy, Coffin admitted that such a God was paradoxically more capable of friendship with humans. Observed Coffin, "We have lost the sense we once possessed of God's nearness. . . . We have lost that feeling of God's actual comradeship, His personal interest in and presence with us, which was so strong in childhood." William Adams Brown echoed Coffin when he called the most "unreal" part of the Psalms "the address to Jehovah as a familiar friend, as intimately known as one's own father or mother." "The vivid sense of God as a determining factor in daily life," Brown continued,

which was characteristic of an older piety, seems strange to many of
the earnest young people of our day.... We have ceased to be partic-
ipants and have become critics of religion, and in the process something has dropped out which has left a gap which for many of us has
not yet been filled.[25]

For many liberals, that gap was apparently filled by Jesus. An immanent
God may have been difficult to visualize as a recipient of prayer, but Jesus
was for liberals both tangible and personal. Jesus exemplified to them all the
best qualities of humanity—love, self-sacrifice, kindness, righteousness, com-
passion, and concern for justice. In this realm there were truly heirs of Horace Bushnell, whose work *God in Christ* argued that Christians should con-
ceptualize God using the character traits of Jesus. Thus, when liberals
thought of God, they used the image of Jesus. Indeed, of the many ways that
liberals and traditionalists differed from each other ideologically, none were
more basic than how they interpreted the statement of Jesus: "I and the
Father are one." Orthodox Protestants had interpreted this to mean that
Jesus was equal in nature to the Jehovah of the Bible. Liberals, on the other
hand, reversed the direction of the analogy; for them, this statement meant
that one obtained glimpses of what God was like by looking at Jesus. After
the Kantian revolution, one could not know in an objective, factual sense
what God was like, but the Christian used the character of Jesus to think of
God.[26]

The fullest explication of this aspect of liberalism came from G. Walter
Fiske, junior dean of the Oberlin Graduate School of Theology and author
of *Finding the Comrade God*. In a chapter entitled "Our Need of Christ to
Make God Seem Personal," Fiske laid out the spiritual task of Christocentric
liberalism, as this movement has been called. Because God is immanent,
invisible, and intangible, Fiske said, "it is hard for us to know him as a
person.... This is what Jesus of Nazareth does for us. He lived for us the
human life of God. He made God visible, vocal, and tangible to men." Expressing his Kantian epistemology, Fiske continued, "[A]ll of God that we
are capable of perceiving we find interpreted to us in the person of Jesus
Christ." He concluded:

We must know Jesus, therefore, in order to feel sure that our God,
whose Presence we feel, is really a Person. Only through knowing
Christ are we led to realize that our God is not a mere aggregation of
awful forces and impersonal cosmic power, but a throbbing, thinking,
feeling, loving Personal Presence of Efficient Good Will.

The Cosmic Power was made personal to liberals in the words and the life
of Jesus.[27]

This heartfelt devotion on the part of liberals to Jesus has been dismissed as an irrational mix of nostalgia and sentimentality.[28] Whatever its sources, however, Jesus clearly undergirded the devotional life for many liberals. We may find it difficult, Fosdick said, to relate to the unknowable God of modern liberalism. However, we can still "love him, be loved by him, and company with him as an unseen friend" by seeing "the divine quality of that Presence revealed in Christ." Lyman Abbott, in recounting his own pilgrimage from the transcendent religion of his father to Christocentric liberalism, wrote in the third person:

> He had thought of God as a great king, sitting upon a great white throne, and he tried to send his prayers up thither by a kind of wireless telegraphy.... But now, when he kneels to pray, he first reads something from the Gospels, then forms in his mind a picture of Jesus, sits down by the side of the man and talks with him and prayer becomes easy conversation.

The problem of a dispersed deity was solved for Christocentric liberals by devotion to Jesus.[29]

Devotion to Jesus may have helped solve the communal element in prayer, that is, the part of prayer consisting of conversing with what otherwise would have been for liberals a vague deity. However, this solution was not as effective when it came to preserving the petitionary element in prayer, for prayer for things was addressed not to Jesus but to the Father, and an abstract deity did not square well with notions of petitionary prayer. The idea of petitionary prayer, Schleiermacher had claimed, "conflicts with our primary and basal presupposition that there can be no relation of interaction between creature and Creator." For Kant and the Germans, the theological argument against prayer had been conclusive; one did not ask things from an infinitely wise and infinitely good deity, since such a God would not wait for prayer in order to grant good gifts to his children. Henry Thompson, in fact, the original formulator of the prayer-gauge challenge, had raised this objection during the prayer-gauge debate. The question was a difficult one: Why would an omnipotent, benevolent God make the bestowal of blessings contingent on prayer rather than simply giving them?[30]

Typically, defenders of petitionary prayer had answered this objection with an analogy from human parenthood: Just as a parent enjoys having the child ask for things and then providing them, so the argument went, God as our Heavenly Father does the same. Jonathan Edwards posed this question and replied that God instituted prayer "so he will be glorified and acknowledged by his creatures" as "the Author and Fountain of all good." J. Oliver Buswell drew on this tradition in the 1920s. Parents could provide for their children mechanically and indirectly, Buswell said, but "we desire and intend that they shall bring their wants to us, that we may have the personal pleasure of satisfying their needs." Similarly, God desired that his children come to him personally in order to obtain blessings that otherwise would not occur. He has "planned to answer prayer, supplementing and superseding mechanical processes of nature," Buswell concluded, "in order to reveal Himself as our Heavenly Father, 'giving good things to them that ask him.'" Rosalind Goforth, clearly one of the most enthusiastic proponents of petitionary prayer around the turn of the century, justified her prayer life using the image of parenthood: "I am convinced that God has intended prayer to be as simple and natural...as the intercourse between a child and his parent in the home. And as a large part of that intercourse between parent and child is simply asking and receiving, just so is it with us and our heavenly Parent."[31]

For liberals, the child-parent analogy as a rationale for prayer was not very helpful. The Heavenly Father of liberalism, while immanent, was also unobtrusive. Rather than the maintenance of a childlike heart as the ideal state of the Christian, liberals conceived of the Christian life as one of growth into maturity, which for them entailed a measure of independence from God. The goal of life for liberals was the attainment of character. For Christians to attain character, they had to learn to make decisions for themselves, to mature into adults who did not seek instructions from God concerning every matter. Thus, God limited himself in dealing with his children, remaining in the background, so to speak. This "unobtrusiveness of God," as Henry Churchill King termed it, was necessary for our spiritual training. As Walter Fiske explained in "Our Need of an Unobtrusive God":

> The eagle forces his eaglet to fly alone; so a wise father accustoms
> his growing boy to make his own independent choices, with a limited
> amount of guidance. Thus the invisible God unobtrusively keeps in
> the shadow, lest he cripple our freedom and paralyze our faith.

God, Fiske said, "is not some overbearing tyrant... effectively dictating even the common details of our life." The liberal God gave his children "democratic freedom, opportunity for real initiative, moral elbow-room" so that they could mature into responsible, independent adults.[32]

For liberals, then, a childlike relationship with God was something not to be maintained but to be *outgrown*; in particular, Christians were to outgrow the idea of getting things from God. Going to God with trivial material requests was childish in the worst sense of the word. When we were children, Fosdick said, "prayer was an Alladin's lamp by rubbing which we summoned the angels of God to do our bidding, prayer was a blank check signed by the Almighty which we could fill in at will and present to the universe to be cashed." Unfortunately, Fosdick said, "there are some who still think of prayer in terms of childish supplications to a divine Santa Claus." Such

Christians profess to being childlike, when in actuality they are merely *child-ish.* "Childishness in prayer," he concluded, "is chiefly evidenced in an over-weening desire to beg things from God."[33]

The modern notion of an immanent God, rooted in German idealism and coupled with the liberal emphasis on mature character, was bound to make petitionary prayer problematic for liberals, just as it had for the German idealists. Not surprisingly, the theological argument against prayer frequently appeared in liberal prayer writings. Fosdick wrote: "[W]hen anyone believes in the whole of God, is sure that he has a wise and good purpose for every child of his, and for all the world, prayer inevitably becomes not the endeavor to get God to do our will, but the endeavor to open our lives to God so that God can do in us what he wants to do." The idea that God "refuses to work his will save as some man cooperates with him," Fosdick concluded, implied "imperfect goodness in God" and should be avoided.[34]

The liberal idea of God affected petitionary prayer in another way. A more abstract, spiritualized deity was a less localized deity, one that played no favorites among humans. Here the liberal doctrine of the brotherhood of man becomes relevant. Another key element of classic liberalism was the idea that, as James M. Campbell put it, "men are brothers all; equally dear to the All-Father." In the Old Testament, asserted Campbell, God was por-trayed as a partisan deity. But the God of the New Testament was "the Universal Father, to whom every one of His children is equally dear." God was "everybody's Friend," a "world God, in friendly relations with suffering, struggling men everywhere." Campbell's statement represented classic liberal ideology as a whole. As Bowne said, "every life is included in the divine plan; and every life is as intimately near and present to the divine thought and care."[35] For liberals, a completely immanent God implied a universal religion, with no distinctions between a "saved" and a "lost" group of people.

This universality of the liberal God had an important implication when applied to prayer for physical needs. In a world of cause and effect and finite number of goods, to ask God for a material object often meant that that object was not available to another person. Similarly, praying for a change in the weather for one's personal need entailed that this might inconvenience someone else who would prefer quite different weather. When Rosalind Go-forth prayed for a rainstorm to keep the Chinese woman at her house to sew clothes, there were undoubtedly other persons who were inconvenienced by it. In other words, prayer for changes in the created order often required a God who played favorites, an idea perfectly acceptable to traditionalists who divided the world into the "saved" and the "lost." As E. M. Bounds said, "while God's providence is over all men, yet His supervision and administration of His government are peculiarly in the interest of His people." This assumption underlay the conservative emphasis on answered prayer.[36]

Liberals, however, believed that, as Fosdick put it, God "has no pets, he plays no favorites." A miracle on behalf of one person rather than all implied that God was inconsistent in his working, favoring some people over others. Yet as William Adams Brown wrote in his work on miracles, "to us consistency is the highest virtue for a moral being." To pray for a material benefit that may result in loss to another did not square with belief in a consistent, universal Father who did not play favorites. The words of Charles Reynolds Brown, dean of Yale Divinity School, suggest the claim on God's personal favor that prayers of this sort required:

> I do not believe for a moment that the through traffic of the divine
> purpose, as carried upon the great trunk lines of cosmic activities,
> will be shunted off on some siding at any hour to give the right of
> way to the local train of my own personal desires simply because I
> am on my knees.[37]

James Campbell spelled out for his readers what the universality of God implied for prayer: "Since the world is governed in the interest of all God's children, it is not seemly or right for any one of them to claim a monopoly of his favor, and ask him to change his arrangement to meet his individual desires and needs." Campbell went on to give an example of a mother who asked her son to pray for nice weather for a picnic, to which the boy replied, " 'Perhaps it would be a great deal better for the farmers to have it wet, and why should it be fine just for our outing?' " Since their interests had to be balanced with those of farmers, it was best to simply pray that they would choose one of God's fine days. "This is in a nutshell," concluded Campbell, "the philosophy of prayer for weather, and for prayer for temporal things in general."[38]

For liberals, then, the belief in an immanent God rooted in German idealism and loving all humans equally led them to question praying for tangible things. Walter Fiske observed that "our idea of prayer depends upon our idea of God." As the liberal thought of God moved away from traditional orthodoxy, so did the liberal doctrine of prayer.[39]

Veneration of Science

Another formative ideological factor in the liberal doctrine of prayer was the liberal veneration of science. Since God was seen to be immanent in human cultural development and revealed through it, liberal Protestants looked to modern culture for revelation of what God was like—and an important part of modern culture was science. Liberal Protestants, therefore, tended to grant modern science sacrosanct status as a determiner of what was and was not possible in the religious realm. Fosdick proudly described liberalism as "the endeavor to rationalize religion; it starts with science and with this new world-view which science brings and, taking that as test and standard, says,

We will have nothing in our religion contrary to that." Unlike their orthodox counterparts who tended to resist new developments in science associated with Darwinism, early liberals were determined to grant science free sway and shape their theology around whatever conclusions scientists claimed to reach.[40]

This mindset was exhibited in 1899, when William Newton Clarke, author of the seminal text of liberal systematic theology, gave a series of talks on Christianity at Johns Hopkins University, one of the most prominent of the "modern" universities set up on the German model dedicated to free scholarship. In the course of his lectures, Clarke asked these secular scholars to set the rules by which Christian theologians would work. "Make clear and intelligible and irresistible whatever you discover, and urge it upon us with a persistency," he pleaded. "Establish the right way of mental work as the only way that shall be welcome anywhere. Illustrate sound, strong thinking for us, until it shall be a matter of course that we must make it our own. Make it impossible for us to live thinking confusedly and incorrectly."[41] Clarke thus pledged allegiance to the emerging scientific and intellectual establishment.

Such a willingness to let science set the intellectual boundaries appears throughout classic liberal writings. Earlier Protestants had accepted and sometimes venerated science, but only when the latter's conclusions squared with the supposed verities of Christian theology. Religious liberals, on the other hand, accepted the conclusions of science as themselves part of the revelation that God had given. William Adams Brown explained:

> To the old theologian science may be a useful tool, but only insofar
> as it helps us to recognize a revelation which is complete without it.
> To the new theologian, science is itself a part of revelation. It is
> God's way of helping man to a trustworthy knowledge of Himself,
> through the disclosure it brings of the nature of the world which is
> God's creation.

Liberals could wax rather effusive about the new scientific spirit of the age. Adapting a well-known psalm, George Gordon wrote:

> The mood of the age is upon us all; whither shall we go from its
> spirit, or whither shall we flee from its presence? . . . If we ascend up
> into heaven, it is there; if we make our bed in hell, it is there; it is
> with us in the darkness and in the light; it is the shadow of God in
> the mind of educated man; as the shadow of God we must behold it.

Harry Emerson Fosdick also could stumble over himself in praising science. "Science has developed saints and martyrs," he claimed, "whose selfless and sacrificial spirit is unsurpassed even in the annals of the church." Echoing

Gordon's biblical imagery, Fosdick said that "a new eleventh chapter of the Epistle to the Hebrews could be written on the heroes of scientific faith."[42]

The result for religion of this veneration of science was obvious: the old conception of the supernatural on which petitionary prayer was based had to go. Science, said Fosdick, "has searched religion for contraband goods, [and] stripped it of old superstitions." Miracles headed the list of contraband goods. Thus, the liberals' high regard for science required a reformulation of the supernatural. George Gordon claimed that "the natural order is supreme; and we do not dream that God will work miracles in our behalf." We are "beset behind and before and on either side by a natural order fixed as fate." "Our world is a universe," William Adams Brown concluded, "and all that it contains must somehow fall into place as parts of a single consistent system. The division of territory which underlay the older treatment of the supernatural is no longer possible for us." Their veneration for science required that liberal Protestants reconstruct Christian supernaturalism to fit a modern one-tiered universe.[43]

Part of the liberal impetus to place modern science on a pedestal and adapt Christianity to it sprang from liberal apologetics. Simply put, liberal Protestants had no way to explain a religion that the best and brightest of society disbelieved. Liberal apologetics was based on the argument from religious experience; that is, Christianity was true because it was experienced personally to be true. The conditions of proof, said William Adams Brown, were the same in religion as in any other department of knowledge:

> To prove a doctrine true it is necessary to show (1) that it is able to win the allegiance of the men and women of the greatest moral and spiritual insight, and (2) that it is able to hold this allegiance in spite of the changes which wider experience and enlarging knowledge may bring.... Looked at from this point of view, the argument for the Christian idea of God appears at its full strength.

The fact that the best and brightest in Western culture gave assent to Christianity was important evidence of its truthfulness. "It is no valid argument against it that so many still reject it," Brown continued. "All that is necessary in order to prove our faith reasonable is to show that the Christian experience is increasing."[44]

Liberal Protestantism was thus committed to a "conquer or die" apologetic scheme. In order for Christianity to be verified, it had to be accepted by a respected and increasing segment of American society. Clarke claimed, concerning this liberal form of evidentialism, that "this power in Christianity to win the response of the best in man is good evidence that the voice is indeed the voice of truth." If the best and brightest disavowed Christianity, it would be shown to have been defective. Clearly, modern scientists were among the cultural elites who must not be given cause to sneer at Christianity. Thus, it was crucial for liberals that Christianity be presented in a form that could retain the assent of this crucial portion of American society.[45]

Concerning prayer specifically, the supposed wave of the future had been clearly traced by the sociologist James Leuba in his influential 1916 book *The Belief in God and Immortality*. Leuba surveyed the "experts" of modern society (historians, physicists, biologists, sociologists, psychologists, and philosophers), asking them, among other things, whether they believed in "a God to whom one may pray in the expectation of receiving an answer." In each group, less than half professed to believe in a God that answered prayer. More important, in each group, the level of belief was lower among the more distinguished, prominent members of the field. Leuba's study seemed to suggest that the trajectory of modern thought lay away from the traditional idea of petitionary prayer. Such doubts concerning petitionary prayer had to be taken into consideration by liberal Protestants who sought to maintain Christian allegiance among society's best and brightest.[46]

Social forces were at work here as well as intellectual ones. Mainline Protestantism was the "establishment" at the turn of the twentieth century but was faced for the first time with ideological and cultural pluralism. As George Marsden has observed, mainline Protestants had two choices. They could cling to a traditional, exclusivist religion with claims to absolute truth and thereby give up aspirations at dominating the larger society consisting of those who believed otherwise. Or they could maintain cultural dominance by broadening their definition of Protestantism to include all "religious" people, even scientists.[47] Liberal Protestants chose the latter course.

These factors taken in isolation, however, could easily distort the liberal Protestant accommodation with science into a disingenuous attempt to maintain cultural dominance and cling to the status quo. In fact, liberal Protestants could play the role of a dissenting minority in American society as well. As many historians have chronicled, the liberal Social Gospel was a prophetic, although for the most part moderate, criticism of the American economic status quo. Even in the intellectual realm, liberals were not merely the lackeys of science. Concerning a doctrine that was really important to them, such as the freedom of the human will, liberal Protestants were willing to go to the wall to defend their beliefs against scientists who argued for determinism.

The liberal reformulation of the supernatural, then, was motivated by more than an unwillingness to offend scientists. In fact, divine immanence can be said to have worked on both sides of the equation. It was one factor leading liberals to venerate science as God's revelation, and it also led them to discount traditional miracles as an idea that needed defending. Scientific *and* religious reasons led them to reformulate the supernatural, and the two were inextricably intertwined. Gordon wrote that "just as the scientific conception of law tends more and more to reduce miracle to a bare logical possibility, so the religious conception of the immanence of God in his universe tends more and more to make miracle superfluous." In a universe in which all things represented the immediate hand of God, liberals saw no need for miracles.[48]

Nevertheless, the liberals' veneration of modern science was tremendously significant for their ethic of prayer, for it committed them to formulate a description of prayer to which scientific elites could give assent. The traditional Protestant notion of petitionary prayer required a universe open to intrusion from without, something that did not square well with modern science. In formulating their ethic of prayer, liberal Protestants would, by the logic of their assumptions, feel the pressure to adapt petitionary prayer to the naturalistic constraints of modern science.

Biblicism

Liberal Protestants' understanding of the world, God, and modern science in terms of divine immanence may be seen as "push" factors leading them away from traditional notions of petitionary prayer. One more important element was the absence among liberals of one "pull" factor—biblicism—that kept other modern Protestants within the historic American prayer tradition.

The strongest justification for petitionary prayer in historic Protestantism had been the Bible. The analogy from parenthood, while useful, was just that—an analogy. As an argument, it had limited persuasive power. The idea that God would allow some disaster to befall a person that he would have prevented had that person prayed for protection was hard to square with a Christian conception of God. Ultimately, prayer was a mystery that Christians had solved by presenting one simple fact: the Bible taught it. Furthermore, implicit in the frequent citations of biblical examples of answered prayer by traditionalists was the assumption verbalized by C. A. Van Anda: "Since the Bible is the Word of God, every answer to prayer there recorded is the history of an event which actually took place." Thus, the conservative Baptist *Watchman-Examiner* exclaimed that "the Bible account of answered prayer is the best we can have." Protestants had traditionally defended petitionary prayer not only by citing biblical examples of answered prayer but by showing Scripture passages that instructed Christians to pray. The Bible instructed Christians to pray for needs of all sorts, traditionalists believed, therefore, petitionary prayer had to be reasonable and efficacious.[49]

Thus, J. Oliver Buswell stood squarely in the Protestant tradition when he began his chapter on intercession with the subheading "The Scripture Commands Intercession." The implication was, of course, that intercession was therefore reasonable and beneficial. The Princeton stalwart Benjamin Warfield, not one to ride the evangelical bandwagon concerning remarkable answers to prayer, declared that the Scriptures "authorize, or rather require, us to pray both for external and internal blessings; for rain and drought like

Elijah; for the healing of sickness like the elders of the Church; for the healing of sin-sick souls like Christians at large." Scripture tells us, he said, that "God answers prayer. And that equally, and equally readily and equally easily, for internal and for external things." We may not be able to understand how or why God would make blessings contingent on prayer, said orthodox Christians, but the teaching of Scripture plainly establishes it.[50]

The importance that biblicism ultimately had for modern Protestants who retained the traditional emphasis on petitionary prayer was best exhibited by Leander Chamberlain. A New England native and a graduate of Yale and Andover Seminary, Chamberlain had impeccable Protestant credentials but considered himself thoroughly up to date as well. He served as a minister in Congregationalist and Presbyterian churches in New England, New York, and Chicago until 1890, when he embarked on a full-time career as a Christian statesman. He helped found the Brooklyn Institute of Arts and Sciences, took part in various cultural and diplomatic endeavors, and served on a variety of national and international church boards and committees. When he wrote *The True Doctrine of Prayer* in 1906, he was serving as the president of the Evangelical Alliance, which had been founded in 1867 as a cooperative endeavor among American Protestant denominations that sought to demonstrate that spiritual unity underlay their diversity. Although strong in the late nineteenth century, by the time of Chamberlain's presidency the Alliance's influence was waning. Still, it served as a forerunner to the Federal Council of Churches and was an important symbol of mainstream Protestant unity in the days before the liberal-conservative schism.[51]

Chamberlain thus represented the unified Protestant evangelical front that still existed in the first two decades of the twentieth century. American Protestantism before the First World War was generally a halcyon period of cooperation between liberals and conservatives, an era that historian Ferenc Szasz has called the triumph of evangelical america. William McLoughlin, portraying the same phenomenon in less glowing terms, wrote that "since 1890 the liberals and conservatives of evangelical Protestantism had been running like men in a three-legged race." Despite underlying theological tensions, conservative pastors like John Roach Straton and Mark Matthews affirmed a vigorous social Christianity, while supposedly conservative concerns such as Prohibition received enthusiastic support from liberals.[52]

This mix of traditional and more liberal elements was manifested in Chamberlain's doctrine of prayer. The book was written, in the typical apologetic mode of the day, for "those who hold prayer to be impossible because of the reign of law" or for those who, "having been bred in the theory that prayer is only of subjective value, have grown weary of the habit." Chamberlain's preface promised to readers who were perplexed by prayer in a world of science "possibilities of answer to prayer quite beyond anything they have imagined." In traditionalist language closely resembling that of the pietistic evangelicals of his day, Chamberlain defended the prominence of petition in prayer:

> It by no means suffices that out of requests to God, and the assurance that those requests are attentively heard, there comes to the praying one a sense of filial relationship and a realization of most blessed communion with God. The fabric of prayer itself falls, the very foundation disappears, the instant that prayer is denied an objective power. . . . If prayer has valid warrant, that warrant must include results directly secured and objectively actual.[53]

However, Chamberlain's book also displayed unmistakable signs of liberal influence. First, divine immanence ran throughout the book. God, he asserted, was "immanent in nature," so that "all things and all events in nature are God's acts . . . there are no second causes." Second, universalism pervaded the work. The object of the Lord's Prayer, Chamberlain said, was "the realized fatherhood of God and brotherhood of man." The "Kingdom" was to be "the universal fellowship of men." Chamberlain's list of items to pray for was a litany of Social Gospel concerns such as "the maintenance of worldwide justice and peace, with liberty under law; the harmonizing of racial instincts and interests; fair wages for labor faithfully performed; the honest acquisition of riches; the consecration of wealth to social service," among other things. Chamberlain concluded:

> No purely selfish petition can be prayer. In so far as the asking soul is unmindful of God's love for all the members of the human family, and thus omits to honor the common bond, the plea is void. All prayer from instructed souls must be with dominant recognition of the Fatherhood of God and the consequent brotherhood of men.

Clearly, some emerging liberal elements informed Chamberlain's thinking on prayer.[54]

Finally, Chamberlain seemed to venerate modern science and concede to it the right to judge the proper scope of prayer. He seemed to imply that miraculous answers to prayer were not appropriate for modern times because "today God distinctly speaks through science." Chamberlain extolled the virtues of modern science in religious terms, sounding every bit like a modern liberal:

> [God] himself has given modern science her spirit of inquiry. His breath has inspired her understanding. Her discoveries are discoveries of his works and ways. It is in accordance with his will that now

science gives new significance to the speech which day utters, and higher meaning to the knowledge which night shows.

If modern science—God's revealer of truth to modern humans, according to Chamberlain—ruled out short cuts, should Christians cease asking for changes in the created order? Chamberlain's rhetoric would seem to lead him to limit traditional notions of petitionary prayer.[55]

However, despite his rhetoric concerning the brotherhood of man and veneration of science, Chamberlain claimed that "all conceivable possibilities of honest individual experience are within prayer's permitted range . . . no domain is excluded." How could this be? Chamberlain's recourse was to the Bible. He began his book with the scriptural injunctions to pray, showing himself to be a traditional biblicist. He cited a psalm as the very words of God: " 'Call upon me in the day of trouble.' " He continued: "Through Jeremiah Jehovah declares, 'For I know the thoughts that I think toward you. And ye shall call upon me, and ye shall go and pray unto me.' "[56]

So then, Chamberlain believed in answered prayer of all sorts. He even gave a litany of answered prayers in the Bible for everything from renewed character to the victory and defeat of armies ("brotherhood of man" notwithstanding), the staying of pestilence, and the bringing of rain. In traditional fashion, Chamberlain maintained that petition lay at the heart of prayer. Using Scripture as his guide, he concluded that "all the Hebrew terms as also all the Greek terms translated 'prayer' have appeal as their central idea. . . . In the Scriptural treatment of prayer, supplication holds the sovereign place." In the final analysis, then, for Chamberlain, biblicism led him to affirm the traditional view of prayer as petition even when other elements in his thinking might suggest otherwise. Modern science and a God who did not play favorites might seem to have made petitionary prayer superfluous, but the Bible proved otherwise. "Why then," Chamberlain asked in closing, "should special and subordinate pleas be made? The recurring answer is still in place:—Because God has so permitted and enjoined."[57]

Unlike Chamberlain, more thoroughly liberal Protestants did not derive their logic from Scripture. They stood on the modern side of the divide created by the concept of historicism. Although they considered the Bible to be a vehicle of God's revelation, it was not normative in a theological sense the way it was for traditionalists. Rather, Scripture was the ongoing, progressive record of an immanent God's continuous revelation in history, as recognized by biblical authors.[58] The fact that Scripture recorded Elijah praying for rain and having his prayer answered meant for liberals that Old Testament Jews had not advanced to a scientific awareness of weather patterns. It did not serve as an example to be followed by modern Christians. Since revelation was progressive, and the human race had advanced since biblical times, it would be expected that modern Christians would have advanced their conception of prayer beyond the level practiced by biblical people who had no conception of natural law. Liberals needed justifications for petitionary prayer other than mere Scriptural warrant.[59]

For mainstream Protestants like Chamberlain, the "pull" factor of biblicism could counteract the "push" factors of immanence, universalism, and veneration of science that made petitionary prayer, as traditionally defined, problematic. Liberal Protestants did not feel restrained by the biblical view of petitionary prayer. They were, however, deeply infused with a desire to put forth a more spiritual conception of the world and of God, one thoroughly in harmony with modern thought. Eventually, their ethic of prayer would reflect the modernist impulse.

FIVE

✛

A Sane Mysticism
The Christocentric Liberal Ethic of Prayer

In light of the American liberal understanding of God and the world elucidated in the previous chapter, one might expect liberal Protestants, like the
German idealists before them, to have abandoned traditional petitionary
prayer altogether. In reality, however, the liberal expurgation of the supernatural element in prayer occurred quite gradually. Before 1920, a significant
segment of liberal Protestantism sought to retain the traditional confidence
in petitionary prayer even while asserting a devotional ethic in harmony with
modern nonsupernaturalistic thought. Not until the 1920s did a full-fledged
ethic of prayer largely stripped of petition begin to become prominent within
American liberalism.[1]

Before proceeding further, I must make some qualifications concerning
the term "liberal" as I use it in this chapter and the next. American Protestant liberalism was a diverse movement. Historian Kenneth Cauthen attempted to accommodate this diversity by delineating two dominant types of
liberals. So-called evangelical liberals, or Christocentric liberals, said
Cauthen, "stood squarely within the Christian tradition" while adapting it to
modernity. A second group Cauthen classified as "modernistic liberals" since
"they were basically determined in their thinking by a twentieth-century
outlook" and grafted onto that outlook certain elements of the Christian
tradition. The widely used textbook *American Christianity*, by H. Shelton
Smith, Robert Handy, and Lefferts Loetscher, exhibited a similar approach
in its chapter entitled "The Christocentric Liberal Tradition."[2]

William Hutchison has since attacked such a scheme of classification as
artificial, pointing out that all liberals shared what he calls the modernist
impulse—the tendency to deny separate categories of Christian and secular
and therefore a willingness to adapt Christianity to modern culture. While
Hutchison's point concerning a certain epistemological agreement among all
liberals is well taken, it remains true that many moderate liberals displayed
a certain evangelical spirit and a desire to retain as much of the inherited
orthodoxy as possible that set them apart from more critical modernists such
as Shailer Mathews and Douglas Clyde Mackintosh. Martin Marty, for in-

stance, has called the former group of liberals "people of faith with pastoral hearts." These evangelical liberals, or Christocentric liberals, receive the spotlight in this and the next chapter.[3]

Most notable in this group were Lyman Abbott and Harry Emerson Fosdick (in his early years, at least), two influential popularizers of evangelical liberalism, and I give their writings on prayer particular attention. By the early twentieth century, Abbott was a venerable founding father of liberalism who reached a wide audience through his magazine the *Outlook*. Fosdick, like Abbott, was more a popularizer than a theologian, but his writings clearly embodied many of the principles of this moderate faction of liberalism. Historians have called him a "representative Christocentric liberal," and Reinhold Niebuhr considered him to be "modern evangelical liberalism personified."[4]

The attitude of these evangelical liberals toward prayer was somewhat analogous to the struggle among the New Theologians of the late nineteenth century to describe the nature of Christ, as explained by Daniel Day Williams. The Andover liberals, Williams wrote, were "sensitive to scientific prestige. . . . If a position seemed unscientific, that is in definite conflict with science, it was not held for long." They had committed themselves to the naturalistic principles of historical criticism of the Bible that would eventually lead liberals to reinterpret the nature of Christ. However, Andover liberals abandoned a traditional supernatural Christology gradually. Their writings, observed Williams, expressed "the hold which belief in the miraculous and supernatural personality of Jesus still possessed over them." Ultimately, said Williams, their doctrine of Jesus "preserved the evangelical language, but gave it a content which showed at every point the struggle which theology was passing through." Concerning Christology, Williams concluded, Andover was "at the transitional stage between supernaturalism and naturalism in liberal theology. . . . They wavered between emphasis on the natural humanity and the supernatural divinity of [Jesus]." Or, as Robert Bruce Mullin observed concerning the Andover liberals' attempts to preserve the biblical portrait of Jesus, "like jugglers, liberal-leaning theologians tried to keep all of their concerns aloft at once. This unfortunately gave to such discussions a frustrating lack of logical consistency."[5]

A similar wavering between the natural and the supernatural appears in the evangelical liberal prayer writings in the first two decades of the twentieth century. On the whole, evangelical liberals sought to retain as much of the traditional inheritance concerning prayer as possible while remaining within the acceptable bounds of modern thought. At times, they suggested a scientifically tenable explanation of how intercessory prayer and prayer for healing could be practiced in a modern, nonsupernaturalistic universe; this is the subject of chapter 6. Concerning prayer as a whole, they sought to retain traditional faith in petitionary prayer as a legitimate enterprise while at the same time avoiding any semblance of conflict that that belief might precipitate with modern science. The resulting ambivalence concerning petitionary prayer was best expressed in the liberals' own terms as a sane mysticism.

Oberlin Seminary's Walter Fiske called his book on prayer "a sane mysticism as a cure for a cold rationalism." Liberal writings were peppered with phrases such as "instructed minds," "intelligent Christians," and "sane Christians," by which they meant those who had harmonized their religious thinking with modern thought. For example, S. Parkes Cadman, a liberal Congregationalist, charged the fundamentalist Reuben Torrey with "clinging to obsolete traditions which have been discarded by the *sane*, reverent, and constructive scholarship of Christianity." The God of the Old Testament was, to *Christian Century* contributor Arthur B. Patten, "unthinkable to the *normal* modern mind." The aim of liberalism, said Fosdick in retrospect, had been to make it possible to be "both an *intelligent* modern and a serious Christian."[6] What liberals meant by these terms, among other things, was that "sane" people saw the world in non-supernaturalistic terms; they employed a "true naturalism." The implication was, of course, that those who retained the idea of a two-tiered, supernaturalistic universe were unintelligent, fanatical, or perhaps even insane.[7]

Liberal Protestants were vitally concerned with renewing spirituality in modern life. However, said Arthur Patten, "what we are seeking is not a reversion, but rather a conversion of both materialistic science and of medieval mysticism. Science should be reverent, and mysticism must be reasonable." The Christocentric liberal ethic of prayer sought to correct two extremes. On the one hand, there were those modern, "sane" people who thought well but were coldly rational and needed a dose of mysticism. On the other hand, there were those traditionalists in the church who had plenty of mysticism but clung to supernatural modes of thinking.[8]

Evangelical liberals sought to keep the devotional intensity—the "mysticism," so to speak—of traditional Christianity but add to it the "sanity" of modern thought. The liberal Methodist James M. Campbell, summarizing the liberal enterprise concerning prayer, said, "one of the most important services which the Christian teacher of the present day can render is to recover faith in the potency of prayer. And this he can do only by bringing the entire subject of prayer into harmony with modern thought and life." This chapter looks first at ways that Christocentric liberals remained "mystical" in a traditional Protestant sense by affirming faith in petitionary prayer; I then discuss how the liberal ethic of prayer accommodated modern thought.[9]

Evangelical liberal devotional writers such as Fosdick, Abbott, Henry Churchill King, and others sought to avoid the critical attitude concerning petition that other liberals beginning with Schleiermacher had displayed. Within the broad liberal religious tradition there had been those who, seeing nature as unalterable, followed their convictions to their conclusion and confined petitionary prayer to internal, subjective objects. This school of thought was best represented in an oft-cited remark by the British broad churchman James Martineau: "God's rule of action in nature we have every reason to regard as unalterable; established as an inflexible and faithful basis of expectation; and, for that reason, not open to perpetual variation on the suggestion of occasional moral contingencies." However, he continued, "behind and amid all these punctualities of law abides, in infinite remainder, the living and unpledged spirit," a spirit that sought companionship with its creatures and provided spiritual comfort. In other words, prayer did not change the external world, but it offered the individual important subjective benefits. The nineteenth-century American Baptist Noah Davis (see chapter 1) concurred: "[W]e are constrained to the conclusion that prayer for an extraordinary natural event is strictly unwarrantable, and indeed a presumptuous offense in any but the ignorant."[10]

Such a view of prayer had proponents within early-twentieth-century American liberalism. George Coe, whom Fosdick credited with providing counsel for his book *The Meaning of Prayer*, restricted prayer to the personal, subjective world, claiming that "praying about such matters as the weather has no effect upon the weather at all, and praying about life and death, health and disease, has no effect upon them except what science recognizes as the influence of the mind upon the body." Even one of the seminal textbooks of classic liberal theology, William Adams Brown's *Christian Theology in Outline*, voiced the modern sentiment concerning prayer:

> In the realm of the physical it is true that while our prayer may
> work no change in the laws which express God's method in this
> realm, and fence in the specific event which is in question in our
> prayer, it may yet produce a change in our attitude to the event, and
> so in its significance for our life.

This was prayer in harmony with modern thought.[11]

While such an understanding of prayer existed in the early twentieth century, most of the liberal spiritual writings before 1920 followed the example of the other textbook of liberal theology, William Newton Clarke's *Outline of Christian Theology*, which asserted an ethic of petitionary prayer more in keeping with traditional American Protestantism. "We must not deny the possibility of God's intervention in natural occurrences in answer to requests from his children," Clarke maintained. While Clarke acknowledged that God ran the universe by general laws, he also said:

> The ability of the free God to alter the course of events if he will is
> by all means to be held fast. . . . Though our faith in his steady gov-
> ernance grows so strong and serene that we do not ask him to alter
> the course of events, still his power to do so is essential to a clear
> and restful doctrine of providence.

Clarke thus sought to reinterpret Christianity along modern lines but also keep a window open for petitionary prayer in the traditional sense.[12]

Evangelical liberals, following Clarke, were careful to maintain the doctrine of prayer as efficacious in the external world. Prayer was more than a subjective enterprise; for prayer to mean anything, it had to have an objective effect on more than just the individual praying. A well-known nineteenth-century remark attributed to George Meredith best represented the subjective understanding of prayer: "He who rises from prayer a better man, his prayer is answered." It was a statement that Christocentric liberals in the early twentieth century commonly rebutted. For example, the popular pastor and author William Dawson commented on Meredith's remark:

> That some poor creature on the rack of anguish may draw a moment's ease from the sweet voice of some woman praying at his side, and from her cool hands laid on him in outflowing sympathy, is comprehensible enough. . . . If that be all, clearly prayer needs no explanation, for there is nothing to explain. It contains no mystery. It is not a secret. It is a matter of psychology, a matter even of physiology.

Christian prayer, he argued, must have an effect outside of the individual praying. Similarly, Henry Churchill King asserted, "we cannot admit that the scientific viewpoint compels us to turn prayer into what is simply a kind of spiritual gymnastics. If religion is to be possible at all the reality of effective relations between God and men cannot be denied—relations that involve actual response on God's part."[13]

Harry Emerson Fosdick's *Meaning of Prayer*, the capstone of evangelical liberal writings on prayer, was equally zealous to defend the traditional notion of petitionary prayer. The idea of prayer as a reflex action, merely beneficial to the person praying, Fosdick likened to a parable: "Two boys were sent into the fields to dig for hidden treasure, where all day they toiled in vain; and at evening, coming weary and disappointed home, they were met by their father. 'After all,' he said to comfort them, 'you did get something—the digging itself was good exercise.'" Many today, Fosdick complained, see prayer as mere spiritual gymnastics: "They lift the dumb-bell of intercessory prayer, not because they think it helps their friends, but because it strengthens the fiber of their own sympathy." This is not prayer but merely meditation, he claimed, and whatever its short-term benefits for those who can no longer believe in petitionary prayer, "this kind of prayer is not likely to persist long."[14]

The fact is, said Fosdick and other Christocentric liberals, for even prayer as communion with God to mean anything, there must be the sense that God hears and may directly answer requests to him. Thus, Fosdick concluded, though petition is not all of prayer:

> Nevertheless this province of petition is important. It is not the
> whole of prayer, but it is the original form of prayer and never can
> be nor ought to be outgrown.... [Petitions] are to the whole domain
> what the thirteen original states are to America; not the whole of it,
> nor the major portion of it, but the primary nucleus of it and the
> initial influence in it.

In this, these liberals stood squarely within the tradition of Austin Phelps
and other mainline Protestants of Tyndall's day, who had adamantly defended the petitionary element as crucial in prayer. Indeed, Fosdick's remarks were strongly reminiscent of J. H. Jellett's preface to his orthodox
response to the prayer-gauge controversy. "If we arrive at the conclusion that
prayer has no external efficacy," declared Jellett, "it is plain that its internal
efficacy must speedily disappear. No man's mind can be beneficially affected
by the constant repetition of that which he believes to be a mere idle form."[15]

Evangelical liberals, therefore, despite the influence of German idealism,
their belief in an immanent God, and professed allegiance to modern science,
claimed to accept prayer's efficacy on all levels. The domain of prayer appeared to be as open to liberals as it had been for Jonathan Edwards and
Austin Phelps, or even for Rosalind Goforth, for that matter. Walter Fiske
even defended the idea of the storm that defeated the Spanish Armada as
an answer to prayer: "Perhaps, you may say, it was a happy coincidence; but
awe-struck England solemnly gave thanks to God for his wonderful help in
that crucial hour." Since "the universe is not a machine with which nothing
can be done," concluded King, "we simply must pray concerning that which
disturbs our peace," be that spiritual or physical. Concluded Fosdick:

> No man can draw a boundary, saying "Within this we may expect
> God to use his laws in answer to our prayers, and without we may
> look for nothing of the kind." ... God is free, so far as the mere pos-
> sibilities are concerned, to answer any petition whatsoever. If a
> prayer is left unanswered, it is not because the reign of law prevents.

This openness to petitionary prayer for tangible objects set these moderate
liberals apart from more radical liberals and kept them in the mainstream
Protestant tradition.[16]

Despite such professions of traditional confidence in petitionary prayer,
however, a number of subtle changes in the Christocentric liberal ethic of
prayer revealed the theological transformations occurring within liberal Protestantism. These distinctives showed that evangelical liberals were trying
their best to be "sane" moderns while retaining the traditional inheritance
concerning prayer. Specifically, the distinctively "sane" element in liberal
prayer writings was this: While paying lip service to prayer as efficacious in
all realms, the liberals in their justification of prayer and their use of ex-

amples focused exclusively on level one prayer—the realm of prayer's efficacy completely in harmony with modern thought. In other words, while proclaiming prayer's objective efficacy, in practical terms they stressed the subjective aspect of prayer, one less vulnerable to modern attacks.

One way that this "sane" aspect can be seen is in the liberal use of "answered prayer apologetics." As explained earlier, traditional Protestants tended to present as evidence for the efficacy of prayer tangible answers to prayer. These were gathered from the Bible and from modern experience—for instance, the case of the recovery of the Prince of Wales in 1871 that precipitated the prayer-gauge debate. Liberal Protestants, on the other hand, with their modern understanding of the Bible, generally ignored "answered prayers of the Bible" apologetics. Furthermore, evangelical liberals had little good to say concerning the attempt to prove prayer by resorting to modern examples of miraculous answers to prayer, an enterprise that clearly had not convinced secular scientists.

How the "evidence" of answered prayer promoted by Arthur T. Pierson and others fared among the skeptics in the modern world was made clear by the University of Chicago psychologist Anna Louise Strong. It will be recalled that Rosalind Goforth gave as one of her instances of answered prayer her search for a key, after which she gave up, asked God to guide her to it, and found it. Strong explained this as nothing more than indicative of a basic law of subconscious activity, that certain memories imbedded in the brain are not strong enough to come to consciousness in the form of a definite recollection. The act of relaxing in prayer was enough to bring them to mind. "It has its correlate," she said, "in the re-remembering of a name by giving up the strenuous attempt to find it, and in the attainment of sleep by ceasing the arduous pursuit of it."[17]

As for those who, like Mueller, prayed for funds without soliciting them, Strong remarked, "the very fact of their trust makes the strongest kind of appeal." Concerning prayer for a change in the weather, Strong remarked, "the fact of coincidence must not be overlooked. There is a tendency to forget the times when prayer was not answered and to remember the time when it was.... The selective nature of consciousness is very great." Strong thus explained the evidence of answered prayer as demonstrating no more than that there were certain psychological laws that prayer taps into: "The percentage of yet unexplained cases is so small that it seems fair to assume that in time all answers to prayer will be seen to come as the result of definite psychic laws." Clearly, evangelical answered prayer narratives did not prove the living God to secular elites.[18]

Like their modern secular counterparts, liberal Protestants—Walter Fiske's remarks about the Spanish Armada notwithstanding—generally saw accounts of answered prayer as unconvincing. "The power of prayer to affect the objective processes of nature," Fosdick observed, "is incapable of scientific demonstration. We never can so completely isolate an event, like a change in the weather, as to prove that nothing but our prayer could have caused it." In a world of complex phenomena, Fosdick was saying, the fact that the wind shifted from north to south after George Mueller's prayer proved nothing, since it was impossible to pinpoint his prayer as the cause of this phenomenon. Accounts and recollections of answered prayer were, these liberals believed, hopelessly subjective.[19]

The *Christian Century*, a good barometer of liberal opinion, mocked those whose "claims to wonderful special providences form the substance of many remarkable testimonies." It gave as a parallel an account of a new sect formed by black believers in Paris, Kentucky. These people believed a severe calamity would annihilate the world on a certain day, and so they gathered to pray in earnest to avert this disaster. The feared day passed with the world still in existence. Therefore, "a mighty shout went up from the gathering which aroused every one in the village. . . . Before the rays of the sun announcing a new day had appeared a new church had been formed, . . . whose creed was announced to be the efficacy of prayer." Dripping with satire, the *Christian Century* editorial made clear its opinion that answered prayer apologetics was considerably less than scientific. Thus, Charles Reynolds Brown claimed in 1924 that the answered prayer narrative, popular in "certain quarters where people chose to live by their happy intuitions rather than by the carefully coordinated results of trustworthy experience, . . . has been largely discredited."[20]

This is not to say that the evangelical liberals had no apologetic of answered prayer—in fact, they did. However, theirs was a demonstration of the efficacy of prayer on a strictly personal level. Christocentric liberals made what had been in traditional Protestantism *one* form of evidence for prayer, its subjective benefits, *the* primary evidence that God answered prayer. The heart of the liberal argument for prayer was that prayer was "efficacious" since the person praying benefited from it. We are, said King, "not looking in the right direction for the answers to our prayers, for evidence of real relation to God" when we seek them in divine interventions and remarkable providences. Rather, evidence of prayer's efficacy lay in "changed attitudes and longings," spiritual growth, and "increasing assurance of spiritual things." Since prayer was chiefly concerned with things of the spirit, said James Campbell, "it is to this sphere of things that we must mainly look for evidences of answers to prayer."[21]

One way prayer's efficacy was proved was in the ethical quality of the lives of persons who prayed. James Whiton, a Congregationalist minister and a member of Abbott's staff at the *Outlook*, asserted: "[I]t requires no special cases of 'answer' to evince the effectiveness of prayer: it is attested by the ethical development of mankind." Prayer's efficacy was also proved by the sense of comfort and divine presence it brought to the person praying. The archetypal Christocentric liberal answered prayer apologetic was the testimony of William Dawson, who recalled an instance of answered prayer during the illness of a child:

> Out of the past years such hours return upon me; times when my
> back was to the wall; when I was beaten down into the dust and
> earthly hopes lay ruined; when all my life hung tremulous above the
> sick-bed of a little child; when another life, dearer than my own,
> trembled in the balance and the shadow of death lay upon my
> house, ... then I prayed, "being in agony." Then I prayed, and knew
> myself mystically consoled, as though God took my bruised life to
> His bosom, and I rejoiced to "feel God's greatness flow round my in-
> completeness, round my restlessness His rest." To have prayed thus,
> and prevailed thus, though it be but once in many years, is to be-
> lieve in prayer forevermore.

In the context of American answered prayer apologetics, Dawson's testimony is noteworthy because he never mentioned the fate of the child. The answer to his prayer was not the healing of the child but rather the comforting presence of God that prayer produced. The fact that this realm of prayer's efficacy was internal did not make it any less scientific, according to Dawson. "Nothing proved by science," he claimed, "is more plainly verified than that prayer is the supreme dynamic of the church."[22]

Evangelical liberals buttressed their answered prayer apologetic with pragmatism. Whatever the intellectual problems may be with prayer, they said, one cannot deny that it works, and that is all one needs to know. The Andover liberal Theodore Munger advised: "[L]et the theories go, and trust the fact." Abbott admitted that he knew very little theoretically about how prayer worked. Yet he retorted:

> What do you know about the laws of electricity? Very little. Why,
> then, do you ride in a trolley-car? We pray for the same reason that
> we ride in the trolley-car. The trolley-car brings us to our destination;
> the prayer gives us the inspiration of comfort, illumination, and
> strength for daily needs.

However it happened, prayer produced an exemplary life and so should be practiced.[23]

William Dawson thus proposed to his readers a prayer-gauge, in a liberal sense. "Make the experiment of prayer," he suggested.

> Mark off some hour, or some half hour, of each busy day as your
> own, dedicated solely to the private occasions of the spirit. ... You
> will be stronger for it, more composed in mind, more certain in aim,

sweeter and more patient in temper, and as you walk the thronged roads of life once more, you will bring perfume and purification in your very presence.

Dawson concluded: "[W]e have but to make the experiment of prayer to discover its eternal efficacy."[24]

Of course, whether this liberal version of the answered prayer apologetic was convincing depended on what one was trying to prove. That praying yielded positive effects few would have denied; but that this proved that in prayer one actually communed with a personal deity was another matter. While accepting the liberal "answers" as legitimate, secular scientists saw no reason to conclude from them that prayer was anything more than what John Tyndall and others had long considered it to be—spiritual gymnastics. Anna Strong, for instance, was perfectly willing to grant that those who prayed received a mysteriously quickened life from doing so, and that prayer was a universal reality, for, she said, "the desire to fall back on the lesser tension of the subconscious, or, if you please, upon what the individual conceives as the higher and calmer unity of all life, is irresistible." The spiritual peace and comfort that believers experienced in prayer were due, she said, "to the relief of conscious tension and the falling back upon the subconscious organization." Praying could even bring specific virtues and moral qualities to the practitioner who sought them. "It is quite comparable as to methods and results," Strong maintained, "with the attempted cure of the drink habit by hypnotic suggestion. There is the same emphasis of desire in one direction, the same removal of all inhibiting ideas by suggestion, and the same result." For skeptics, Christocentric liberal answered prayer apologetics proved a living, personal God no more than did the "proofs" of conservative Protestants.[25]

There was an important difference, however, between the two apologetic enterprises. Many of the instances cited as answers to prayer by traditionalists—a change in the weather, for example—would have been scoffed at by modern intellectuals. There was no such affront to modern science in the liberal answers to prayer. The answered prayer asserted by the liberals was in fact the kind of prayer that Tyndall had approved of when he said: "It is not my habit of mind to think otherwise than solemnly of the feeling which prompts prayer. It may, as alleged, be necessary to man's highest culture." Francis Galton had concurred: "[A] confident sense of communion with God must necessarily rejoice and strengthen the heart, and divert it from petty cares." The difference was a matter of the interpretation of the phenomenon, not the phenomenon itself. Herein lay one of the qualities that made the liberal ethic of prayer a *sane* mysticism. While maintaining proximity to the prayer tradition of American Protestantism, which asserted prayer's external efficacy, liberals in practice shifted their apologetic of prayer away from external phenomena and defended it in a way consistent with modern thought.[26]

Christocentric liberals sought to reduce the tension between traditional notions of prayer and modernity in another way. While maintaining in word the importance of petitionary prayer, in practice they moved petition to the periphery of prayer. This scaling down of the petitionary element in prayer was exhibited in the liberal idea of prayer as a battlefield. In his chapter "Prayer as a Battlefield," Fosdick called prayer the innermost form of "a fight for character." Through prayer the Christian overcame base desires, examined and purified motives, and aligned him- or herself with God's will. "Prayer," said James Campbell, "is the soul's battle ground where victories are won." The traditional notion of wrestling with God in prayer, said Campbell, was "a travesty." The Christian did not wrestle with God, rather he was to "wrestle with himself to overcome deadness and obstinacy of heart." Prayer was the process by which the Christian struggled with self to achieve character.[27]

While the elements of introspection and meditation had always been parts of Christian prayer, the liberal stress on prayer as a battlefield represented a subtle shift in emphasis. Simply put, traditional Protestants had seen the battle for character as *preparation* for prayer, while liberals saw it as prayer itself. For instance, Austin Phelps gave as one of the reasons Christians did not experience a dynamic, satisfying prayer life the fact that they were too occupied with the cares of the world. "How wearily do we often drag this great earthen world behind us, into the presence of God!" he exclaimed. "Is not our first petition, often, an ejaculation for the ornament of a meek and quiet spirit?" One should instead settle down and collect one's thoughts first before going to God in prayer. Phelps recommended the instructions of the Puritan divine Jeremy Taylor, who had called prayer "the issue of a quiet mind, of untroubled thoughts." The man of the world had to leave temporal matters behind and calm his thoughts before praying, instructed Taylor. Then when "his spirit is becalmed," his prayer "ascends to heaven upon the wings of a holy dove, and dwells with God, till it returns, like the useful bee, laden with a blessing."[28]

Fosdick also cited Jeremy Taylor, but his response to Taylor's understanding of prayer was indicative of change. "Jeremy Taylor may call prayer 'the peace of our spirits, the stillness of our thoughts,'" but, Fosdick said, "Taylor's definition is inadequate. Prayer is a fight for the power to see and the courage to do the will of God." Taylor had certainly believed that mastering self and submitting to God's will were important to the Christian; he simply saw them as occurring *before* one prayed. William Dawson claimed that "in prayer we re-collect ourselves." Traditional American Protestants would have said that *before* prayer we re-collect ourselves. As the Methodist William Kelly declared, noting the subtle change some were making, "the chief end of prayer is not, as some would have us believe, that we may learn submission to the will of God. We are supposed to have subjected ourselves to him before we pray for things."[29]

In the evangelical liberal understanding of prayer, then, what Christians would have typically labeled meditation tended to crowd petition out of prayer. In explaining "battlefield" prayer, Fosdick cited the examples of the missionaries Andrew Gordon and David Brainerd. Yet in each case, Fosdick imparted a slight change in meaning to the events. Gordon was beset with backbiting and envy, but, he said, "by dint of perseverance in prayer, God has given me the mastery to a great degree; I did not wish to give it up, so I besought him to give me that wish; he did so, and then I had the promise of his fulfilment." Gordon thus phrased his "battlefield" with backbiting and envy in the context of petition. In his thinking, his struggle was not so much an internal battle; rather he petitioned God to give him the desire to master envy, and God sent the answer to the prayer. It was not so much Gordon's own internal effort as it was a supernatural act of God that gave him victory. Fosdick, however, cited Gordon's experience as an example of gaining self-mastery in prayer. Similarly, Fosdick cited Brainerd, who, after prayer, re-called, "my joints were loosed; the sweat ran down my face and body as if it would dissolve." For Fosdick, this was evidence of prayer as an internal struggle for character. However, in Brainerd's own accounts, his intense struggle in prayer was over his *petitions* to God for the salvation of the Indians. In each case, the change in meaning was subtle, but revealing.[30]

Along with the Christocentric liberal answered prayer apologetic and the notion of prayer as a battlefield, a third, closely related element in these liberal prayer writings marked them as distinctively "sane" by modern standards. The nature of prayer's efficacy, whenever it was explained, was shown to be understood in a way consonant with modern thought. Traditionally, when Protestants asserted that prayer was efficacious, they typically meant not only that it changed the person praying, but that it somehow it led God to intervene in the world in a direct manner to alter its working or its elements, either in a spiritual or a physical sense. Christians addressed a request to God, which brought about a change independently of the individual praying. This is what Austin Phelps had in mind when he called prayer a real force in the universe, and it is also what Tyndall understood when he proposed the prayer-gauge.

In evangelical liberal writings, however, prayer's efficacy was typically described in another fashion. Like islands in a sea that were rooted in subterranean continents, Christians sought the immanent God within their subconscious, and their communion with him produced spiritual and moral strength that in turn produced a direct, indeed "objective" effect in the real world. Thus, when James Morris Whiton claimed that petitionary prayer had "objective effects" in the world, he meant something quite different than Phelps had. "Verbal expression," he said, "has much to do with both clearness of thought and the concentration of attention and will. . . . The confession in words of our wants to God enables and pledges us in a clearer consciousness to work out more reverently and patiently the Divine conditions of their supply." Thus, Whiton concluded, petitionary prayer had an effect in the world by "clarifying moral insight, deepening reverent convictions of responsibility, and dedicating self more thoroughly to Divine ends, which can be accomplished in the world no sooner or more fully than men devote themselves to their fulfilment." Prayer's effects were on the individual praying and flowed from there out into the external world.[31]

A similar explanation of prayer's efficacy was given by Fosdick. Like traditional defenders of prayer, Fosdick maintained that prayer was "not a form but a force. Prayer really does things." However, what prayer did in Fosdick's description of it was galvanize individuals to change the world themselves. For example, said Fosdick, David Livingstone cried "O God, help me to paint this dark continent white." As a result, "there was an invasion of the world by God through Livingstone." Fosdick concluded that "no one can set clear limits to this release of divine power which the effectual prayer of a righteous man can accomplish." Once again, Fosdick's change in meaning was subtle but telling. In the Bible, the "effectual prayer of a righteous man" referred to Elijah asking God to alter the weather in Palestine. In Fosdick's paradigm, the mode of efficacy was strictly along level one lines: the effect of prayer was on Livingstone, who in turn had a real effect on the world. Traditional Christians, of course, would have agreed that prayer galvanized its practitioner into active service, but they would not have seen such an effect as an example of prayer's *external* efficacy.[32]

Of course, what was important about this notion of the "efficacy" of prayer was that it was the one aspect of prayer most amenable to modern "sane" Americans. By focusing almost exclusively on what traditional Protestants had called the internal function of prayer, Christocentric liberals were able to present a rationale of prayer for intelligent Americans that did not require traditional supernaturalism. At the same time, the liberals' lingering evangelical sentiments led them to assert the traditional rhetoric concerning prayer as a petitionary exercise for which no domain was excluded. Like those who had struggled with a supernaturalistic Christology, moderate liberals writing on prayer before 1920 kept a foot in both the traditional Protestant world and the naturalistic world of modern thought.

The wavering over prayer that this seeming double-mindedness could produce was amply exhibited in the pages of Lyman Abbott's *Outlook*. At times Abbott seemed to negate the element of petition in prayer altogether, defining prayer as a state rather than an act. "True prayer," he claimed, in language reminiscent of Kant, "is not a continual appeal for things that we want, but a continual expression of our willingness to accept what our heavenly Father sees we need." Later Abbott gave examples of what constituted prayer: "expression of gladness, sorrow for our faults," and "aspiration for higher living," all of which could lead some readers to conclude that petition played no part in prayer. Indeed, Abbott called prayer "the intermingling of your life with God's life" and claimed that "they who love pray unceasingly, and unceasingly God answers them."[33]

It is understandable, then, that Abbot received a letter in 1913 from a reader who asked if prayer were no more than earnest desire. No, replied Abbott, prayer involved petition. "The boys in a school may earnestly desire a holiday, but their earnest desire for a holiday is not a petition to the teacher for a holiday." Similarly, prayer was not merely desiring to control one's temper, rather it was "a request for spiritual aid in getting this control." Prayer, then, did involve petition, but apparently only in the spiritual realm. The Christian was to pray for "moral excellence," a request that would invariably be granted.[34]

Those who prayed, said Abbott, received "counsel and comfort" and "help from an unknown source." Like other liberals, Abbott gave an example of answered prayer quite similar to that given by William Dawson. Abbot pictured in typical Victorian fashion a child and his mother praying for a baby sister: "If baby sister is sick and the prayer is, 'God make baby sister well,' the burden of a childish anxiety is lifted off the child and is lightened for the mother." Abbott made no comment concerning the prayer's efficacy in making baby sister well; its effect strictly concerned the internal state of those praying.[35]

Abbott was also adamant about the close relationship between prayer and work, and he asserted that in fact prayer changed things through human agencies. Concerning prayer for the sick, for example, Abbott said: "God has stored the earth with remedies for disease." Essentially, then, Christians answered their own prayers for healing by finding and using the remedies that God had provided in creation. In fact, Abbott said, "men are always praying without knowing it; they are silently asking for things, actively striving to get them." The real prayer for bread, he maintained, was being done by those who till and plant, reap, grind, and mix and bake. "As men have learned to ask, God has given; and asking has meant a study of the soil, invention of new implements of agriculture, more intelligent methods of work." Abbott concluded that "the whole world is organized to answer prayer, and if one puts one's self in the spirit and submits to the teaching which the earth and society offer him through all manner of opportunities, the answer to prayer is unerring and inevitable."[36]

This was hardly the meaning of petitionary prayer in the traditional sense. Abbott seemed to be wiping out petitionary prayer in terms of asking God for a change in the created order beyond what the pray-er could achieve, making prayer simply a subjective spiritual exercise in preparation for real work. That, at least, was what one subscriber to the *Outlook* concluded. In response to Abbott's comments, this subscriber wrote: "[M]ay I call attention to another recent volume which contains suggestions along the lines you have followed." The book was Joseph Henry Crooker's *Church of Tomorrow,* a much more radical statement (compared to Abbott's Christocentric liberalism) of the need of Protestantism to adapt to changing times. The subscriber relayed a lengthy passage by Crooker:

> All the prayers of all the saints could never span the river with a bridge, nor move a train the smallest fraction of an inch, nor produce a more abundant harvest.... To attempt to produce these results in the world of matter by the use of any except physical means is an act of impiety.... The simple fact is that God has not given human desire a mechanical efficiency in the physical world.

The real value of prayer, Crooker argued, is that it "so influences us in the unseen realm of our existence that we become better equipped mentally, physically, or spiritually, as the case may be, to secure by our own endeavors the blessings we crave."[37]

This was prayer understood completely along naturalistic lines: Prayer had no efficacy in the material world, but it could inspire the pray-er to more actively work to change the world. And though Abbott's remarks had inspired his reader to recommend Crooker's statement of prayer, Abbott himself was not prepared to go that far. Crooker's remarks had some sense to them, Abbott replied, "but he who would limit the resources of prayer would limit the power of God." Instructing another reader who had lost faith in petitionary prayer, Abbott showed himself to be more traditional than most liberals by drawing on the Protestant biblicist theme: "The Bible justifies praying for things," he counseled. A small but important window was left open to the possibility of objective answers to prayer as traditional Protestants had conceived of them. Abbott's teaching on prayer thus displayed a mix of traditional and modern elements and illustrated the liberal Protestant penchant for keeping a foot in both traditional and modern camps.[38]

With this understanding of the liberal ethic of prayer as at once "sane" and "mystical," much of the apparent success of Christocentric liberal prayer writings—and in particular Fosdick's *Meaning of Prayer*—can be explained. *The Meaning of Prayer* represented the moderate liberal ethic of prayer in its most polished form. There was nothing completely new in this book; all of Fosdick's emphases had been laid out by Abbott and other liberals before him. However, Fosdick systematized the liberal ethic of prayer and communicated it in his characteristically crisp and vivid style. As I noted earlier, religious observers have seen Fosdick's devotional books, and especially *The Meaning of Prayer,* as tremendously popular and influential. Union Seminary professor John Knox remarked that "no finer books on the meaning of Christian devotion have been written in the last several generations." Many Americans claimed that reading this book saved their Christianity.[39]

The key to this book's success, in addition to Fosdick's widely acclaimed skill in communication, was its ability to speak to Americans across the ideological spectrum of the early twentieth century. As we have seen, the liberals' primary audience was modern, socially minded, active Americans for whom traditional Protestantism was an impossibility. They were those beset by what Fosdick called modern perplexities—namely, that "the reign of law seems to rule out the activity of Providence." This audience was personified in *The Meaning of Prayer* by Florence Nightingale. "When we were children," Fosdick explained, "many of us doubtless prayed as Florence Nightingale said she did." We prayed for specific objects and expected them to come to pass. However, said Fosdick, we moderns can no longer pray this way.

> What is it that has changed this childlike spirit in our prayer? Is it
> not our increasing knowledge of the reign of natural law? So Miss
> Nightingale came to say in contrast with her childhood's point of
> view, "God's scheme for us is not that he should give us what we
> ask for, but that mankind should obtain it for mankind."

Nightingale, of course, went on to perform pioneering work in alleviating human suffering. The liberals' message to "sane" modern readers in the Florence Nightingale mold was essentially this: Yes, the good that will occur in this world will do so by human initiative, not divine fiat; but prayer is a vital means of energizing us to actively change ourselves and the world.[40]

Moreover, the evangelical liberal ethic of prayer for modern readers was a breath of fresh air compared to traditional prayer writings that typically sought to put all Christians in a certain spiritual mold. In contrast to a Protestant devotional classic such as Matthew Henry's *Method of Prayer*, Lyman Abbott asserted, "there are as many forms of prayer as there are petitioners, and every form . . . is good and acceptable." One could not specify one method for all to use. Fosdick was vitally concerned not to let active, healthy-minded modern readers—the "thinkers and workers," in his phraseology—turn away from Christian spirituality. There has been a tendency, he said, to create an impression that prayer is reserved for a certain mystical temperament. This must be changed.

> If prayer is so interpreted that it is left as the possession of those
> only who are of the emotional and mystic temperament, many of the
> most useful folk on earth, in whom practical and intellectual inter-
> ests are supreme—the thinkers and the workers—will feel themselves
> excluded from the possibility of praying. We touch here one of the
> most crucial matters in our study of prayer. *Every man must be al-
> lowed to pray in his own way.* It is far from being true that the most
> valuable temperament in religion is the mystical. God needs us all.

Fosdick thus concluded that "there are as many different ways of praying as there are different individuals."[41]

The Christocentric liberal ethic of prayer's appeal to early-twentieth-century Americans can be demonstrated in "The Praying Football Hero," a 1925 *Literary Digest* feature article.[42] This piece told the story of the captain of the Army football team, Edgar William Garbisch, who, the author observed, "is no recluse, given over entirely to study and meditation. He is a virile, active young man—an example of muscular Christianity." Garbisch had viewed religion as "something apart, something away from my life in general. It seemed a growth on the outside. I could not become interested, and I could not believe in it as a vital portion of life." However, he continued,

> I began to wonder and study and read about the power of prayer. I read *The Meaning of Prayer* by Harry Emerson Fosdick. That remains now one of the greatest books in my life. . . . Through prayer, religion became a real thing for me. It became a part of my actual life, which is the only way I can see that it is of real use.[43]

Garbisch was a typical active, nonreligious, worldly minded modern American who had no use for religious dogmas concerning heaven and hell, biblical inerrancy, and the like. Yet the liberal ethic of prayer appealed to him in a practical, down-to-earth way. He eventually arranged to lead the Army football team in prayer—not a sectarian prayer, of course, but one shared by "Protestants, Catholics, and others." They did not pray for victory. "It was simply that we asked God to permit us to go into action with a clean heart, acquit ourselves like men, give our best all the time and maintain a Christian, sportsmanlike attitude throughout the game." Their prayers proved efficacious in the ethical realm, so to speak. Garbisch said: "I don't think all season that we had more than two or three penalties for holding. . . . And there wasn't a single penalty all season for unsportsmanlike play."[44]

However, such were not all of prayer's effects. Indirectly, it had an impact on the external world. Prayer improved the team's results on the gridiron, for because of their praying spirit, claimed Garbisch, "you couldn't beat that bunch. We had a spirit after that that was unbeatable." Though the team had no great stars, it was beaten only once all season, "and then by Notre Dame, the greatest team of them all." Garbisch's example demonstrated the liberal ethic of prayer's practical appeal among modern Americans and how it had "objective" efficacy in the real world. The Christocentric liberal ethic of prayer, then, appealed to Americans who harbored intellectual doubts and were impatient with old religious constraints.[45]

Yet as has been demonstrated, the evangelical liberals did not burn their bridges behind them. For one thing, the main theme of the moderate liberal understanding of prayer—prayer as essentially communion with God—was not drastically different from that of traditional Protestantism. The Princeton conservative Benjamin Warfield, for example, although he adamantly maintained due to biblical precedent the possibility of level three answers to prayer, argued that communion with God was the most vital aspect of prayer. Even the Keswick holiness writer Henry Frost closed his book on prayer with the words: "[W]hat a marvelous experience it would be both for him and us if we should so come, and if when he had asked us what we might desire we should say, 'Nothing, Father; I am just loving Thee, that is all!' " Christocentric liberals, then, were not departing from tradition by asserting that prayer's primary importance was communion with God that produced ethical and spiritual benefits. The subtle changes discussed here that indicate the ideological revolutions occurring within liberal Protestantism are more apparent in historical hindsight than they were to Protestants of the day.[46]

Furthermore, though not dwelling on such things, liberals repeated the traditional rhetoric and justification of prayer in all domains of life. The farmer could still pray for rain and the mother for her sick child without being rebuked by moderate liberals. Fosdick's list of sources at the end of *The Meaning of Prayer* exemplified a broad approach to prayer, citing books by Andrew Murray and Austin Phelps on the one hand and Anna Louise Strong on the other. Evangelical liberal writings on prayer in effect functioned as a type of devotional Rorschach test; what one got out of them depended upon one's presuppositions. Or, to borrow a political analogy, liberal Protestants were devotional "centrists" whose stance on prayer could appeal to groups on opposite sides of the supernaturalist spectrum. Modern Americans hedged in by the reign of law could gain new insight into how prayer was still a practical, effective discipline in modern life, while traditional Protestants could read Fosdick and rest assured that here was a modern liberal who still testified that God was free to answer any petition whatsoever.

The successful "cross-over" nature of the Christocentric liberal ethic of prayer was evidenced by the commendation *The Meaning of Prayer* received from mainstream Protestants. The book's preface was written by John Mott, the paragon of early-twentieth-century moderate mainline Protestantism, and even conservative Protestants had few negative words for Fosdick's book on prayer. Most revealing was an address on prayer given at the gathering of Baptist conservatives at a preconvention conference at Buffalo in 1920, generally considered one of the early manifestations of the fundamentalist movement. The speaker noted that everyone believed in the subjective effects of prayer, but asked: "[A]re there objective effects through prayer as well as subjective?" Does prayer change conditions, cure illness, avert danger, bring blessings? "Baptists of the past evidently believed so. They took the Bible seriously and believed what it said." The speaker went on to cite "amazing and miraculous answers to prayer." For instance, he said, "Joseph Clark on the Congo prays as the boat filled with cannibals approaches, and a wind rises that blows them off." Here then was a conservative Protestant with a strong view of petitionary prayer, concerned about moderns who were undermining it. Therefore, it is noteworthy that the speaker cited in the span of his talk, in addition to E. M. Bounds and others, a paragraph from *The Meaning of Prayer* by "Doctor Fosdick." Even William Bell Riley, paragon of Baptist fundamentalism, cited Fosdick as an authority in a 1919 article for the *Moody Bible Institute Monthly.*[47]

Indeed, it seemed that the only Protestants to grumble over the Christocentric liberal ethic of prayer were, not surprisingly, those pietistic Christians in the Keswick holiness tradition who strongly emphasized answered prayer. For example, in 1915, Charles Blanchard claimed that there were Protestants writing on prayer who did not really believe that prayer had any effect on the action of God. They "teach that God does not answer prayer," he said, and so "sin against the souls of men" by causing them not to pray. Keswick writer Robert C. McQuilken referred not-so-cryptically to *The Meaning of Prayer* when he complained about "books on prayer which beautifully discuss its philosophy and altogether omit any testimony to the kind of praying that gets miracle results."[48]

McQuilken's grumbling was itself an indication of the success evangelical liberals had in reaching traditional Protestants even while addressing the concerns of the so-called cultured despisers of religion. In fact, despite the traditional rhetoric concerning prayer as efficacious on all levels, moderate liberals essentially had focused almost exclusively on subjective, internal prayer. In the fluid state of American religion before the 1920s, these liberals were able to bridge the gap between modern Americans informed by a world of science and conservative Protestants for whom prayer rested on traditional supernaturalism. In other words, their ethic of prayer was "mystical" enough for the traditionalists but "sane" enough for the moderns.

Six

✛

The New Belief in Prayer

Healing and Intercession
in Liberal Protestantism

The previous chapter explored ways in which evangelical liberals exhibited a concern to retain as much of traditional prayer as their ideological convictions would allow while subtly adapting to modern thought. A more obvious indication of the ambivalent nature of Christocentric liberalism was the eagerness with which these liberals latched onto new developments in science to undergird the traditional faith in intercessory prayer and prayer for healing. These two elements in the Christocentric liberal ethic of prayer—prayer for bodily healing and intercessory prayer—require separate attention because the ideological context surrounding them changed drastically in the early-twentieth century.

In 1909, Ray Stannard Baker claimed that a "great wave of idealistic philosophy" was sweeping over the nation, altering the way Americans thought of matter and spirit. While Baker's frame of reference was obviously limited, other sources, both secondary and primary, indicate that certain segments of society in early-twentieth-century America became, if not exactly bastions of Emersonianism, at least amenable to idealistic interpretations of reality. The idealist influence, according to historian Raymond Cunningham, was felt from the rarefied circles of the Harvard philosopher Josiah Royce to more popular and influential movements such as Christian Science and New Thought.[1]

Many early-twentieth-century observers claimed that scientists were moving away from the materialistic excesses of some nineteenth-century elites back to a more open acceptance of spiritual factors in the universe. Yale's Charles Reynolds Brown said: "[W]e are witnessing a tremendous reaction against that hard, narrow materialism of a generation which now humbly confesses itself to have been too hasty in its judgment and altogether incomplete in the offer it made of a competent philosophy of life." James Campbell maintained that while "in the not far distant past" the scientific spirit was critical, analytic, and destructive, "the pendulum is beginning to swing back toward a simple and rational faith in the reality and power of prayer." In

keeping with the spirit of the times Edward Scribner Ames, a psychologist
of religion, penned an article entitled "Ernest Haeckel and the Passing of
Naturalism" in 1919 in which he claimed that the recent death of the famous
German scientist "marks the passing of the last of his school of thought. . . .
We are emerging from the bondage of Haeckel's notion that to be scientific
involves accepting this philosophy of Naturalism."[2]

The Episcopalian Samuel McComb spoke for many when he titled a 1910
article "The New Belief in Prayer." "We are witnessing at the present time
a resurgence of faith in prayer," he claimed. "This instinct, which for a
generation and more has suffered a great eclipse, chiefly through the ab-
sorbing interest in the natural sciences and the critical temper which they
produce, is now at length reasserting itself and is coming to its own." As a
result of the new idealism of the day, claimed McComb, we are witnessing
"the returning springtide in the spiritual world." He continued: "Renan
spoke with prophetic insight when he said that if the nineteenth century
were materialistic and skeptical, the twentieth would prove idealistic and
believing. . . . There are signs of a revival of a belief that is more than traditional in the reality and value of prayer."[3]

McComb was correct in calling this new belief in prayer "more than traditional," for this was no mere return to traditional supernaturalism. It was
instead a new way of conceptualizing prayer. McComb himself was a committed liberal who attacked the virgin birth, sided with the Episcopalian
modernist Algernon Sidney Crapsey in his famous heresy trial, and had no
place for miracles in his worldview. As Edward Scribner Ames remarked, "it
is true that the passing of Naturalism is accompanied also with the passing
of Supernaturalism." Nature was seen to be uniform; all proceeded according
to laws of cause and effect, with no divine intervention in the universe. The
"new belief in prayer," however, lent support to petitionary prayer by incor-
porating mental as well as physical phenomena as causative factors in the
universe.[4]

In general terms, the "new idealism" represented something of a reversal
of the understanding of matter and spirit that had underlain the prayer-gauge
debate of the nineteenth century. Scientists and many orthodox Protestants
of the nineteenth century had viewed the physical, natural world as "hard,"
while thoughts and ideas were thought of as "soft." Thus prayer, which was
a mental act, worked by inducing God to step into this chain of cause and
effect. For example, during the prayer-gauge debate J. H. Jellett had said:

> Now, it will be conceded on all hands, that prayer can produce an
> external effect only in one way—namely, by determining the appear-
> ance of the Divine volition in the series of antecedents. Prayer is not
> of the nature of a physical cause. It cannot produce a physical effect
> by the introduction of a series of purely physical phenomena. It is a
> petition addressed by man to God, and can act only, like any other

petition, by influencing the will of the person to whom the petition is addressed.

Since the physical, impersonal part of the universe proceeded according to a sequence of *physical* causes and effects, it was not the prayer itself that altered events but *God* who might, in answer to the prayer, effect a change in the created order.[5]

If, however, thoughts themselves were "of the nature of a physical cause," to use Jellett's phrase, then prayer may have uses independent of a personal, transcendent God. That is in fact what certain Americans came to believe in the early twentieth century. According to the new idealism, the physical world was "soft" and ideas were "hard." The really effectual things in the universe were thoughts; matter was plastic and could be molded by the mental. The essence of the new idealism was the idea that, as W. P. Paterson explained, "the human mind can do unsuspected work in a world in which all facts are ultimately mental." As McComb asserted, "our thoughts are not dead, inert things; they are living forces that tend to find expression in corresponding physical states." This understanding of thoughts as living forces formed the basis of the new belief in prayer.[6]

At its most popular level, the new idealism manifested itself in the New Thought of Ralph Waldo Trine, whose book *In Tune with the Infinite* first appeared in 1897 and enjoyed continued success for years thereafter. Trine's subtitle summarized the goal of New Thought: "Fullness of Peace, Power, and Plenty." According to Trine, "the realm of the unseen is the realm of cause. The realm of the seen is the realm of effect." The "supreme fact of the universe" was a benevolent Spirit of Life and Power that lay in back of everything. Humanity's purpose was to realize its oneness with Infinite Life and open up the floodgates for this Life to flow into individuals and empower them: "To come into harmony with it and thereby with all the higher laws and forces, to come then into league and to work in conjunction with them, in order that they can work in league and conjunction with us, is to come into the chain of this wonderful sequence," claimed Trine. "This is the secret of all success."[7]

According to Trine, one could tap into these spiritual reservoirs of power by realizing that the idea of gravity applied to the unseen world as well as to the visible world. There are laws of spiritual attraction; faith draws spiritual forces to the individual in direct proportion to the strength of his or her faith. This had a direct impact on physical health. Since the Infinite Spirit was health and goodness, by thinking good thoughts one could link up with the infinite and allow its healing water to rush through oneself and wash out any ill health. Thus, advised Trine, we must assert mind over matter, think positive thoughts, and not allow bad thoughts to lodge in us. By mastering such techniques, we could recover the supposedly miraculous healing powers that Christ displayed when he awakened faith in the person to be healed, thus allowing the healing power to flow into that person. Such "divine" healing was open to all, for, Trine maintained, "any power that is possible to one human soul is possible to another."[8]

Basic to Trine's enterprise was the idea that thoughts were real factors in the mental world that had tangible effects. "Every thought you entertain," Trine claimed, "is a force that goes out." A thought was a real *thing* that "invariably produces its effect before it returns." Yet Trine was adamant that there was nothing sectarian or supernatural about this. All proceeded according to laws of the spiritual world; each individual could gain immediate benefit from realizing and capitalizing on the spiritual resources that underlay the physical world. Trine thus closed by prescribing a regimen of daily devotions in which believers spent a few moments each day in quiet allowing "God" to take possession of their soul.[9]

New Thought ideas as a basis for prayer also appeared among those educated, respectable middle-class Americans who constituted liberal Protestantism's main audience. For instance, Ellen Burns Sherman's "Evolution of Prayer," published in the venerable *North American Review* in 1912, was vintage Trine. Like everything else, Sherman argued, our notions of prayer need to evolve with changing ideas. Fortunately, the discovery of the powers of the subconscious had thrown open the doors to modern prayer. Indeed, it was common knowledge now, she claimed, that "before going to sleep one may give an order to his subliminal self to wake him up at a given hour and be confident that the command will be obeyed." If the subconscious mind could do so much, she said, surely the possibilities of the subconscious in prayer were immense. Each originating thought had an energy of attraction, Sherman explained, that drew the powers of the universe to it. Thus, she concluded, "when you have a thing in mind, it is not long till you have it in hand."[10]

In 1921, the popular Protestant author and minister J. Edgar Park asked in the *Atlantic Monthly*, "Is There Anything in Prayer?" Yes, he concluded, in the new idealist sense of the word. "There are laws governing the organization of unsatisfied desires, which must be observed." Prayer was simply the proper organization of one's unsatisfied desires. It is "an activity of the will and mind and feeling which makes us the natural channel through which good effects flow to those for whom we pray." Thus, for example, a mother whose son is doing poorly in school "replaces the picture of failure, which threatens to become fixed in her mind, with a more vivid and living picture of success." As a result, "in the thousand ways, known and unknown, in which the mother's mind touches the mind of the child, . . . faith in his powers now flow in upon the will of the child."[11]

Such a mental influence, Park believed, may even aid in healing of physical illnesses of another person, for "who can tell in what numberless ways the minds of those who love touch one another, all unseen even by the argus eyes of science? Miracles occur, and the tide of life returns into sluggish

veins, when the desire of life is kindled through the touch of kindred minds."
Park was thus willing to grant "prayer," in this modern sense of the word,
significant power in the physical world. However, he was careful to distance
such a conception of prayer from traditional Christian supernaturalism.
"There is no dogmatism in such prayer," he said. "The claim is simply made
on the universe."[12]

Louise Willcox answered the question "Shall We Pray?" in similar fashion
in *Harper's*. "We are uncertain what God is like," she said, "and we no more
feel sure that Heaven is a city in the sky." Shall we cease to pray, then? No,
Willcox said, for "the law of cause and effect goes on beyond our sight . . .
in the unseen world as in the seen." Each deed and thought goes on forever,
for all things are ultimately connected. Hence, even though no *person* hears
prayer, "the whole universe hears it." One's prayer, Willcox claimed, "leaves
just a tiny dent on the great, inert mass of matter. . . . If we desire, the answer
is there, unrealized perhaps, but as necessarily existent in the universe as
the circle the pebble makes in the pond." Our prayer may be no more than
the lifting of a casual thought and "flinging it out beyond the bound of one's
petty human vision," but because the universe was basically mind, not matter, Willcox believed, we could have faith that the desire would ultimately
be answered.[13]

The "cultured despisers of religion" who constituted an important audience for liberal Protestants, then, did not necessarily abandon belief in prayer
when they left Christian orthodoxy. Indeed, the potential of prayer in accordance with the new belief in mind power was seen as virtually unlimited by
some in this group. In the future, claimed one writer in the *North American
Review*, "when we see a comet coming our way we may be able to pray our
planet out of its course as easily as we steer a ship out of the course of
another and avoid a collision." This remark was made not by some socially
marginal mind-cure proponent but by Edward S. Martin, a founding editor
of *Life* magazine and assistant editor of *Harper's* in the early twentieth century. Clearly, the new idealism had made significant inroads in middle-class
America.[14]

The fact that ideas of prayer shaded by New Thought were popular among
writers in the *Atlantic* and the *North American Review* indicated that this
was no quack philosophy on the fringes of society. In fact, openness to the
possibilities of mind-power existed among the modern-day arbiters of reality,
the scientists. Though it was only a semirevolution at best, certain influential
scientists around the turn of the century lent credibility to the new idealism.
Samuel McComb, therefore, claimed that a spiritual reaction had taken place
against the "hard, if brilliant, materialistic philosophy" of a generation ago,
and he named numerous examples. "Men of the highest distinction in the
realms of thought, imagination, and practical enterprise, such as Tennyson,
Meredith, James, Myers, Stevenson, Lodge, Lecky, H. M. Stanley, and Cecil
Rhodes, joined their voices to the chorus inviting us to pray." Of these

names, I will discuss two here who illustrate the turn away from materialism that some intellectuals were taking.[15]

The most important American intellectual who turned away from a so-called bare materialism was, of course, William James. A pioneering psychologist who claimed immense prestige among the American public, James illustrated the contribution this budding science made to the new belief in prayer. He was, according to historian Donald Meyer, the "chief authority" for those espousing New Thought ideas. In a field in which most scientists were searching for ways in which mental phenomena were determined by physical and biological causes, James represented those who sought to reverse the direction of influence—he explored ways in which mental states affected physical reality. James called the discovery of the subconscious "the most important step that has occurred in psychology since I have been a student of that science." After surveying hundreds of testimonies of religious experience for his book *The Varieties of Religious Experience*, James concluded that the "subconscious self" was a real psychological entity much more extensive than scientists had realized. On its farther side it is linked up with the "MORE," which western civilization typically referred to as "God." People may differ in how they describe this "MORE," James concluded, but, "that the conscious person is continuous with a wider self through which saving experiences come . . . seems to me literally and objectively true as far as it goes."[16]

By tapping into this reservoir of spiritual power, individuals gained power, not only spiritually but physically. In prayer, said James, "something ideal, which in one sense is part of ourselves and in another sense is not ourselves, actually exerts an influence, raises our center of personal energy, and produces regenerative effects unattainable in other ways." Anyone who viewed the phenomena objectively, believed James, had to conclude that prayer had a real effect on physical well-being. In a remark that would be cited almost invariably by liberal Protestants, James said that, "as regards prayer for the sick, if any medical fact can be considered to stand firm, it is that in certain environments prayer may contribute to recovery, and should be encouraged as a therapeutic measure."[17]

James thus criticized the closed-minded, "sectarian" scientists of his day who refused to accept the mounting evidence for the power of spiritual forces. "I can, of course," said James, "put myself into the sectarian scientist's attitude, and imagine vividly that the world of sensations and of scientific laws and objects may be all." But, he continued, "the total expression of human experience, as I view it objectively, urges me beyond the narrow 'scientific bounds.'" The rigorously materialistic view of modern science, James mused, "might one day appear as having been a temporary useful eccentricity rather than the definitively triumphant position which the sectarian scientist at present confidently announces it to be." James preferred to call himself a "crass supernaturalist" because he believed that "transmundane energies, God, if you will, produced immediate effects within the natural world." James was no supernaturalist in the sense that traditional Christians were, but the fact that one of the nation's most eminent thinkers would call himself one indicated a significant development in intellectual circles. As Robert Bruce Mullin has observed, "more than any other figure, James gave intellectual credibility to the new search for evidence of the spirit world." Moreover, it was extremely important to those seeking to pray in harmony with modern thought that they had an advocate among America's intellectual elite.[18]

Another prominent intellectual figure lending credibility to the new belief in prayer was Sir Oliver Lodge, a highly esteemed British physicist. Lodge's experiments concerning ether and electromagnetic radiation paved the way for the theory of relativity. He was knighted in 1902 and served as president of the British Association for the Advancement of Science in 1913. Lodge's interest in science was sparked by hearing John Tyndall speak at the Royal Institution in London, and Tyndall, as the symbol of critical, hard, unsentimental scientific method, remained one of Lodge's heroes. Lodge even wrote the entry on Tyndall for the *Encyclopedia Britannica*. It seems ironic, then, that one of Tyndall's heirs would do as much as any other scientist to renew modern Americans' faith in the benefits of petitionary prayer.[19]

As a young physicist, Lodge became interested in reports of psychic phenomena and befriended the Cambridge classical scholar Frederick H. Myers. Myers had founded the Society for Psychical Research in 1882 to scientifically explore the possibilities of telepathy, telekinesis, mediums, psychosomatic healing, and other forms of mind power. In 1884, Lodge served as an independent scientific witness to a demonstration of telepathy and was convinced that the phenomenon was legitimate. He joined the Society for Psychical Research, and, as its president after 1900, his sterling scientific reputation lent legitimacy to the enterprise. Lodge also struck up a friendship with William James, beginning in 1889 when James brought a purported medium, Mrs. Piper, to England for evaluation. Lodge and James became long-time colleagues in the attempt to verify and explain psychic phenomena.[20]

As remarked earlier, the openness of men like Lodge and James to mindpower as a causative agent in the physical world represented a half-revolution at best in scientific circles. Lodge had to constantly defend his interest in psychic phenomena to other scientists who considered his views ridiculous; in the scientific world's eyes only his groundbreaking work in physics outweighed his dabbling in such things. James admitted that "the current of thought in academic circles" ran against him. Louis Pasteur's recent germ theory only strengthened the prevailing scientific school of opinion that physical illness was rooted in unalterable biological factors, not in mental ones. However, the fact that certain prominent scientists were willing to accept such phenomena was of great importance to liberal writers on prayer. Liberal

Protestantism, as I have shown, was a movement shaped by the assumption that nothing in religion should stand in disharmony with modern science. The practical effect of the new idealism among some respected scientists, then, was to provide a small, albeit temporary window of opportunity for liberal Protestants to affirm level two and level three prayer while still being scientific in the modern sense of the term.[21]

The importance to liberal Protestants of men like Lodge was expressed in a 1920 *Christian Century* article "Sir Oliver Lodge and Religion," by the Disciples of Christ minister H. D. C. Maclachlan. In an open letter to a liberal colleague, Maclachlan asserted his impeccable modernist credentials. "You cannot believe more completely than I in the 'scientific point-of-view,' or the necessity of clearing away the undergrowth of superstition," he said. "To science belongs the task of determining all matters of empirical fact, and to oppose the authority of church or Book to its seasoned conclusions in such matters is to play the role of a very futile Mrs. Partington."[22]

However, Maclachlan went on, "I cannot follow you in your conception of the supernatural." Maclachlan's colleague disbelieved in miracles, seeing them as a mere husk needing to be stripped away from the ethical kernel of Christ's teaching. Maclachlan, however, believed that "supernormal phenomena . . . are of the essence of Christianity." If you take the miracles out of Christianity, "you remove its prime postulate and change not only its form, which is admissible, but its nature." Hence the importance of men such as Oliver Lodge to Maclachlan. Lodge represented, said Maclachlan, a

> rapidly growing number of eminent men of science who stand for the scientific endorsement of the very kind of supernatural for which I am pleading. In other words, if he and his co-workers are right, one does not, in order to be strictly scientific, need any longer to desupernaturalize the Christian tradition, since the very things that were formerly a stumbling block to faith are now in good scientific standing.

Even the miracles of Jesus—indeed the resurrection itself—posed no problem to the new science. "No one can read a page of the New Testament without feeling that he is breathing exactly the same atmosphere as that in the Reports of the Psychical Research Society." The postresurrection appearances of Jesus were "typical 'phantasms of the dead,' and if they occurred today would at once be submitted to the Society for Psychical Research for verification." Thus, concluded Maclachlan, due to the efforts of those on what was to him the cutting edge of science, "I can believe in the supernatural in the old religious sense."[23]

This was clearly *not* supernaturalism in the old religious sense, which had supposed a dualism between God and the created world. Maclachlan's beliefs, he maintained, were "not at all inconsistent with an ultimate oneness of

Reality." Moreover, the explanation of Jesus' miracles as due to him being ahead of his time in his knowledge of mental science—a popular belief of the day—was just as antithetical to orthodoxy as the denial of the miracles themselves. The purpose of the gospel miracles, in orthodox teaching, was to show Jesus as uniquely the Son of God in a way that no other human being was. If, however, Jesus was simply "the Greatest Teacher of Mental Science the world has ever seen," as Ellen Burns Sherman called him, then his gifts were available to anyone who perfected these principles. All of this was explained by Princeton seminary's Benjamin Warfield, who throughout his lifetime displayed a keen nose for even the faintest scent of heresy (in this case, the aroma was pungent). Attributing the miracles of Jesus to the use of mind-power, he said, "tends to obliterate the category of the miraculous altogether, and in the long run to assimilate the mighty works of our Lord to—we put it at its best—the wonders of science, and Him, as their worker, to—we still put it at its best—the human sage."[24]

Traditional supernaturalism or not, the effect of the new idealism among some eminent intellectuals was to give those concerned with maintaining petitionary prayer in a world of science a foothold on which to stand. Maclachlan told his liberal colleague: "You still pray, of course, but you would confine the possible answer to a sort of reflex spiritual influence." Maclachlan wanted more room for petitionary prayer than simply that it benefited the pray-er spiritually. The new science opened the door for "objective" answers to prayer. Maclachlan concluded that "to be scientific, therefore, after this newer pattern, one need not . . . try to make oneself believe that prayer loses nothing in value, if the answer to it be merely subjective." With the sanction of men like James and Lodge, objective answers to prayer were once again possible, even for those who wished to remain scientific.[25]

The affinities between the new idealism and liberal Protestantism are obvious. Liberalism was itself rooted in German Idealism, and it was a small step to substitute for the Infinite Spirit, or Mind, of New Thought the personal, immanent All-Father of liberalism. Applying the insights of the new psychology, New Thought, and mind-cure to Christian doctrines of prayer offered liberal Protestants a way to maintain belief in petitionary prayer on levels two and three without resorting to traditional supernaturalism.

The primary arenas in which the new belief in prayer manifested itself in liberal Protestantism were healing and intercession. Healing made its deepest inroads among liberals in the Episcopal Church. Episcopalians had long been open to the idea of physical healing. In the 1870s, one of the first American Protestants involved in the faith healing movement had been the Episcopalian minister Charles Cullis. Cullis's healing ministry was of the traditional sort; physical healings were a result of divine intervention in the physical world in response to prayer, and he based his beliefs on the teachings of Scripture. In other words, Cullis and the faith healers of his generation were traditional supernaturalists.[26]

In the twentieth century, however, a very different type of healing movement emerged in the Episcopal Church, one founded squarely on modernistic principles. Whereas the healing movement of Cullis and others was, in historian Robert Bruce Mullin's term, "thaumaturgic," that is, miraculous, the new form of healing was strictly therapeutic. The emphasis was not on wondrous miracles but on therapy in keeping with sound scientific theory. This was the Emmanuel Movement, and the movement's founder, Elwood Worcester, was a frank modernist who wrote a number of critiques of supernatural Christianity. In 1906, Worcester, rector of Emmanuel Church in Boston, began a ministry dedicated to the cooperation of clergy and medical professionals in the ministry of healing. Its basis was an assumption that such healing had to be grounded in modern scientific theory. Old theories of divine intervention were, in their worldview, incomprehensible. Rather, the new idealism opened up for them a new understanding of the healing power of religion.[27]

The Emmanuel Movement's primary spokesperson was Worcester's colleague, the aforementioned Samuel McComb. Born in Ireland and educated at Oxford, McComb wrote a number of articles explaining how the new idealism reinvigorated belief in prayer for physical healing. His 1918 essay "Prayer: Its Meaning, Reality, and Power" won the Walker Prize in Scotland's international competition of articles on prayer. Since human nature was a unity of spirit and body, McComb argued, "all diseases are at once physical and mental." That being the case, prayer played just as important a role in the individual's recovery from disease as did medical treatment. "Statistical inquiry has shown," McComb said, "that patients who are prayed for, and who know that they are being prayed for, have a better chance of recovery than those who ignore this spiritual help."[28]

There were limits, however, to these modern level three prayers. Prayer for the body was one thing, but prayer for the weather was something quite different. Though William James recommended praying for healing, he asserted that "the case of the weather is different. . . . Everyone now knows that droughts and storms follow from physical antecedents, and that moral appeals cannot avert them." James's Protestant admirers, McComb among them, made the same distinction. "The pious man," he maintained, "will not pray for a violation or suspension of any of these fixed expressions of the divine will which we call 'the laws of nature.' " Wherever the will of God is expressed unmistakably, he said, such as in "the law of gravitation, or of the succession of the seasons, or of the finality of death as a temporal event, prayer has no place." External nature was uniform and inviolable. Thus, McComb concluded, though many untenable claims had been made in the name of religious faith, prayer was not capable of "changing, as by a miracle, the face of nature." Edward Martin's hopes of changing the orbit of earth through prayer notwithstanding, those in the therapeutic healing movement walled off external nature from the realm of prayer. In the human biological sphere, however, therapeutic healers maintained that prayer was legitimate and efficacious.[29]

As well as from McComb and the Emmanuel Movement, the Christocentric liberals discussed in chapter 5 freely borrowed from the insights of William James and the new idealism to explain prayer for healing. Indeed, Lyman Abbott, Harry Emerson Fosdick and other leading liberals rarely wrote on the issue of prayer and physical ailments without the name of William James, if not an actual citation from him, appearing. For them, the new idealism was a new way—with quasi-scientific legitimacy—to maintain the traditional faith in prayer's objective efficacy.

Sometimes the link between the liberal ethic of prayer and New Thought was quite overt, as when William Dawson defined prayer as "the effort to bring the human soul into tune with the Infinite." Usually, however, reliance on the tenets of the new idealism only emerged when liberals discussed certain forms of petitionary prayer. In "A Medical Estimate of Prayer," Lyman Abbott quoted extensively from a doctor who expounded on "the therapeutic value of prayer." "It matters not what are one's theological conceptions," he concluded, "the effect is the same." Later, when addressing how one should pray in a case of illness, Abbott essentially waffled, but he closed with the remark: "[T]here is medicine to the spirit as well as to the body, and medicine to the spirit is sometimes medicine to the body."[30]

Fosdick also employed the tenets of therapeutic religion on occasion. In one of his earliest works, Fosdick waxed optimistic about the possibilities being explored by psychical research. "It may be," he said, "that great light will break upon us from this quarter, and that, as Frederick Myers prophesied, a few generations hence it will be impossible for any man to doubt the appearances of Jesus to His disciples after Calvary." Indeed, Fosdick was open, like other moderns, to explaining the gospel miracles in light of the new idealism. Jesus "had faith and demanded faith," Fosdick asserted, "and wherever the faith-attitude can be set in motion against the fear-attitude and all its morbid brood, the consequences will be physical as well as moral." After citing William James's recommendation of prayer as a therapeutic measure, Fosdick explained that, "prayer is the inner battlefield where men often conquer most effectively all the unwholesome specters of the mind that irritate the spirit and make the body ill." Far be it from he, Fosdick, to tell the faithful that prayer for physical ailments was useless in a world of science.[31]

Among liberal devotional writers, James Campbell, the Methodist, waxed the most enthusiastic about the therapeutic value of prayer for physical ailments.[32] "The church of to-day," Campbell complained, "is being shorn largely of her power because she is not exercising her healing ministry." She was losing ground to Christian Science and New Thought because she failed to meet the physical needs of people. The church's prayer meetings, Campbell advised, "ought to be 'testimonial meetings,' at which those who have been sick in body and in soul shall bear witness to the healing, restoring power of the Living Christ." As to the method of such healing through prayer, however, Campbell was clearly modern. The laws of suggestion work freely during prayer, he said. More important, through prayer "we virtually give an invitation to the Infinite Life, with which connection has been made, to enter the soul, and work within it and through it all his healing, recreative power."[33]

This is not to say that these liberals were themselves exemplars of the new "therapeutic spirituality" that became a fixture of twentieth-century religion. Although historian Donald Meyer has called Fosdick's 1943 work *On Being A Real Person* "pure therapeutic psychology," in the period before 1920, at least, mainstream liberal Protestantism and the therapeutic religion of Samuel McComb were clearly two separate entities. The most that can be said is that the evangelical liberals borrowed from the insights of the new psychology and New Thought when it was useful to do so but never emphasized such elements in their ethic of prayer.[34]

One element that kept Christocentric liberals, with their strong notion of a personal God, at a polite distance from New Thought forms of mind-cure was the latters' undermining of a central aspect of personality: arbitrary will. Mind-cure made physical well-being contingent on the observance of certain unalterable universal laws, thereby expunging the variable of a willful God from the healing equation. In the orthodox Protestant understanding of prayer, one may pray properly and still not receive the thing asked for, since God had a will and chose whether or not to grant the petition according to his own purposes. New Thought sought to purge this unpredictable element from the equation. Donald Meyer writes:

> Nothing betrayed this redirection of orthodox theology more plainly than mind cure's invariable omission of the idea of God as Will. Will, or Sovereignty, implied the gap between ruler and ruled, the inevitable danger that the ruled could never succeed thoroughly in searching out the purposes of the ruler. Mind cure's translation of "omnipotence" as "all-power" lacked this essential characteristic of Will—irreducible inward mystery. Will manifested what mind cure wished to expunge—the arbitrary.

In mind-cure the focus was not on God but on technique. If mind-cure failed, it was because the practitioner failed to properly utilize the principles.[35]

In Protestant circles, Samuel McComb evinced the same impulse. "Whatever is hard and exclusive and arbitrary about the notion of personality should be dissolved away in the vision of universal forces that are operative in the smallest as in the greatest things on earth," he declared. The effectiveness of intercessory prayer, according to McComb, was not dependent on whether or not God, to whom the prayers were directed, chose to make them effective. Rather, there were "laws which connect soul with soul, and all souls with the Universal Soul." And intercessory prayer was simply making the most of those universal, unwavering laws.[36]

Moderate liberals before the 1920s, however, resisted somewhat this downplaying of the arbitrary will of God in petitionary prayer. The issue was a bit problematic for them, since, as noted earlier, consistency in the deity was a prized trait. Nevertheless, they maintained that a willful God chose according to his own purposes whether or not to grant the answer to prayers. In citing William James's recommendation of prayer for healing, James Campbell was careful to note that "nothing is said by him to warrant the belief that the recovery of the sick will always take place in answer to prayer." For Campbell, God was still arbitrary, an unpredictable variable in the prayer equation. Physical healing depended on God's purposes, which entailed more than physical health. "Not all who pray for the recovery of others have their prayers answered," he said, for "God always subordinates physical to spiritual interests. He is more concerned about our souls than about our bodies; about our character than about our comfort."[37]

Campbell's comments revealed the major distinction between evangelical liberals and proponents of therapeutic spirituality. While sharing certain ideological assumptions, they differed on the purpose of prayer and religion in general. For therapeutic religionists, health was an unquestioned good, an end in itself. McComb, claimed that "disease is an evil. . . . Health is normal; disease is abnormal." For mainstream liberals, *character* was the goal of life, and physical well-being was subsumed under that larger purpose. "The healing cult that is annexing itself to the office of the preacher," George Gordon said, was an "evil tendency," because it looked at human beings from a physical rather than a spiritual perspective. "The human person," he maintained," is "essentially a spiritual being, one whose most serious concerns are those of character. The claims put forward in behalf of psychic healing are in favor of an inferior interest." A request to God for physical healing, then, may or may not be answered, depending on whether or not it would further the spiritual and moral interests of the person. "The fruits of character," said Lyman Abbott, "cannot be realized until the seeds of nobility have had time to grow," and sometimes it is physical hardship that is required to produce inward character.[38]

Moreover, these liberals were heirs to the evangelical zeal of the late nineteenth century that had launched such crusades as the Student Volunteer Movement and the Social Gospel. They believed as strongly as did revivalistic evangelicals that the purpose of the spiritual life was to empower the Christian for effective service. Fosdick's *Meaning of Prayer*, therefore, was followed five years later by *The Meaning of Service* (1920). The Christian should experience communion with God in prayer, said Walter Fiske, but "it is a woeful waste of spiritual forces unless this experience brings fresh power into their lives." And this power was not for better health but for more effective Christian service. Prayer generated spiritual energy, but we must "apply the energy we have thus generated, and over some sort of invisible high-tension wires to carry it to the field of human service." Just as Keswick holiness evangelicals pictured the Christian as a soldier in God's service, so too the liberals saw the Christian life in terms of active, sacrificial service. "Just what ought to be thought of a man," asked Abbott derisively, "who accepts the pledge of Almighty God for all the resources of infinity to enable him to serve his fellow-men, and asks to use it that he may get ease and luxury for himself?" He answered, "[W]e are here, if we are really in the Christ spirit, not to ask for the best office, the easiest place, the largest wealth, but to ask for the best opportunity for the largest service."[39]

The attitude of many liberals toward therapeutic religion may thus be characterized by the suggestion of *Christian Century* editors Herbert Willett and Charles Clayton Morrison recommended that Christians utilize the insights of the new idealism "without adopting the theories of those who make physical healing central in their religion." When God *did* choose to answer prayer for healing, the method used was not supernatural intervention but the therapeutic effect of prayer upon the body. Though mainstream liberals were not outright proponents of therapeutic religion, the important function that the new idealism served in the liberal ethic of prayer should not be overlooked. Liberal Protestants, while remaining within the bounds of a culturally legitimated science, were able to affirm the traditional Protestant faith that prayer could bring about the healing of the body, even if their rationale for it differed from that of traditionalists.[40]

In addition to prayer for bodily healing, American Protestants traditionally believed in and valued intercessory prayer—that is, prayer for the needs of others. This faith was exemplified in John Mott, a mainline missions statesman, leader of the YMCA, and the epitome of mainstream Protestantism in the first half of the twentieth century. Mott was, like most mainstream Protestants of the day, a theological moderate; while he differed from conservatives in refusing to exclude liberal Protestants from fellowship, Mott himself remained essentially orthodox in belief. Mott was intensely concerned with spreading the influence of Christianity across the world, and he saw intercessory prayer as the key ingredient in this task. "Beyond question," he wrote in 1909, "prayer is the mightiest force which any Christian can wield in this world." At a time, he claimed, when "rationalists in Europe and in our own country have been loudly asserting that prayer does not have achieving power, that it does not bring things to pass objectively," Mott maintained that intercessory prayer was the key to the success of the gospel in the world. The opening of mission fields, the overcoming of opposition, the raising of workers and money all depended on the intercessory prayers of Christians. "The energies of God are released in answer to prayer. Everything vital to the missionary enterprise hinges on prayer."[41]

Mott, ever the organizer, urged churches to institute a strategy of intercessory prayer, complete with posted maps of the world and daily schedules and prayer bands within the local church. In 1916, the mainstream Association Press published *The Discipline of Prayer*, which closed with a weekly schedule of intercessory prayer. Each day had a specific denomination, national need, and continent to pray for. Mott claimed that interest in intercessory prayer, spurred by the onset of World War I, was worldwide. "The multiplication of Calls to Prayer and of Prayer Cycles, and the formation of Prayer Bands and of Leagues of Intercession," he said, all demonstrate the commitment among American Christians to intercessory prayer.[42]

Evangelical liberals were heirs to this tradition and valued intercessory prayer. Moreover, if their ethic of prayer was to resonate within the rest of mainline Protestantism, it would clearly have to affirm intercession. But to the modern consciousness, traditional notions of intercessory prayer were untenable. For one thing, the theological argument against prayer was most heavily felt there. "That God should deliberately withhold from a man in China something that he is free to give him ... until it occurs to me to ask him to bestow it," wrote Fosdick, "plainly involves a thought of deity with pagan elements in it." If God were good and wise, he would not wait for the prayers of another before blessing someone. A more spiritual, less anthropomorphic conception of the deity did not square well with such aspects of traditional notions of intercession. Moreover, in the one-tiered universe of modern science, the idea of praying to a God "up there" who in turn intervened in the life of another was problematic. Liberal Protestants, however, maintained a belief in intercessory prayer; they simply explained it on the basis of the new idealism rather than using traditional supernaturalism.[43]

The new idealism changed the way the geometry of intercessory prayer was visualized. According to the traditional understanding of intercessory prayer, to put it crudely, the Christian prayed "up" to God, who sent a response "down" to another person on earth. A typical example of intercessory prayer, related by Henry Frost in *Effective Praying*, illustrates this understanding of intercession. Henrietta Soltau, a worker at the China Inland Mission training school in London, sensed an uneasy spirit one night that kept her from sleeping. She determined that God wanted her to pray for something, so she knelt in prayer. There came into her mind a party of missionaries that was on its way to China. At once she had the conviction that these friends were in danger and so she prayed for their protection. Her heart was eased, and she returned to bed. Later, Soltau received a letter from one of the missionaries. As it turned out, at the very time Soltau was moved to pray, the missionaries were sailing through a dangerous storm on the Indian Ocean. The missionary, too frightened to pray herself, had cried to the Lord, "O God, lead Miss Soltau to pray for us!" Soon after, the storm abated. For orthodox Protestants, such an instance was evidence of a transcendent, personal God who closely governed the people and events in the world.[44]

Proponents of the new idealism, however, would not have doubted this story (though they would have questioned the calming of the storm as an answer to prayer). Rather, they would attribute such an incident to the tremendous powers of mind and telepathy that the new psychology was only beginning to discover. The missionary's distress, formed into a prayer, somehow sped through a "subliminal consciousness" directly to her friend in London, prodding her to pray. Rather than intercessory prayer being based in a kind of triangular imagery, the thought itself was deemed to have direct power. In a kind of Occam's Razor applied to intercessory prayer, modern idealists simplified the equation by eliminating a personal, active, transcendent God from the equation.[45]

J. Edgar Park explained the new imagery of intercessory prayer in these terms. In traditional intercession, such as a mother praying for her child, he said, the case is looked upon as a triangle—"the mother and the child are at the base angles; God is at the apex. The mother sends up a prayer to God, which God considers, and, if it seems good to Him, sends down the answer to the child." For a growing school of religious thinkers, however, the process was "not so much a triangle as a straight line." The prayer itself traveled directly from the mother to the child, becoming a "natural channel through which good effects flow to those for whom we pray."[46]

W. P. Paterson, explaining what he called the theosophic conception of prayer-force, said:

> We are all living in a great ocean of mind power wherein the waves of mentative action are passing on all sides. The vibrational activity set up in our mind at the time of a deep and earnest sentiment passes on its vibrations to this ocean of mind-power, producing currents or waves which travel on until they reach the mind of other individuals who reach them as if by induction. Thus our religious influence passes on to other people who are receptive to our feelings.

Liberal Protestants who wished to justify intercessory prayer simply inserted the Christian God into Paterson's model. God was the "ocean" that surrounded individuals and through which the thoughts of one person emanated to another. McComb explained:

> All souls live in God and through Him. He is their unifying bond, the fundamental ground of their existence. Hence they lie open to His influence, and to the influences of other souls which energise in harmony with Him. Thus we can understand, in a certain measure, how prayers, or wishes of ours, rising up in the Divine mind can reach and influence other spirits.

A contributor to the *Baptist* put it in coarser terms: "[I]ntercession is the wireless message sent by my soul to another through the ether of God's love."[47]

Evangelical liberals invariably used such ideas to defend intercessory prayer. Even though, as McComb admitted, " 'orthodox' science, generally speaking, rejects the existence of such facts," nevertheless there were some "competent and highly-trained specialists" who were convinced that the mind could reach other minds through mental action. The community represented by Lodge and James was, moreover, the only school of modern science that allowed for intercessory prayer as an efficacious enterprise, and its claims were seized on by liberals who wished to retain this aspect of prayer.[48]

How could one justify praying for others in a world of scientific law? a reader of the *Outlook* asked Lyman Abbott. First, Abbott replied, "by praying for another we change our attitude toward that other" and so learn if there is anything we can do for that person. Of course, that was not what traditional Christians had meant by the efficacy of intercessory prayer. Thus, Abbott continued:

We know too little about the spiritual influences at work in the world to know that they may not be directed to a given end by a sincere desire, simply expressed. . . . There is much in recent investigations to justify belief that there is an undefined and incomprehensible wireless telegraphy by which spirit affects spirit.

In other words, research in the field of the new psychology, Abbott hoped, might prove to be the savior of intercessory prayer.[49]

James Campbell more overtly used the new psychology to undergird intercession. Writing in 1915, he optimistically asserted that "psychical research" had almost established telepathy as a proven fact.

It would perhaps be putting the matter too strongly to speak of telepathy as an established scientific fact; it is, however, a feasible hypothesis, in behalf of which there is a strong presumptive proof. The conviction prevails and grows that we can project our thoughts into the minds of others, and that they in turn can transfer their thoughts to us.

Thus, he claimed, prayer "is seen to be in harmony with the laws of mind and with the established scientific principles." Armed with the backing of science, Campbell was quite explicit about intercessory prayer as an exercise in mind-power under the auspices of a personal, immanent God. Prayer was "a distinct kind of psychic energy flowing out from the praying soul into the world's life—a sublime form of telepathy by which impulses and suggestions are transmitted to those who are 'psychologically attuned' to the one who prays." There was nothing un-Christian about this, however, Campbell maintained. Telepathy simply was God's method of intercessory prayer. It "affords Him a medium through which to work; supplies conditions which enable Him to do things which otherwise would have been impossible." Intercessory prayer, Campbell believed, creates a new atmosphere around those we pray for. It sends "into the polar sea of human life a warm gulf stream of altruism, which will raise the moral temperature." There was no need, Campbell believed, to resort to traditional supernaturalism to explain intercessory prayer.[50]

Harry Emerson Fosdick devoted a section of *The Meaning of Prayer* to affirming intercessory prayer's viability in a world of science. Persons, Fosdick claimed, "are not separate individuals merely, like grains of sand in a bag, but, as Paul says, are 'members one of another.' . . . We all run into each other, like interflowing rivulets with open channels, above ground and subterranean, connecting all of us." Thus "even telepathy may prove to be true." Fosdick closed by citing the remarks of his mentor, George Coe, employing the analogy of spiritual gravity, a common metaphor in the new idealism:

"All things are bound together into unity. I drop a pebble from my hand; it falls to earth, but the great earth rises to meet it. They seek a common center of gravity, determined by the mass of one as truly as by that of the other. You cannot change any one thing without changing something else also. The man who prays changes the center of gravity of the world of persons. Other persons will be different as well as himself, and he could not have produced this difference by another means than this union of himself with God."

Such remarks bore unmistakable resemblance to Ralph Waldo Trine, who had claimed that he who "lives in the realization of his oneness with this Infinite Power becomes a magnet" in the spiritual world.[51]

Given their traditional Protestant background, many of the Christocentric liberals themselves perhaps continued to visualize intercessory prayer in traditional ways, even while borrowing insights—or, to put it more aptly, grasping at straws—from a tenuous science in order to reassure modern skeptical Americans. Whatever the case, the significance of the new belief in prayer was that liberal Protestant devotional writers before 1920, while keeping in step with modern thought, barred neither prayer for bodily healing nor intercessory prayer from Christian experience. Traditional "mystical" Protestant readers who visualized intercession in triangular imagery would find their simple faith in the importance of praying for missionaries affirmed in liberal writings. Even those who prayed for healing would find this practice allowed for by liberal writers. "Sane" moderns, on the other hand, would find nothing obscurantist and unscientific in the liberal understanding of prayer—provided they were willing to accept the new belief in suggestion, telepathy, and other such things that some scientists were advocating. The incorporation of New Thought elements into evangelical liberal teachings on prayer, then, made old practices possible under new justifications and comprised an important element in the "sane mysticism" of the liberal ethic of prayer.

SEVEN

✢

The Religion of a Mature Mind

Liberal Devotional Teachings in the Early Twentieth Century

Liberal Protestant devotional writers of the early twentieth century not only attempted to justify petitionary prayer in a world of science; they also sought to encourage a *life* of prayer in the busy modern world. The daily devotional life, a staple of Protestant spirituality, had to be maintained in the twentieth century. However, while their conservative counterparts held fast to the historic Protestant norm, liberals, in keeping with their reinterpretation of Christianity for a modern age, departed significantly from traditional Protestant devotionalism.

Protestant Christians, with their notion of the priesthood of the believer, have historically emphasized the importance of maintaining a personal devotional life. Early Protestants were expected to pray often in private, and failing to pray was serious business. Martin Luther's lieutenant Philip Melancthon considered the neglect of prayer as great a sin as stealing or murder, while *Pilgrim's Progress* author John Bunyan listed as the first step in nine stages of apostasy the abandonment of "private duties and closet-prayer."[1]

The Puritans who came to America are well known for their strict religious observances. In addition to church attendance and small group meetings, Puritans were instructed to follow a daily regimen of both family and individual devotions. Morning and evening family devotions consisting of Scripture reading, a brief exposition by the father, prayer, and the singing of a psalm, were considered essential to inculcating religious instruction and a spirit of piety in the youth. As Roger Clap advised: "[D]o not neglect Family Prayer, Morning and Evening. And be sure to read some part of the Word of God every day in your families." As important as family devotions were to the Puritans, however, private prayer was just as crucial to the Christian's spiritual well-being. "You say you have been at prayer in the family," warned the Reverend John Cotton, "but hast thou been so by thy self? If not, I say not that thou wantest grace, but I feare that thou wantest a spirit of prayer. . . . It is a suspicion of hypocrisie, if a man's gifts be only family gifts." Individual devotions basically followed the same pattern as family devotions.

Bible-reading came first (along with a devotional manual, for some), then came meditation—a time of intense self-examination, confession, and applying the Scriptures to oneself—and prayer culminated the exercise. Like family devotions, "secret prayer" was to be done in the morning and the evening. Of course, it is impossible to determine to what extent these instructions were followed by the faithful. Charles Hambrick-Stowe, the leading student of Puritan devotional disciplines, however, believes such a lifestyle was characteristic of many Puritans' lives.[2]

New Englanders of the eighteenth century continued this tradition of religious devotion. Cotton Mather called secret prayer "the duty and practice of every serious Christian." He urged his congregation to "resolve, that after this day, you will not let any day pass you, without going alone before the Lord and laying before Him the requests of your souls, for grace, and for glory, and for every good thing." Jonathan Edwards claimed that the consistent practice of private prayer was a distinguishing mark of a sincere Christian and that those who neglected it showed themselves to be hypocrites, lacking regeneration. "Let us be much employed in the duty of prayer," he concluded. Nathanial Niles, a Congregationalist preacher of the second half of the eighteenth century, exclaimed, "[L]et all be exhorted to a constant attendance on the duty of secret prayer. Attend it frequently, attend it fervently."[3]

The regimen of individual and family devotions continued among nineteenth-century Protestants. Calls for family devotion, not surprisingly, were common in Victorian society.[4] The Andover Ministerial Association reminded heads of households of their duty to inculcate piety in their children through family devotions. "We beg leave to recommend," the clergy advised, "that the family set apart a stated hour, morning and evening, for devotion." The Methodist minister Jacob Moore instructed his readers: "Family prayer is your duty as well as secret prayer; and if you would prosper in your spiritual concerns, you must perform them both." "Let all heads of families pray morning and evening in their families, and read the holy Scriptures," urged the Reverend Benjamin Trumbull. "By no means excuse yourselves from these duties."[5] Well-organized family devotional manuals proliferated in the nineteenth century to guide fathers through the devotional process, though such works were by no means unique to this period.[6]

Important as they were, family devotions did not take the place of private prayer. Religious leaders of the nineteenth century displayed a strong concern that individual devotional standards remain high. For instance, James Bennett wrote a pamphlet for the New England Tract Society detailing instructions for private devotion. Bennett insisted on a regimented system of personal piety. "The proper place, time, method, and spirit of secret worship require attention," he said. As to method, Bennett's regimen was a familiar one: Bible-reading, self-examination, and prayer, with a devotional book to close. Moreover, Bennett instructed, "the time of retirement should be duly regulated." Morning devotions should be done before breakfast, and evening prayers should be performed well before drowsiness set in. As for duration, Bennett said, "perhaps the medium, most generally suitable, is an hour at morning and evening . . . Though some may not be able to employ more than half an hour, what Christian could endure less?" The Princetonian Archibald Alexander, writing for the American Tract Society, concurred. "He is the best Christian who prays most," Alexander maintained. "One hour spent in prayer, will accomplish more good than many employed in study or labor."[7]

The Methodist minister William Thatcher was adamant about the need for private prayer daily. "The neglect or deficiency of any person in this invaluable means of grace," he cautioned, "cannot be commuted by any, or all, the other religious services which we can perform. God will not accept any other service as a substitute for secret prayer: it must be well attended by those who would inherit eternal life." As for how long to spend so disposed, Thatcher wrote, "when you enter into your closet, *take sufficient time. . . .* As sure as you slight him in prayer, he will slight you." Methodist as well as Reformed Protestants maintained that the true Christian would practice lengthy daily devotions.[8]

Mid-nineteenth-century American Christians of all stripes agreed on the need for morning and evening devotions. Charles Finney, as one would suspect, demanded that Christians spend much time in prayer. His autobiography was laced with personal accounts of hours spent in agonizing prayer both morning and night. He also recounted an instance where he reproved a "miserable backslider" who had allowed family devotions to wane. "You must establish family prayer, and build up the altar that has fallen down," Finney warned the man. In his *Lectures on Revivals of Religion*, Finney dwelt at some length on the importance of consistent praying. He advised that "if you mean to pray effectively, you must pray a great deal." The true Christian, Finney believed, had "callous knees" from praying so much. On the opposite end of the theological spectrum, the teaching concerning daily devotions was generally the same. James Freeman Clarke, spokesperson for progressive Unitarianism, maintained that the Christian life "must be maintained in its fulness by constant prayer. . . . It is therefore proper and useful to fix certain hours for prayer, and those who do not do this will not be likely to find time for prayer." Furthermore, Clarke said, "the morning and evening have always been regarded as the most suitable seasons."[9]

On the eve of the twentieth century, this devotional ethic remained strong among religious leaders, as the writings of John Mott demonstrate. Early in his career as a Christian statesman, Mott wrote tracts for the Young Men's Christian Association instructing young Christians on various issues in the Christian life. Two of them, "The Secret Prayer Life" and "The Morning Watch," dealt with the devotional life largely in the same manner that earlier Protestants had. "Each person should have regular, stated seasons for private prayer," Mott declared. He recommended prayer three times a day, the most important of which was the morning watch. "By the observance of the morning watch," said Mott, "is commonly meant the spending of at least the first half hour of every day alone with God in personal devotional Bible study and prayer." There are Christians, Mott acknowledged, "who say that they do not have time to devote a full half hour or more every day to such a spiritual exercise." This was nonsense. Any Christian who tried it would find that this was the best possible use of one's time. "Form an inflexible resolution to keep the morning watch," Mott concluded. "It will prove most dangerous and disastrous to permit any exceptions."[10]

Twentieth-century Protestants, therefore, had a strong inheritance concerning daily devotional expectations. Yet according to contemporary observers, Christian devotionalism had fallen on hard times in the bustling American society of the late nineteenth and early twentieth centuries. With the emergence of the middle class and a consumer culture, Americans were seen as too busy pursuing the good life to devote much time to the cultivation of Christian spirituality. "Protestants," writes Donald Meyer, "were learning how to spend and consume, having produced and saved as Calvin and Wesley had urged." Sinclair Lewis's fictional depiction of George F. Babbitt, the quintessential American businessman, so successfully captured the spirit of the 1920s middle-class culture that the name Babbitt has become part of the English language. Lewis walks the reader through a typical day in Babbitt's life full of business calls, lunches at the club, and booster meetings. Except for a Sunday morning church service, religion is conspicuously absent from Babbitt's life.[11]

Robert and Helen Lynd, in their pioneering sociological study of Muncie, Indiana, described what they saw as a decline in traditional Christian piety among the townspeople. The Lynds concluded: "It is generally recognized in Middletown that the 'family altar,' the carrying on of daily prayer and Bible reading by the assembled family group, is disappearing." The Lynds' perceptions were shared by devotional writers across the theological spectrum, who noted the "awful rush of modern life," in the words of the evangelist William Biederwolf. "We do not live in a praying age," lamented Reuben Torrey. "We live in an age of hustle and bustle, . . . an age of human organization and machinery, of human push, and human scheming, and human achievement; which in the things of God mean no real achievement at all." Newton Theological Institution professor George Horr, writing in the liberal journal *Biblical World*, observed that "it is not nearly so easy to find a place in the home life for family worship as it was a generation ago. Home life has been becoming increasingly complicated." William Adams Brown concluded: "One of the outstanding facts in the religious life of our generation has been the decline in the practice of prayer."[12]

Such lamentations concerning the state of piety must be taken with a grain of salt. It is perhaps part of human religious nature to view the previous generation as a model of piety and decry the sorry state of the present one. Puritan divines were well known for their jeremiads contrasting their back-slidden flock to the sterling founding fathers. Charles Hambrick-Stowe notes:

> From the first decades devout New Englanders complained in diaries
> and sermons that there was 'not so much Prayer in New England' as
> there ought to have been—that people were "not gaining much in
> private duties, in Prayers, Meditation, Reading, and daily Examina-
> tion of a man's own heart."[13]

In the early nineteenth century, Benjamin Trumbull echoed his Puritan forebears, claiming that "it is lamentably evident, that prayer and family religion are exceedingly neglected, and rapidly on the decline." In the mid-nineteenth century, Amherst College professor W. S. Tyler sounded much like Torrey or Brown in castigating the declining piety of his day:

> Ministers themselves fall in with the current, and wear themselves
> out in the preparation of polished sermons, with too little prayer for
> the presence of that Spirit who alone can give power to a sermon....
> The house of God, the prayer-meeting, the closets, and the con-
> sciences of Christians, do they not all bear witness to a sad derelic-
> tion of duty in this respect?

The devotional writers of the early twentieth century were not unique, then, in decrying the sorry state of spirituality in their day. Indeed, the idea that the rush and bustle of life is unique to the present age seems to crop up in almost each generation. As A. T. Pierson astutely observed, "to an attentive eye, the world is constantly coming to new crises."[14]

Nevertheless, some significant social changes were occurring in Torrey's and Brown's age. Industrialization and urbanization seemed to be creating more regimented lifestyles for middle-class Americans. Charles Blanchard spoke for many when he explained the problem that modern life posed for traditional devotionalism:

> There is probably no one fact in modern life which has more seri-
> ously interfered with family prayer than the early and late trains
> which have become necessary in view of the complexity of modern
> life. When men lived and worked in their homes, for themselves,
> conditions were radically different from those which at this time ex-
> ist. Men are now cogs in wheels and the wheel cannot turn if cogs
> are absent or broken. The result is that in every great city in the
> world, thousands of people, young, middle-aged and old, hasten from
> their homes in the morning and return to them late at night. How

shall these persons share in the home prayer which used to charac-
terize every Christian household? How shall they even have the time
required for deliberate and effective personal prayer?

Whatever the reality of the uniquely busy lifestyles of the modern era that
made devotions difficult, twentieth-century devotional writers *perceived* this
to be a problem that had to be addressed.[15]

For many Christians, resistance to modernity was the appropriate response. Conservative, pietistic evangelicals in the Keswick holiness tradition—the same Christians who stressed remarkable and frequent answers to
prayer—addressed this issue, as one might expect, by steadfastly resisting the
encroachment of modern culture. Just as their understanding of petitionary
prayer showed an intensification of the historic Protestant faith in the power
of prayer in the midst of modern unbelief, their devotional ethic promoted,
if anything, an increased attention to the prayer life in the face of modern
lifestyles.

Conservative evangelicals thus articulated a devotional ethic that made
no allowance for the busy lifestyles of modern Americans. These writers
asserted without exception that, as E. M. Bounds put it, "our devotions are
not measured by the clock, but time is of their essence." Bounds was most
adamant about the need for a time-consuming devotional life. "We must
demand and hold with iron grasp the best hours of the day for God and
prayer," he wrote, "or there will be no praying worth the name.... Much
time spent alone with God is the secret of all successful praying." This theme
permeated the writings of Andrew Murray, the patriarch of Keswick spirituality, who wrote that "there can be no converse with a holy God ... *unless
much time is set apart for it.*" His book *The Prayer Life* was devoted to
helping combat the sin of "prayerlessness," which he saw as the central
blight of the modern church. Reuben Torrey pronounced with typical bluntness:

> The Christian who doesn't spend much time in prayer, is disobeying
> God, just as much as the man who steals, or commits adultery, or
> murders. The same God who said: "Thou shalt not commit adultery,
> thou shalt not steal" also said: "Continue steadfastly in prayer." One
> is a commandment just as much as the other; and you are a sinner if
> you don't keep the commandment; you are disobeying God; you are
> a rebel against God if you don't spend much time in prayer.

Such writers were reluctant to specify just how much time one should spend
in devotions, for they believed the question itself exuded the wrong spirit,
but in general these devotional writers seem to have regarded one hour as
an appropriate *minimum* for the Christian, half of that spent in reading the
Bible and half in prayer.[16]

Like traditional Protestants, Keswick holiness writers were adamant about the need to pray in private, and in the morning. Samuel D. Gordon, an itinerant speaker and prolific writer on devotional themes, remarked concerning those who would settle for praying in the midst of the day's activities: "You can pray anywhere, on a train, walking down the street, measuring calico, chopping a typewriter, dictating a letter, in kitchen or parlour or shop. But you're not likely to, unless you've been off in some quiet place, with the door shut." Though prayer in the evening was expected as well, devotions *had* to be done in the morning, according to these writers. One of the early heroes of Keswick spirituality, George Mueller, recalled in his widely read memoirs wasteful early years when he would sleep in until six or seven in the morning. After getting serious about spirituality, however, Mueller discovered that he could get by on six hours of sleep and thus procure "one, two, or three hours in prayer and meditation before breakfast." American evangelical writers echoed Mueller's advice in spirit, if not in exact detail. "Every child of God," Reuben Torrey declared, "should set apart the first part of the day to meeting God in the study of His Word and in prayer." To those who would protest that they felt more like praying in the evening than in the morning, Torrey replied, "when we feel least like praying is the time when we most need to pray."[17]

In articulating such a time-intensive devotional ethic, Keswick devotional writers spotlighted the examples of past saints of the church as exemplars of the devotional life. One of Bounds's numerous books on prayer included a chapter entitled "Great Men of Prayer," which gave a roll of saints, such as Luther, Wesley, and Francis Asbury, who allegedly devoted two hours a day to private prayer. Stories of prowess in prayer made their way through evangelical circles, with George Mueller and Hudson Taylor, of course, being particularly popular examples. S. D. Gordon claimed that Taylor rose in the middle of the night for an hour of prayer. William Biederwolf, however, had Taylor rising at three in the morning for two hours of prayer and staying up for the rest of the day. The most astounding example, given by both Bounds and Torrey (in strikingly similar wording), was that of John Welch, a Scottish Reformer who Torrey claimed "counted that day ill-spent in which seven or eight hours were not used alone with God in prayer and study of His Word." The lesson to be learned from such great men of prayer was clear. Modern lifestyles notwithstanding, the Christian should emulate these heroes of prayer from the past. Concerning Welch, Torrey wrote: "I do not suppose that God has called many of us, if any of us, to put seven or eight hours a day into prayer, but I am confident that God has called most of us, if not everyone of us, to put more time into prayer than we now do."[18]

Not surprisingly, pietistic evangelicals also displayed a fiercely biblicist devotional life. They believed that, in Torrey's words, "there is no true prayer without the study of the Word of God." Devotions were in essence a dialogue between the Christian and God, with the words of the Bible serving as the script. Gordon wrote: "Bible reading is the listening side of prayer. In the book God speaks to us. In prayer we speak to God." The Keswick Christian's prayer life was thus done with an open Bible on his or her lap. Every page, even every verse, of Scripture contained a promise to claim, a commandment to obey, a godly life to emulate, or a poor example to avoid. By immersing oneself in the text of Scripture, the Christian would have ample material for meditation and prayer. Andrew Murray called this approach to Scripture "prayerful Bible study," and it comprised, along with intercessory prayer, the heart of the pietistic evangelical's devotions. "The Word of God," concluded Bounds, "is the fulcrum on which the lever of prayer is placed."[19]

With the Bible so central to the devotional life, much time had to be spent in reading it. Thus, Torrey complained of a "neglect of the Word of God" because few Christians spent an hour a day in Bible study, and S. D. Gordon advised that for reading the Bible "one must get at least a half hour daily when the mind is fresh." Just as these pietistic evangelicals had their pantheon of prayer heroes, they recounted famous exploits of Bible-reading as well. Hudson Taylor claimed late in life to have read the Bible cover to cover every year for his last forty years, while the missionary Jonathan Goforth allegedly had read the New Testament sixty times in a span of six years. The devotional spirit of Keswick evangelicalism was summed up perfectly in a statement by one of its proponents, Robert Horton: "The Bible of anyone who has lived the life of which we are concerned is yellow with the years, thin at the edge with the constant turning of the pages. . . . Without this use of the Bible, the devotional life becomes unhealthy, ascetic, morbid, extravagant."[20] Thus, a biblicist, time-intensive devotional ethic persisted among conservative Christians well into the twentieth century.[21]

Like their conservative counterparts, liberal Protestants of the early twentieth century wrote extensively on the devotional life; but they reached quite different conclusions. The most concerted effort among liberal Protestants to encourage the devotional life occurred in 1919, the year the *Christian Century's* Daily Altar movement was launched. The previous year, the *Christian Century* had published a daily devotional guide entitled *The Daily Altar* by editors Herbert Willett and Charles Clayton Morrison. Throughout 1919, weekly issues of the *Christian Century* encouraged readers to purchase the volume, printed advertisements for it, and published numerous letters from readers testifying that *The Daily Altar* had revived the devotional life for them. In addition, each *Christian Century* issue began with a printed prayer.

Morrison explained the importance of the Daily Altar movement in a February editorial. "The remarkable response to the appearance of the devotional volume, 'The Daily Altar,' has, we believe, deep significance as to the hunger of multitudes of souls for some sane and inspiring guidance in the things of the spiritual life." No book has ever been produced by our press, he continued, "which has won so quickly and so spontaneously the grateful approval of its readers." In the compiling of this volume, Morrison explained, he and Willett "conceived their task not merely as the making of a *book*, but as the initiating of a *movement*." *The Daily Altar* was to be "the means of establishing family and personal religious exercise in an age in which a revival of the old-fashioned family worship is practically impossible."[22]

In light of *The Daily Altar's* stated purpose of re-establishing Christian devotionalism, it is noteworthy how different the devotional expectations of Willett and Morrison were compared to the historic Protestant norm. The book was intended to provide Christians with "a few moments of quiet and reflection" in the midst of "short and crowded days" in order to maintain a daily prayer life. To be precise, devotions in *The Daily Altar* took about one and a half minutes to complete. Also in 1919, Joseph Fort Newton, a frequent contributor to the *Christian Century*, devoted two articles to urging daily devotions among his readers. In each, he recommended ten minutes a day as sufficient to establish and maintain the spiritual life.[23]

The prescriptions in the *Christian Century* accurately represented the devotional expectations of liberal Protestants in general, which had been set forth a few years earlier by Lyman Abbott. In 1913, Abbott received a question from a reader in the *Outlook*: "Would you advise the setting aside of certain times for prayer and then praying at that time whether we felt inclined to do so or not; or would you say that we should pray only when we feel moved, as it were, to do so?" Abbott replied: "If we do not set aside certain times, we shall soon discover that we have no time." Companionship with the Father "can be attained only by a habit of seeking him, talking to him, listening to him," and habits can only be formed by regularly repeated actions. Therefore, Abbott advised his readers to "take a little time every day to form a habit of communion with the invisible." The time given to this exercise could be at any hour, but Christians were to "give to communion with your Father a few moments" sometime during the day. These two elements, a "few moments" and flexibility regarding the time of day, set the pattern for liberal devotionalism.[24]

Fosdick's daily devotional guides, for example, applied Abbott's strictures in concrete devotional form. *The Manhood of the Master* (1913) contained a Scripture passage and a one-paragraph comment on the passage. This would have typically required about one to two minutes to complete, plus whatever time one took to pray afterward.[25] In addition, there was a weekly passage by Fosdick that required roughly fifteen minutes to read, presumably on Sunday. *The Meaning of Prayer*, published two years later, followed the same format but expanded it to include a short prayer for each day. It required about two minutes, plus a fifteen- to twenty-minute weekly reading. Fosdick's third devotional, *The Meaning of Faith* (1917), lengthened the format to about three minutes in length, including the prayer, and extended the weekly readings to about twenty-five to thirty minutes. *The Meaning of Service*, published three years later, scaled back the devotional length to about two and a half minutes per day and a twenty-minute weekly reading.[26] Another liberal devotional, William Adams Brown's *The Quiet Hour*, contained meditations and a prayer on a passage of Scripture that lasted about ten minutes. For the liberal Methodist James M. Campbell, author of *The Place of Prayer in the Christian Religion*, to practice daily devotions meant "to stoop down and quaff a cupful of the water of life before rushing out into the fray."[27]

Moreover, while Protestants had traditionally been quite strict about times and durations, for the liberals flexibility in devotions was crucial. "Every man must be allowed to pray in his own way," asserted Fosdick. "There are as many different ways of praying as there are different individuals." Consequently, "the time involved in the deliberate practice of prayer may indeed be brief or long," depending on the person. Seeing the brief time that most Christians spent in prayer, one "might cry out against such ill proportion." But one should not, because "the length of time is not the decisive matter in prayer." William Adams Brown echoed Fosdick in his book *The Life of Prayer in a World of Science*. Christians needed to develop a regular habit of daily prayer, he believed. However, he said, "the time involved will vary greatly for different people.... How long we stay is between us and God. It is the quality that counts, not quantity." Moreover, though one should have daily prayer, "the question when to take it, each must decide for himself what his time of prayer shall be—whether it shall be morning or evening, or some time snatched from the pressure of the day's work." Since we lead busy lives, Brown advised, we may need to be creative in how we go about it. He thus cited approvingly the example of a friend who prayed on the train to work as he gazed into the faces of the other passengers, trying to imagine how they would appear to the eye of God.[28]

Liberal devotionals also, in comparison to traditional Protestantism, displayed a sparse biblical content. As mentioned earlier, Fosdick's devotionals began with a passage of Scripture. The length of the passage steadily diminished from his first devotional book to his last. In *The Manhood of the Master* (1913), the Scripture passage was typically five to ten verses, roughly the same length as Fosdick's comment on the text. In subsequent devotionals, Fosdick's comments increased, and a prayer was added, while the amount of Scripture decreased. In *The Meaning of Faith* and *The Meaning of Service* (1917 and 1920, respectively), for instance, the Scripture passage is usually less than five verses. This whittling down of the scriptural element in devotions was epitomized in Willett and Morrison's volume. Devotions in *The Daily Altar* contain a short paragraph on a theme for the day, a related Scripture verse, a passage of poetry, and a brief prayer. The Scripture is given without context and adds little to the subject at hand.

While traditionalists considered the Bible to be the fuel for prayer, William Adams Brown advised the Christian to seek "inspiring and beautiful thoughts" about which to pray: "Thought must be allowed to roam freely," he said, "taking up one by one the familiar events and experiences of daily life." In this way, claimed Brown, not just Scripture but "all of life may become the raw material for prayer." Poetry was an especially useful medium for liberal devotions. *The Daily Altar* contained devotions on such topics as "The Treasures of Books" and "The Charm of Poetry." Poems by Emerson, Tennyson, Longfellow, and others dot the pages of the book. Concerning family devotional content, George Horr wrote:

> The repetition of choice poems is also appropriate. The writer will not soon forget a certain twilight time on a Sunday when, during the family worship, the little seven-year-old daughter of the house re- peated Longfellow's "Sifting of Peter." The gracious words falling from those sweet girlish lips wove throughout the little group new ties of love to each other, and of devotion to Christ.

Such an event would hardly have passed for devotions in traditional Prot- estantism.[29]

Clearly, liberal Protestants' understanding of devotions, like their notion of petitionary prayer, was rooted in a spirit of adaptation. As we have seen, liberal Protestantism purported to begin with the dictates of modern thought and adapt religion to that. The same went for devotions and modern life- styles. In other words, just as liberals adjusted their theology in accordance with intellectual trends, they adapted Christian devotionalism to cultural trends.

The sociologist Thomas Symington performed a comparative study of re- ligious liberals and conservatives in the early 1930s. Conservatives, he con- cluded, believed that the highest calling would be to go into Christian service and that "the main purpose of life is to pray and read the Bible." By way of contrast, Symington quoted the words of a liberal: " 'I take my life as I find it, trying to find the best in each situation.' " This mood of cheerful adap- tation—of "evangelizing the inevitable," to quote the title of a 1917 *Christian Century* article—permeated liberal devotional writings. Fosdick praised the "splendid enthusiasm for work" that was "the prevailing temper of our gen- eration" and that modern practices of prayer needed to accommodate. Willett and Morrison prefaced *The Daily Altar* by saying that "for the mood of our time the lengthy and more formal exercises of household devotion of former days cannot be revived. Nor," they continued with characteristic buoyancy, "need this fact be deplored." *The Daily Altar* was their adaptation of Chris- tian devotions to the inevitable busy-ness of modern life, for, as Morrison declared, "the revival of the prayer life of the church must be no return to obsolete and discarded habits of devotion." James M. Campbell's suggestions for family devotions represent the best articulated statement of the liberal spirit of accommodation concerning devotions:

The habit of family worship will not be recovered until it is adapted to existing conditions. The long and leisurely and often dreary exercises of our forefathers are no longer suitable. What is needed is something brief and bright; the repeating it may be of a few favorite texts, and the lifting up of the heart in a few words of prayer. . . . In many instances it will be that or nothing. But let no one despise any method that maintains the religious unity of the home.

Campbell's message was clear: The patterns of modern life are a given. Any devotional system must start with this in mind and make the best of the situation.[30]

The scaled-down devotional expectations of Protestant liberalism were rooted in more than just a spirit of adaptation, however; they also stemmed from liberal theology. Indeed, it was the liberals' understanding of divine immanence that ultimately made it possible for them to alter traditional devotional requirements. Traditional Protestants had typically explained daily prayer as providing spiritual power to help the Christian through the day—as a way of recharging one's spiritual battery, so to speak. Liberals also justified the prayer life as providing spiritual power for living. Prayer, wrote William Adams Brown, "can furnish us with supplies of energy which will reinforce our limited powers and make us adequate to meet whatever strain the day may bring." Walter Fiske of Oberlin Seminary claimed that prayer released spiritual energy that was dammed up in our commonplace life. "The life of power," he concluded, "is the life that lets God in." But liberal Protestants had a different conception of how this divine power was best appropriated.[31]

For traditional Protestants, the importance of devotions presupposed that God was in a sense separate from the world and that his power had to be appropriated supernaturally through the specific channels of prayer and Bible study. For liberals, however, since God was conceived as immanent within the world, every place in the world, from the inner chamber to a crowded train, was seen to be equally filled with God's presence. Therefore, while the believer still needed divine power to live the Christian life, such power was more readily available, and through a wider variety of means. For liberals, empowerment from God was thus more like a windmill than a battery. The power they received to live a godly, effective life was seen to be continuous rather than sporadic; it came throughout the day. Moreover, just as the empowering wind may blow from many directions, spiritual power for liberals could come in various ways in addition to the specific channels of private prayer and Bible study.

Borden Bowne, in spelling out the liberal doctrine of God in *The Immanence of God*, applied the doctrine of immanence to the spiritual life. "The undivineness of the natural," he claimed, was "a great source of the weakness of the religious life. . . . We must discern the divine presence and agency in life as a whole." This meant that we should not expect some irruption from outside (as in the supernatural filling of the Holy Spirit, in traditional Christian thinking) to make us godly but should instead "study the order of life, and avail ourselves of all the normal means of influence for developing character." Religion, according to Bowne, "knows no distinction of secular and religious, but pervades all life, and perpetually offers unto God in living sacrifice as its continual spiritual worship the daily round with all its interests." The Christian will come into communion with God in prayer, of course, but also in work of all kinds. "We shall find God everywhere, not merely in unmediated and miraculous manifestations." As James M. Campbell put it more succinctly, "the world is a temple, any spot thereon an altar."[32]

The doctrine of divine immanence thus helps explain the short, flexible devotional ethic of Protestant liberals. If it is the case that "any spot on earth may be a holy temple where worshipping souls may hold communion with the unseen and immanent Father," as Campbell claimed, then the traditional Morning Watch would seem to have much less significance. This was manifested in Campbell's own teaching on private prayer. "It is a sad day for the church," he wrote, "when those who compose her fellowship do not take time for private devotions." Yet for Campbell private devotions did not require a literal inner chamber. He continued:

> While outward seclusion is an advantage for quiet, refreshing converse with God, it is not a necessity. We can find God in the crowded street car as well as in nature's solitudes; we can make a little sanctuary in the heart, where we are as much alone with him as in the most peaceful sylvan retreat.... Outward separation is often unattainable, inward separation never is."

Campbell's flexibility in devotions was bred from a confidence that fellowship with God was equally attainable all throughout the day.[33]

William Adams Brown, who as we have seen also advocated devotions on a train, titled one of his chapters in *The Quiet Hour* "The Encompassing Presence." His introductory poem expresses well the liberal sentiment underlying Christian devotionalism:

> Afar I sought thee in the radiant sky,
>   But thou art near.
> In every breeze that sings its lullaby
>   Thy voice I hear.
>
> So let me feel Thy presence day by day
>   In wind and sod,
> That every bush I meet upon my way
>   Shall glow with God.

For liberals, a special time of devotions was simply one small aspect of an entire day spent in an empowering fellowship with God. As God's presence was discerned in every breeze and every bush, the blades of the windmill were constantly turning and generating new supplies of spiritual power. That being the case, a specific time of private devotions would obviously take less importance, and a few moments spent therein could set the Christian on the right track for the rest of the day.[34]

The windmill analogy also helps explain the sparse biblical content of liberal devotions. In the "windmill" vision of the spiritual life based on divine immanence, God had many more means of communicating to humans than just the words of the Bible. "The supreme value of the Bible," wrote Walter Fiske, "is not merely to find God there, but to gain inspiration to find him here." When William Adams Brown called the Bible "the great manual of the devotional life," he meant something very different than did traditionalists such as Reuben Torrey or S. D. Gordon. The Bible was "an exhaustless reservoir" of themes for fruitful meditation, but it was not the only reservoir: "Any book that tells the story of God's self-revelation in nature and in history, and of man's response to that revelation in worship, may be a devotional book." Thus, claimed Brown, "though the Bible is the best book of devotion, it is not the only book."[35]

This meant that liberals were not tied to the text of Scripture in the prayer life, as were traditionalists. It is thus no accident that the poetry is usually longer than the Scripture passage in *The Daily Altar*. While Willett and Morrison believed that God "spoke" in the Bible, they also maintained that "the attentive and expectant soul will hear Him speaking in conscience, in a good book, in a little child, in friendship, in sorrow," and in a host of other ways. "Our soul must learn to hear Him in all the orderly on-going of life," they concluded. Brown summarized Christian devotions in this way: "Let us realize that we are in a world full of wonderful and ennobling things, and yield ourselves up to the contemplation of them." Such a remark exemplified the "windmill" approach to devotions.[36]

The novelty of this "windmill" mentality of the liberals should not be pressed too far.[37] Christians have always believed that God is present in all of life and that believers should pray without ceasing, and liberal writers valued a special time of private prayer as well. Moreover, many traditional Christians have gained inspiration from poetry, while many liberals undoubtedly spent much time studying the Bible. Still, liberal devotional writings expressed a distinctive vision of the Christian life based on an emphasis on God's immanence unrestricted by a strong doctrine of sin and human separation from God. For traditional Christians, morning devotions were a time for the Christian's spiritual battery to be charged with divine energy, a supply that would have to sustain the believer as he or she emerged from the inner chamber and withstood the onslaughts of the world, the flesh, and the devil. As Dwight L. Moody had remarked concerning daily devotions, "any man or woman who does this faithfully cannot be more than twenty-four hours away from God." For liberals, on the other hand, a cheerful face on the train, a good book, or a beautiful sunset were all instances of spiritual breezes by which God's presence continually recharged the Christian's spirit.[38]

To some readers, this liberal devotional ethic may seem to reflect the liberals' penchant for pasting a spiritual veneer on whatever modern culture threw their way. It would be a mistake, however, to dismiss liberal devotionalism as merely a lowering of standards to accommodate the Babbitts of the early twentieth century. One must keep in mind the doctrine of divine immanence on which it rested. What liberals were actually asking their readers to do was not simply to "quaff a cupful of the water of life before rushing out into the fray," but rather to transform their vision of the fray itself. For them, the goal was to see through the mundane reality of daily life to the benevolent, loving, personal spirit of God that permeated it all, to make every day Sunday and all of life prayer. This could be, perhaps, just as demanding a task as spending an hour a day shut up in the prayer closet. George Coe, the liberal Methodist professor at Northwestern University, wrote a book on the Christian life, *The Religion of a Mature Mind*. Maintaining a "spiritual interpretation of the universe" on a crowded New York City streetcar required a truly mature mind, as well as firm commitment to the task. Liberal devotionalism, therefore, can best be seen as a sincere attempt to awaken the churches of early-twentieth-century America to a more fervent, life-changing piety.[39]

EIGHT

✚

Modernism and Prayer in the Twenties

In 1926, Harry Emerson Fosdick returned to the subject of petitionary prayer in his book *Adventurous Religion*. His discussion of the subject, however, must have surprised some of the traditional faithful who had enjoyed *The Meaning of Prayer*. As we have seen, when Fosdick discussed level three prayer in *The Meaning of Prayer* (requests for changes in the natural order), he maintained that such prayer in the external world was still legitimate and answers were possible. "God is free," he had asserted, "so far as the mere possibilities are concerned, to answer any petition whatsoever. . . . No man can draw a clear boundary, saying, 'Within this we may expect God to use his laws in answer to our prayers, and without we may look for nothing of the kind.' "[1]

Eleven years later, however, Fosdick himself drew a firm boundary on prayer. He bemoaned "the futile and dangerous extension of prayer to realms where it does not belong. . . . Prayer is a poor reliance if one is mainly intent on managing the external world. That is not the realm where prayer operates. Prayer will not alter the weather." Praying for changes in the external world, Fosdick maintained, was equivalent to primitive magic, and "the sooner science breaks up that kind of sacramental magic, pulverizes that vain reliance on supernatural sleight-of-hand, the better."[2]

Fosdick now seemed to disparage not only level three prayer, but petition in general. Whereas in 1916 he had maintained that petition, while not central to prayer, was still its original and important element, he now railed against "the pious blasphemy of telling God what we think he should do, or reminding him of gifts to be bestowed which he would unhappily otherwise forget." Real prayer, he said, "ceases clamorous petition and becomes affirmation." Liberal Protestants, he claimed, "do not think that God so plays favorites and, like a celestial charity organization society, doles out small gifts upon request to improvident applicants." What was prayer, then? It was "not crying to a mysterious individual off somewhere," but rather "fulfilling one of the major laws of the spiritual world and getting the appropriate consequences." Prayer was "silent companionship with the Unseen." Those who practiced such prayer gained poise, perspective, and balanced, unified personalities. "What do we believe about prayer?" he asked. Citing the remark of George Meredith that earlier liberals had typically reacted against, Fosdick answered: " 'He who rises from his knees a better man, his prayer is answered.' " Fosdick closed his discussion of prayer by citing, of all people, John Tyndall as one who avowed the benefits that praying had on one's personal well-being.[3]

Clearly, Fosdick's teaching on prayer had changed to reflect a more thoroughly modernistic point of view. It is unclear whether many other liberal Protestants personally changed their understanding of prayer in these decades. Undoubtedly, the spirit of prayer exuded by the evangelical liberals continued to exist after 1920, as evidenced by the continued popularity of *The Meaning of Prayer* throughout the twentieth century. However, Fosdick's 1926 depiction of prayer signaled the presence of a modernistic outlook that, while expressed earlier, became much more common in 1920s liberalism. The Detroit pastor Gaius Glenn Atkins wrote in the 1930s that "in 1890 the 'liberal' was debating whether there were two Isaiahs; in 1930 the extreme 'modernist' was debating whether there was a personal God." This was an exaggeration, but nevertheless pointed to a real tendency within Protestant liberalism as "modernistic liberals," to use Kenneth Cauthen's term, became increasingly visible.[4]

One factor in the change within liberalism was undoubtedly a more polarized religious climate in the Protestantism of the 1920s. Before World War I, a functional unity between liberals and conservatives had generally prevailed in the northern mainline denominations. World War I, however, led liberals to attack premillennialism as detrimental to the war cause, while fundamentalism as a formal movement solidified in 1920 in the formation of the World's Christian Fundamentals Association. The denominational clashes of the 1920s, of which Fosdick was one of the main casualties, left mainstream Protestantism deeply divided. The result of these conflicts within the church, historian Martin Marty has concluded, "was a deeply, permanently divided Protestantism.... Original-stock Protestantism—from which both sides derived—no longer presented a single front."[5]

This polarizing trend can easily be exaggerated. Many of the most influential Protestants of the day were moderates such as Robert Speer and John Mott who refused to take sides or persecute the modernists. Still, whatever the accuracy of Marty's assessment concerning Protestantism as a whole, liberals and fundamentalists by the mid-1920s clearly perceived themselves as antithetical rivals. The extent of the differences was indicated by an editorial (cited eagerly by fundamentalists) by *Christian Century* editor Charles Clayton Morrison in 1924 entitled "Fundamentalism and Modernism: Two Religions:"

> Christianity according to Fundamentalism is one religion. Christianity according to Modernism is another.... There is a clash here as profound and as grim as between Christianity and Confucianism. Amia-

ble words cannot hide the differences. "Blest be the tie" may be sung till doomsday but it cannot bind these worlds together. The God of the fundamentalist is one God; the God of the modernist is another.

Clearly, the breach between fundamentalist and modernist had become deep by 1924. The descriptions of prayer by Fosdick and other liberals in this decade may have stemmed in part from a reaction to the perceived supernaturalistic excesses of fundamentalism.[6]

The importance of the Scopes Trial of 1925 in this respect has often been stressed. Religious historians have generally seen this event as discrediting fundamentalism in the nation's eyes and thus pushing the movement "underground" for the next few decades. However, Garry Wills has observed that the real casualty of the Scopes Trial was the fusion of progressive politics and evangelical moralism that had characterized not only William Jennings Bryan but also many liberal Protestants. Wills writes this in the context of religion and politics, but the same may be hypothesized in a theological sense. As fundamentalism became more combative and removed from the cultural mainstream, leading liberals of the 1920s were determined at all costs to separate themselves from the taint of obscurantism and supernaturalism that had come to typify conservative Protestantism.[7]

As background to the modernist spirit of prayer, one other development of the 1920s deserves attention. Evangelical liberals, as I have explained, attempted to limit the impact modern science had on prayer by advancing quasi-scientific justifications for intercessory prayer and prayer for healing. By the 1920s, however, logical positivism came to dominate the intellectual world, and the idealistic philosophy on which the "new belief in prayer" had been built was increasingly viewed to be on thin intellectual ice. Men like William James and Sir Oliver Lodge, instead of being precursors to a budding new age in science as some had hoped, were in fact some of the last respectable intellectuals to lend credence to parapsychology and other fringe sciences. In fact, in 1926 Lodge himself was ostracized from the Royal Society because of his continuing interest in psychical research and spiritualism. Robert Bruce Mullin has observed that "speculations and theories that had been respectable in 1905 and had provided a foundation for the empirical grounding of the supernatural were no longer in favor by the 1920s."[8]

Healing movements such as Emmanuel were not so much repudiated as assimilated into popular culture, while the limits of spiritual medicine were more clearly grasped. Though the early years of psychology had produced hopes about the power of the mind in healing, by the 1900s few psychologists believed that mental states alone caused illness. The distinction between functional and organic disorders, the former a legitimate object of mind-cure, was clearer. As one writer commented, prayer did have an effect in the biological world, but only in a limited sense. "In the case of cancer we may indeed pray," but "first of all we seek a skillful surgeon." Concerning the brainchild of Lodge and James, the historian Laurence Moore concluded that "psychical research enjoyed no more prestige among respected scientists in 1970 than it had in 1890. That is to say, parapsychology remained a marginal activity."[9]

The situation was similar with the other aspect of prayer rooted, for evangelical liberals, in the new idealism; intercessory prayer. Belief in the power of thoughts hurled through a spiritual universe, rather than continuing to blossom, became increasingly suspect to the scientific establishment. Historian John Cerullo concludes: "Well into the 1920s there would be only the same (by this time rather tired) assertions that the subliminal self did indeed exist and was indeed telepathic. Fewer people seemed to be listening. . . . There would be fewer and fewer intellectuals of any note even interested in psychical research." Concerning telepathy, the phenomenon upon which the liberals had placed their hopes for intercessory prayer, the psychologist George Stolz—himself a liberal Protestant—declared bluntly:

> The evidence for telepathic marvels is scientifically untenable. The most competent students of borderland psychology reduce the so-called telepathic occurrences to a hopeless jumble of suggestions, unconscious perceptions, chance and coincidence, illusions, defective observation, exaggeration, deliberate or intentional fraud.

By the 1920s, then, a scientifically tenable justification for petitionary prayer on anything but a personal level was considerably weaker than it had been a decade earlier.[10]

Among leading liberals of the 1920s, therefore, the Christocentric liberal ethic of prayer—wavering between traditional Protestantism and modern thought—was neither desirable nor reasonable. Maintaining ties to traditional orthodoxy was less of a concern, and the dominant voice of science was clearer about what was possible in prayer. D. C. Macintosh of the University of Chicago Divinity School thus sounded the modernist theme concerning petitionary prayer when he exclaimed: "The heavens are as brass toward any petition that asks for what is against the laws of nature. . . . There is no place in the best possible kind of world for the arbitrary interruption of the established natural order." Of course, there had always existed liberals such as George Coe and William Adams Brown who ruled out petitionary prayer as a force in the physical world. While before World War I such men represented the extreme in liberal Protestantism, in the 1920s such a belief was more common among leading liberals. In other words, liberal prayer writings of this decade reflect the rise to prominence of a thoroughly modernist party in Protestantism. Those who claimed to speak for the left wing of American Protestantism in the 1920s purged petitionary prayer of its traditional supernaturalist overtones.[11]

In addition to Fosdick's 1926 description of prayer, other representative liberals exuded the modernist spirit concerning prayer. Charles Reynolds Brown, dean of Yale Divinity School, expressed disdain for what he called the magic of prayer, the belief that prayer could be used to alter events. When he was a child, Brown claimed, he thought prayer was "asking for something without giving anything. It was indeed 'getting something for nothing' in open defiance of the law of cost so strictly enforced in all other fields of human effort." However, Brown had come to see that God did not interfere in the natural world. Rather, "the object of prayer must lie within the field where we have reason to expect results from the cooperation of these human wills or ours with the will of the Father." In other words, prayer did not cause God to step in from without; rather "in prayer man mobilizes all the best energies of his own inner life." Again, the "newness" of such an ethic of prayer was not in its emphasis on the subjective, internal aspect of prayer; liberals had always done that. However, while earlier liberals had been reluctant to say that God could not directly answer prayer in the material world, Brown explicitly closed this realm off: "*Everywhere* the method of the divine action in answering prayer is mediate rather than immediate. He helps men to help themselves and to help others."[12]

Another example of a more thoroughly naturalistic ethic of prayer was that of David Trout, a liberal Baptist minister and professor of religious education at Union Theological College. A modern conception of prayer, Trout said, must not be asking God for things. "Magic is a better word than prayer to describe this sort of thing!" The new, scientific idea of prayer was instead "a process by which one's energy is brought into readiness for overcoming the obstacles to the achievement of the true, the beautiful and the good." Prayer was "enthusiastic previsioning" that had "objective" results, Trout claimed, for one who prayed gained poise and self-confidence, which in turn would draw followers, which meant greater resources. As a result, Trout explained,

> The increased enthusiasm, the heightened comradeship, the poise
> and quiet confidence, all the fruits of much prayer, become character
> which, by its charm, increasingly enlists the social and consequently
> the physical forces of the universe until all things become possible to
> him who prays believingly.

This "objective" efficacy of prayer was clearly in full harmony with naturalistic science.[13]

The seminal discussion of the doctrine of prayer among modernists in the 1920s was William Adams Brown's *Life of Prayer in a World of Science* (1927). Brown lacked the crisp writing style and popular appeal of Fosdick, but if *The Meaning of Prayer* represented the Christocentric liberal ethic of prayer before 1920, Brown's work was an accurate representation of the modernism of the 1920s and effectively illustrated the different intellectual climate concerning prayer that had emerged by 1927. In the world of science, Brown maintained, the old "theory of the supernatural," of God as an "arbitrary and incalculable will" shaping the course of history from without, had become untenable. "Science knows no such world of the unpredictable," he said. Moreover, any modern faith in prayer must arise not back from science, but "forward through science to a more assured and satisfying faith."[14]

One important element of the world of science to Brown was psychology. America in the 1920s witnessed a "psychological revival," in the words of historian E. Brooks Holifield. One observer has called the era between 1919 and 1929 "the period of the psyche." Partly a result of the popularization of Freud, the psychological craze in the 1920s set Americans on the path toward achieving psychological wholeness and personal success. The trend was epitomized in 1922 when Emile Coue, the French prophet of personal power through positive thinking, made his American tour. Coue had countless Americans repeating his famous formula, "Day by day, in every way, I am getting better and better." "Adjustment," "mental hygiene," and "connecting" became buzzwords of the culture and found their way into Protestant prayer writings as well.[15]

For Brown, psychology offered a way to re-envision prayer in a world of science. Psychology tells us, said Brown, that "piety is unity." Modern people are troubled because the various elements of their psychological makeup— the conscious and the subconscious—are often at odds with one another. They need to be brought into harmony through focusing on a unitive ideal. Since, said Brown, "the source of our worst evils is the divided self," our chief need is of some influence that will unify the self. "This can be found," he claimed, "only in some reality greater than ourselves that excites our admiration and commands our loyalty. Such an object commanding loyalty is God."[16]

Prayer, therefore, was a means of producing psychological wholeness by focusing on God as the unitive ideal. Brown said that "prayer unites the divided self by bringing about its willing surrender to the supreme principle of unity, which is God." Brown gave various descriptions of what prayer was. Prayer was "the name we give to the practice of the presence of God." It was "the out-reaching of the human spirit to that which is without and above—the instinctive cry of man for some reality that shall satisfy his deepest longings and embody his highest ideals." Or prayer was "the natural expression of what is best in ourselves; the way we realize the larger life which is laid up for us in God." Finally, prayer was "an adventure of faith by which we realize our true nature through contact with a reality greater than ourselves." What was conspicuously absent in Brown's treatment of prayer, in light of historic Protestantism, was any mention of prayer as petition. Earlier liberals would have agreed with all of these formulations of prayer by Brown but would have felt the need to warn against the specter of prayer as merely spiritual gymnastics. Brown apparently felt no such need.[17]

Brown also displayed a more modernistic understanding of intercessory prayer. When we pray for others, he said, "we find our attitude toward them changing." Liberals such as Abbott and Fosdick had said the same thing but had gone on to assert that through some means as yet unknown, intercessory prayer also had an objective effect on the person being prayed for. Brown apparently did not bother to claim such efficacy for intercessory prayer. It was simply, he said, "God's means of revealing to us what he desires for others, so that we can pray for them aright."[18]

In all, *The Life of Prayer in a World of Science* did not contain any distinctively new teaching. Except for a more frank reliance on the insights of psychology in explaining how prayer recreated character, Brown's emphases had been covered in earlier liberal works. However, earlier liberals had typically been careful to postscript such rhetoric about prayer's internal benefits with a "but that is not all . . ." passage. In Brown and other modernists, the "but" had disappeared. In the intellectual climate of modernism in the 1920s, there was no need for it.

Another indication of the change concerning prayer in Protestantism was the understanding of prayer among those on the extreme edge of 1920s modernism. If in pre-World War I liberalism the "radicals" were those who like Coe and Brown walled off the natural world from prayer, in the late 1920s those on the left of center, for example the "Chicago school," were defining prayer in ways that made a personal God basically irrelevant. For instance, Henry Nelson Wieman, professor of philosophy and religion at the University of Chicago Divinity School, wrote a book on practical religion entitled *Methods of Private Religious Living*. In it his teaching on prayer exhibited tendencies even beyond what mainstream modernists of the 1920s such as Fosdick and Brown were displaying.

Interestingly enough, Wieman did not use the word "prayer" in his chapter on prayer. Instead, Wieman accurately called his formulations on communing with God "worship," thereby avoiding any of the petitionary connotations associated with prayer in traditional Protestantism. Worship, said Wieman, "is preeminently probing down beneath all the sham and pose which inevitably accumulate in every man's life with the daily routine. Worship is struggling to cast off all this." In other words, this was the battlefield for character that Fosdick had described earlier but emptied of any association with prayer as traditionally defined. Wieman also separated "worship" from belief in a personal God. "A man does not need to believe in God in order to worship," he claimed. That is, one may be so constituted so as to not be able to believe that a personal being exists to whom to pray. But that was not important. God was simply "that integrating process which works through all the world . . . to maintain and develop organic interdependence and mutual support between all parts and aspects of the cosmos." Wieman continued: "[O]ne can think of this all-encompassing reality as atoms, if he wishes, or electric tension, or use some other such imagery." What was important was that each person worshipped, whether or not he or she used the word "God" when doing so.[19]

Prayer, then, for Wieman was essentially a technique, an exercise in auto-suggestion. It was in fact the epitome of the "spiritual gymnastics" that liberals of the previous decade had reacted against. Wieman advised readers to set aside a certain time each day for private worship. "The best time, we are very sure, is just before retiring at night and soon after rising in the morning." Why was this the best time? Because that was the time that the subconscious was most receptive to input, as any mental hygiene proponent would attest. Ralph Waldo Trine advised his readers to practice positive thinking when they awoke, because the mind was then in its most receptive state. Philip Cabot, who preached the benefits of a devotional life in line with New Thought to readers in the *Atlantic*, was adamant about the need for prayer before and after sleep because that was when the subconscious was most open to influence from the conscious.[20]

Wieman gave a series of steps that should be followed during these times of worship. First, one was to relax and "become aware of that upon which we are dependent." The second step consisted of calling to mind "the vast and unimaginable possibilities for good which are inherent in this integrating process called God," to envision the best possible state of affairs in the universe. Next, one faced the chief obstacle that was preventing this ideal state of affairs from materializing, and analyzed oneself "to find what change must be made in our own mental attitudes and personal habits" to remove this obstacle. The final crucial step—one that Wieman frankly referred to as auto-suggestion—was to verbalize this readjustment of personality and behavior. For instance, Wieman said, one might discover that he or she is haughty toward and seeking a position of superiority toward others. Then one might verbalize, advised Wieman, " 'I am simple, lowly, sensitive and sympathetic toward . . . ' and here again mention explicitly certain individuals." This statement should be repeated many times, said Wieman, in order to "get it rooted deeply and firmly as a subconscious attitude of the personality." "Anyone who will try this method of worship, ending with this practice of auto-suggestion, and continue it for several weeks" concluded Wieman, "will note some remarkable results of great benefit to himself and his associates."[21]

Wieman's understanding of prayer as self-culture was echoed by Shailer Mathews, Wieman's colleague at the University of Chicago and a leading spokesperson for the modernist cause.[22] Although Mathews still used the word "prayer" and thought of it in terms of efficacy, for him prayer was a technique to be mastered, with predictable results. "We hope to make the technique of religion as intelligible as arithmetic," he said. "God" was important to this enterprise, but not as some arbitrary, willful factor in the process. God was, for Mathews, "the sum of all personality-producing and personally-responsive forces in the universe.... These forces, we hold, can be 'tapped,'" thereby producing "happiness, prosperity, achievement, greatest good" in the one who prayed correctly. Mathews summed up prayer as follows:

> You want to get something or do something, and don't know how.
> You feel there are forces, within or without, that would help if you
> could summon them. By conscious effort you make your wishes clear
> and "expose yourself" to the forces. You try to "reach up." You put
> your wishes into words, for they are meaningless otherwise. That, as
> I understand it, is prayer.

Mathews's remarks more closely resembled the teachings of therapeutic religion than that of traditional Protestantism.[23]

Wieman and Mathews were clearly on the modernistic extreme of liberal Protestantism. The *Christian Century*, however, was not. Begun in the late nineteenth century as the *Christian Oracle* by the Disciples of Christ and renamed at the turn of the century, the *Christian Century* had dropped its denominational focus in the 1910s under the editorship of Charles Clayton Morrison. By the 1920s this journal was recognized as the voice of liberal Protestantism in America. As W. A. Silva has written, "through its history *The Christian Century* has reflected and communicated the social and theological agenda of mainline American Protestantism."[24] The best evidence, then, of a merging of liberal Protestant concepts of prayer and modern thought is found in the pages of the *Christian Century*. By the late 1920s, the liberal Protestant understanding of prayer as expressed in this journal was virtually indistinguishable from that of its secular counterpart, religious humanism.

Religious humanism was a movement to the left of Protestant liberalism consisting largely of some Unitarian clergymen and academicians such as John Dewey, Roy Wood Sellars, and Harry Elmer Barnes. If liberal Protestants sought to combine modern thinking with Christianity, religious humanists explicitly left behind Christianity and set their religion within the context of a purely naturalistic worldview. Religious humanists were nontheistic; they did not necessarily rule out God's existence, but the personal God of Christianity had no place in their system. Humanists rejected supernaturalism in any form, insisting that the natural world was the only real world and that humankind had no separate, spiritual identity apart from nature. Although they greatly admired William James, humanists thought that other psychologists such as James H. Leuba, with his emphatic dismissal of supernaturalism, offered a more realistic approach to the study of humanity. Humanists also accepted science as providing the only proper method for describing the universe and interpreting its meaning. Religious humanists, then, differed from modernists in their frank avowal that, as one of them put it, there was no "friend behind the phenomena." The universe was winding down, no divine sanction for human values existed, and it was left to science to determine and make possible the greatest human good in a cold universe.[25]

Nevertheless, religious humanists differed from other humanists such as Joseph Wood Krutch in that they were optimistic about the potential to achieve fulfilling lives and a just society in the midst of a godless universe. In the words of the historian Donald Meyer, religious humanists expressed "the determination to maintain an attitude of cosmic piety, of reverence and awe before the universe." Of these humanists, John Haynes Holmes, an ordained Unitarian minister and pastor of the Church of the Messiah in New York City, was one of the most prominent.[26]

In the fall of 1929, the *Christian Century* published "A Humanistic Interpretation of Prayer" by Holmes and invited responses from its readers. Much of the way most people prayed was archaic and contemptible, Holmes began. "The call to some remote deity in the heavens to give attention to our concerns, a demand that the laws of the universe be suspended for our participation," Holmes said, was useless. However, prayer itself was a worthy endeavor, as long as it was conceived as a psychological and not a theological phenomenon. For Holmes, prayer was "the conscious and deliberate attempt to gain contact with the universe, . . . to merge our lives in the life of the whole, and therewith identify with the cosmic destiny." There was nothing theistic about such an enterprise, he insisted. "From beginning to end, it is an experience within ourselves." Yet such prayer could also have tangible effects, for prayer was "the deliberate formulation in our minds of an idea of something that we need or want" and then the "deliberate direction of our life-forces to the attainment of our desires." In all, Holmes's ethic of prayer could just as well have been called "A Tyndallian Ethic of Prayer," for, as he himself acknowledged, this understanding of prayer was entirely in keeping with that of "that great scientist," as Holmes called John Tyndall. Fittingly, then, Holmes closed with Tyndall's well-known endorsement of prayer as a useful exercise in self-culture.[27]

Holmes's article provoked, in the words of the editors, "a veritable avalanche of comment." The *Christian Century* thus devoted an unusual amount of space to publishing selections from among the "basketfuls of letters" it received. Not surprisingly, Henry Nelson Wieman agreed "enthusiastically" with much of what Holmes said. However, Wieman sought to clarify what Holmes meant. In prayer we seek not contact with the whole universe indiscriminately, but only with "that going on in the universe which makes for the greatest value," which we can best label God. On the whole, most of the published responses to Holmes's article were of Wieman's temper. Holmes, it was believed, was really a closet theist, and Edward Scribner Ames said that Holmes, "like most humanists, is too timid about the word 'God.' " As one writer put it, "all that the Christian philosophy of prayer has ever asked of us is to believe that there is something infinite outside of ourselves which we can rally to our support as we align ourselves with it. . . . In practice if not in terminology, Dr. Holmes seems to us to be a theist."[28]

Indeed, the whole prayer debate seemed to hinge on a semantic difference: whether one prayed to "the universe" or to "God." Holmes pointed this out in his reply to the responders. People who disagree with my interpretation of prayer, he said, say either that I leave out a personal God or that I subtly put him in. Both responses, Homes noted, show that there is really no quarrel between humanism and theism. Humanism throws out all deductive notions about God, all revelation, and bases everything on experience. But as a humanist, Holmes claimed, he still had profound spiritual experiences when he viewed nature, or read the poets, or encountered humanity. When the pulse of emotion was high, he said, "I find it easy to speak as the poets speak, and cry, as so many of them cry, to *God*. But when I say 'God,' it is poetry and not theology." He concluded: "The humanist can pray as well as the theist; and it is time that the humanist proved his right to prayer and thus denied to the theist his monopoly of this profound experience of the inner life."[29]

This understanding of prayer was apparently enough to place Holmes in the *Christian Century* camp concerning prayer, at least according to the journal's editors. Holmes is one of us, the editors concluded in summing up this lengthy discussion, even though he may use the term "the universe" instead of "God." Holmes was, according to the *Christian Century*, "a liberal-modernist and a theist." He sets up a straw man of childish anthropomorphism, the *Christian Century* claimed, but when he talks about prayer he and we modernists are clearly talking the same thing. Holmes posits "an 'infinite center of energy,' 'akin' to ourselves, which 'rallies' to our 'aid,' which is companionable—not leaving us to work 'alone'! That is what *The Christian Century*, at least, means by God."[30]

Seemingly unnoticed in this semantic debate was the fact that Holmes's understanding of prayer was far removed from that of both traditional Protestantism *and* the liberal ethic of prayer promoted in the 1910s. Of the thirty-nine published responses, only two took exception to Holmes's interpretation of prayer itself rather than to how he described the object of prayer. One of them, a Reverend Hobart D. McKeehan, obviously disturbed by all of this cold speculation on the term "God," seemed to voice the protest of the long-departed father of Christocentric liberalism, Lyman Abbott. "John Haynes Holmes is wrong," McKeehan said bluntly. Prayer was an "authentic dialogue between the soul of man and the Father of Jesus." It was "communion with God—God who is Christlike and personal, God who cares, and who hears and answers the earnest petitions of his children."[31]

Another respondent trumpeted the petition-oriented spirit of prayer displayed in traditional Protestantism. Tucked away in the back page of a later issue of *Christian Century* was the response of James W. Schillinger of Marion, Ohio:

> There is something very essential lacking in Mr. Holmes' article on "Prayer." I will supply it. Here it is. "Call upon me in the day of trouble, and I will deliver thee, and thou shalt glorify me." "The effectual fervent prayer of a righteous man availeth much." "Ask and ye shall receive, seek and ye shall find, knock and it shall be opened unto you."

Schillinger's meaning was clear. Holmes and his respondents had left out the heart of prayer as traditional Protestants had understood it—a petition to a supernatural God to intervene in the affairs of life. The fact that the *Christian Century* only saw fit to quarrel over Holmes's description of the recipient of prayer showed how far modernism had moved away from previous Christian understandings of prayer.[32]

A year later, another prayer event recorded in the pages of the *Christian Century* revealed that in intercessory prayer, almost all traces of the supernatural had been expunged. The emblematic instance of intercessory prayer for liberal Protestantism in this period concerned the 1930 London conference on naval armament limitations. The *Christian Century*, in an editorial entitled "Let Us Pray!" urged all Americans to pray for the success of the conference. Such a call to prayer was nothing new; as we have seen, they abounded in American culture, especially during World War I. But while calls to prayer in World War I basically assumed the efficacy of intercessory prayer, the noteworthy aspect of the *Christian Century*'s call to prayer was the lengthy rationale given for it.

Christians were obligated to pray for the conference, editor Charles Clayton Morrison wrote, for "prayer is the most powerful instrument which the spirit of man can use." In his attempt to persuade readers to pray for the London conference, Morrison at first seemed to draw on the possibilities of mind-power in a spiritual universe. Since the universe was "essentially a spiritual system," said Morrison, "shall not Christian men and women speak to the conference through the instrument of prayer?" If humans have discovered the uses and power of radio waves, may there not also exist unknown means to "broadcast" spiritual messages? "Who will say," Morrison mused, "that there is no power to broadcast such messages—aye, to carry them into the very hearts and minds of those who sit at the conference table?"[33] Clearly, the belief in telepathy had not completely waned.

However, most of Morrison's plea for intecessory prayer was closer to the spirit of John Haynes Holmes, who had remarked months earlier, "if our prayers are to be answered, we must answer them ourselves." "Is there a reader of the *Christian Century* whose liberalism has made it impossible for him to act?" asked Morrison. Rest assured, "these words are not intended to be taken mystically. Our faith has an element of calculation in it." Morrison determined that since the *Christian Century* was distributed to about twenty-five thousand churches with an average attendance of three hundred persons, there existed a potential prayer circle of seven and a half million Christians to pray for the London conference. "Is there even an avowed atheist who will say that such prayers would register only zero? We do not believe that there is." Sheer numbers alone would seem to shrink doubts about inter-cessory prayer.[34]

According to Morrison, the prayers of seven and a half million Christians could have efficacy in two ways. First, there existed at the present time, he said, a sense of "spiritual defeatism" concerning the possibility of slaying the war system whose effect was "more sinister than open opposition." A wave of national prayer for the success of the conference would wipe out this defeatism and restore among Americans optimism that the extinction of war could actually be accomplished.[35]

Second, since President Hoover was the initiator and the prime influence on the conference, Morrison advised, prayer should be made for the president. It was feared that Hoover's resolve in the matter was wavering in the face of opposition from conservative presses and advocates of U.S. sea power who were labeling him a pacifist. At all meetings where prayer is made, therefore, said Morrison, "a consistent and unremitting policy [should] be followed of writing to the President assuring him that he was remembered." Why? Morrison explained that "the spirit of God has many ways to bring to bear upon one who is a subject of prayer the grace and benefit of the petition. But there is no surer way than for those who pray for him to tell him so!" Thus, pleaded Morrison, "the White House should be showered with letters and telegrams from the Christian people of the United States from this day on, telling its Christian occupant that our hearts are bearing him up in prayer, and that our hands and purposes are in full support of his course."[36]

Morrison's editorial reflected the modernist understanding of intercessory prayer completely removed from traditional supernaturalism. For those readers who considered the possibilities of mind-power in a spiritual universe, intercessory prayer was justified in this way. For others, the combination of prayer with a letter-writing campaign by seven and a half million people provided the clearest way that such prayer would have objective efficacy. In other words, as the religious humanists and scientific naturalists had been saying for decades, the pray-ers would have to answer their own prayers. The possibility that God would supernaturally alter the state of affairs in direct response to intercessory prayer—something traditional Protestants had as-sumed—was never raised.

Clearly, by the end of the 1920s a wide rift concerning petitionary prayer had opened in American Protestantism between liberals and conservatives, one that had been bridged over before the 1920s by the Christocentric liberal ethic of prayer. Conservative books on prayer, such as Reuben Torrey's

Power of Prayer and the Prayer of Power (1924), Henry Frost's *Effective Praying* (1925), and J. Oliver Buswell's *Problems in the Prayer Life* (1928) continued to maintain the traditional faith in petitionary prayer as a supernatural enterprise. Liberal Protestants, on the other hand, inhabited a different theological universe, and their reflections on prayer clearly revealed this.

A final snapshot revealing the tendencies that had cemented by 1930 was a *Christian Century* symposium entitled "Does Prayer Change the Weather?" The summer of 1930 was a difficult one for farmers in many parts of the nation as a severe drought withered crops across the land. Calls for prayer for rain rang out from churches as well as state legislatures. In response, in September the *Christian Century* asked what it called "a representative group of American clergyman and theologians" the question: "Does prayer change the weather?" The two conservative respondents of course answered in the affirmative. Citing "the record in the scriptures" as evidence, Mark A. Matthews, a conservative Presbyterian pastor, affirmed that God has answered and does answer prayer for rain.[37]

Moody Bible Institute president James M. Gray, the other conservative Protestant polled, carried on the "answered prayer apologetic" tradition in his affirmation of prayer for rain. Gray turned not to Scripture, as Matthews had done, but to recent history for evidence that God answered prayer. "In the judgment of many," he claimed, "current history furnishes numerous marked interpositions of God in answer to united prayer." Gray went on to recommend a recent tract that claimed that God had removed a Minnesota locust scourge in answer to prayer. A subsequent issue of Gray's *Moody Bible Institute Monthly*, in response to the *Christian Century* symposium, published three accounts of answered prayer for rain submitted by the African missionary James W. Bell.[38]

The other seven solicited responses adamantly disavowed level three prayer. The universe was governed according to unchangeable laws, and prayer had no business there. "If prayer affects the weather," asserted the Congregational minister Samuel Harkness, "meteorology ceases to be a science and becomes an article of theology." Walter Horton concurred: "[I]f prayer affects the weather, then my whole conception of the nature of prayer is erroneous. . . . The great effect of prayer is the relief of spiritual drought in the individual human soul." Raising the specter of that symbol of the scientific age, John Tyndall, Horton said in closing that "until Tyndall's 'prayer-gauge' challenge is answered more convincingly than it ever has been so far, one should not expect prayer to affect the weather."[39]

Harry Emerson Fosdick, perhaps reflecting the effects of the bitter religious quarrels of the decade, summed up the modernist position in the most polemical terms. Of course prayer did not affect the weather, Fosdick exclaimed. Prayers for rain were "ignorant travesties" that were "disastrous to true religion." He continued:

Evidently this still needs to be said in this benighted and uncivilized country. The crude, obsolete supernaturalism which prays for rain is a standing reproach to our religion and will be taken by many an intelligent mind as an excuse for saying, "Almost thou persuadest me to be an atheist." If belief in God is still made the basis of such primitive magic, how can observant people avoid the suspicion that faith in God is costing more than it is worth in the case of many believers?

Fosdick's comments indicated the source of his ire; he was vitally concerned with making Christianity believable to "many an intelligent mind," and traditional supernaturalism was an impediment to that. His statement thus recalls once again Winthrop Hudson's observation that Protestant liberalism was a movement devoted to reaching the "cultured despisers of religion" in modern America.[40]

The *Christian Century* symposium thus revealed an important trend in twentieth-century religion. As members of the intellectual and cultural establishment intent on reaching intelligent moderns, the modernists in the pages of the *Christian Century* were distancing themselves from the concerns of grassroots—or in this case, dust bowl—Americans. Henry Nelson Wieman, for example, listed the problems for the farmer in times of drought as "keeping his personal poise and self-control; maintaining the morale of his family; treating his land in the best way known to science in time of drought; making the best possible economic adjustment." This drought was a crisis, Wieman acknowledged, but the farmer who met it in such a way as to wring from it a blessing "will look back to this time and thank God for the turning point in his life which led to green pastures." Such encouragement, while perhaps true, would have hardly seemed comforting to those left destitute by a failed crop. Similarly, the Unitarian pastor Dilworth Lupton testified:

Were I a farmer in a period of drought I could not conscientiously pray for rain. But I could pray God that I meet the situation without bitterness or despair. I could pray for patience. I could pray for a realization that my soul is stronger than anything that can happen to it. And I know that my prayer would be answered.

Many American Christians, however, *were* praying for tangible drops of rain, not just for character and patience. Perhaps one bitter correspondent expressed the sentiments of many to the modernists' advice when he replied to Fosdick:

It has made little difference to Dr. Harry Emerson Fosdick whether it rained or not. . . . Suppose you were younger, Doctor, living in the Shenandoah Valley on a little farm, your apple crop a failure, brooks bone-dry, credit gone, and your girls hungry; and even suppose you entertained the same theories you do now—don't you think physical distress might cause you to forget your sophistication, and that almost unconsciously, oppressed by your children's' wants, you might drift into the country church and find yourself joining silently with others in prayer for a little rain? "Ignorant travesty"![41]

The modernists clearly did not speak for all Christians.

In light of this episode concerning prayer in the pages of the *Christian Century* and its reflection of the modernist ethic of prayer in general, it is tempting to speculate on the tenuous popular success of liberal Protestantism in the twentieth-century religious landscape. As members of an intellectual establishment, the liberal Protestants of the 1920s, it seems, projected their own particular doubts about petitionary prayer onto the screen of American culture as a whole, even when such doubt was not always evident. This was perfectly illustrated by William Adams Brown's assessment of two articles on prayer that appeared in the 1925 *Atlantic*. In the first article, Harvard professor Kirsopp Lake, a true secularist, claimed that "the religion of to-morrow will have no more place for petition than it will have for any other form of magic." Instead, he said, prayer's purpose will simply be "to stimulate and quicken communion and aspiration." In the ensuing article, Glenn Clark, a proponent of the therapeutic benefits of religion in Christian terms, adamantly asserted otherwise, claiming that in the past few months he had seen "an almost continuous stream of answered prayer." Concerning this exchange, Brown claimed, "large numbers of people have been exchanging the attitude of Glenn Clark for that of Kirsopp Lake. Where their fathers and mothers prayed, they philosophize about prayer." Brown's assessment of the situation seems curious, since the editors of the *Atlantic* concluded just the opposite. Clark's article, the *Atlantic* observed in retrospect, was "the most widely appreciated of all recent *Atlantic* papers."[42]

Clearly, American Protestants on the whole in the late 1920s did not rule out prayer for rain as the modernists did. The *Literary Digest*, a kind of *Reader's Digest* of the day, reported the *Christian Century* symposium on prayer and the weather but did so in a fashion that again indicated the growing division between liberal Protestantism and popular culture. It began by noting the majority of those respondents who believed that prayers for rain were futile, but it closed without comment by quoting in full the responses by Matthews and Gray. In addition, a large box appeared prominently in the middle of the page that quoted the biblical testimony from the Epistle of James concerning Elijah's successful prayer for the weather. The *Literary Digest* was clearly taking its stand on the side of traditional supernaturalism.[43]

Even among the readership of the *Christian Century*, those who announced level three prayer to be futile received little support, if the responses to the symposium published in subsequent issues are at all representative of the magazine's general audience. Of the eleven published letters, seven took exception to the liberals and affirmed that prayer for rain was legitimate, two claimed it was not, and two wavered in between. Of course, prayer for rain was not necessarily crucial; relatively few Christians have placed much emphasis on it. Rather, it was what prayer for rain represented—a supernatural God whom one could turn to for divine help in any kind of emergency—that formed an important issue for many Americans.[44]

In retrospect, then, it seems that by attempting to harmonize the Christian doctrine of prayer with the modern scientific worldview, liberal Protestants were making a permanent choice between constituencies that was not apparent at the time. It was widely believed by cultural elites in the early and middle twentieth century that the march of science was destined to extinguish supernatural worldviews. Liberal Protestants were among those who naively accepted the sociologist James Leuba's conclusion, allegedly based solely on his data, that as knowledge continued to increase, the belief in a personal God who answered prayer in objective ways would become extinct.[45] "The slow but inevitable processes of education," Fosdick claimed in retrospect, "were bound in time to put an end to such outdated thinking." Traditional religions such as fundamentalism were believed by many to be, in the memorable words of the historian Richard Hofstadter, "afloat on a receding wave of history."[46] However, it seems in retrospect that the problems that modernity posed for supernaturalism were felt by a relatively small, albeit influential group of Americans.

This is not to say that the liberals were wrong in disavowing petitionary prayer, though perhaps some of them could have done so in more sympathetic terms. As partakers of a worldview profoundly shaped by modern scientific thought, they were simply being true to their own presuppositions. If liberal Protestants erred in any way, it was in naively believing that their nonsupernaturalistic religion would eventually win the day and that rank-and-file Americans would follow the path they blazed. For instance, the liberal Presbyterian John Beauchamp Thompson reflected in the pages of the *Christian Century* on the plethora of prayers for rain by those who "have not paused to grapple with such problems as prayer and the reign of law" and who continued to view God as an Old Testament deity who granted fair weather as a reward for righteousness and poor weather as a punishment for sin. Yet Thompson believed that some day such people would come to a truer notion of both Christian social ethics—in the form of the Social Gospel— and the workings of God in nature.[47]

As the vitality of modern supernatural forms of Protestantism such as Pentecostalism and fundamentalism shows, however, many Americans, along with never having imbibed the values of the Social Gospel, have been less troubled by the problems of prayer in a universe of law than were the modernists of the 1920s. Supernaturalism has proved not as obsolete as Fosdick thought. The expunging of the supernatural from Christianity was vital to the survival of theistic belief among liberal Protestants and their peers who made "modern" modes of thought the arbiter of reality. It would do little, however, to enhance liberal Protestantism's appeal to the religious rank and file, many of whom, it turned out, failed to sense the difficulties inherent in the life of prayer in a world of science.

Notes

Introduction

1 William Thayer, *From Log Cabin to White House: The Life of James A. Garfield* (New York: Hurst, 1881), 419–420. See also Allan Peskin, *Garfield* (Youngstown, Ohio: Kent State University Press, 1978), 599–607.

2 Reddy, *Prayer and Providence in Relation to the Death of President Garfield* (Syracuse, N.Y.: Masters and Stone, 1881), 3–4; C. A. Van Anda, *Prayer: Its Nature, Conditions, and Effects* (Cincinnati: Cranston and Stowe, 1891), 44. Other contemporary observations are found in "Death of President Garfield" *Harper's* 63 (1881), 624, 784–785, 949.

3 *Independent* 53 (1901), 2250. On details surrounding McKinley's death and assassination, see H. Wayne Morgan, *William McKinley and His America* (Syracuse NY: Syracuse University Press, 1963), 520–525. Other contemporary observations are found in "William McKinley," *Outlook* 69 (1901), 160–161, and "The Death of the President," *Atlantic* 88 (1901), 432.

4 Wilson quoted in "How to Pray and What to Pray for in the International Crisis," *Current Opinion* 57 (1914), 341–343.

5 Quoted in "Failure of Prayers for Peace or Victory," *Literary Digest* 49 (1914), 1068; Jefferson, *Old Truths and New Facts* (New York: Fleming Revell, 1918), 87.

6 "Prayer," *Princeton Theological Review* 17 (1919), 87.

7 Calvin quoted in Faye Kelly, *Prayer in Sixteenth-Century England* (Gainesville: University of Florida Press, 1966), 26; Edward Charles Lyrene, Jr., "The Role of Prayer in American Revival Movements, 1740–1860," Ph.D. diss., Southern Baptist Theological Seminary, 1985, 24–25.

8 Kelly, 26–28, 64.

9 Hambrick-Stowe, *The Practice of Piety* (Chapel Hill: University of North Carolina Press, 1982), 177.

10 Mather, *Remarkable Providences* (London: Reeves and Turner, 1683), 256; Clap and the didaetic couplet are quoted in Hambrick-Stowe, 175, 177.

11 "The Duty of Secret Prayer, Publicly Inculcated" (Boston: B. Green and J. Allen, 1703), 32; "Family Religion, Excited and Assisted," (Newport: Widow Franklin, 1707), 10.

12 Turner, *Without God, Without Creed: The Origins of Unbelief in America* (Baltimore: Johns Hopkins University Press, 1985), 36–39. Robert Bruce Mullin, *Miracles and the Modern Religious Imagination* (New Haven: Yale University Press, 1996), 14–25. Mullin observes: "the line between miracle and special providence was never clear-cut" (14–15). On Hume, see Van Anda, 98. See also Henry F. May, *The Enlightenment in America* (New York: Oxford University Press, 1976).

13 *Dictionary of Christianity in America,* edited by Daniel Reid (Downers Grove, Ill.: Intervarsity Press, 1990), 598.

14 "A Demonstration . . ." (New York: Weyman, 1760), 14–16.

15 Edwards, "The Most High a Prayer-Hearing God," in *The Works of President Edwards* (Worcester, Mass.: Isaiah Thomas, 1809), vol. 8, 47; Williams, *The Power and Efficacy of the Prayers of the People of God* (Boston: S. Kneeland and T. Green, 1742); Newton, quoted in *The Study of Spirituality,* edited by Cheslyn Jones et al., (New York: Oxford University Press, 1986), 460. On concerts of prayer, see Lyrene, 60.

16 D. P. Nord, "American Tract Society," in Reid, *Dictionary of Christianity in the United States,* 52–53.

17 "Prayer a Privilege," in *Practical Truths* (New York: American Tract Society, [1852]), 37.

18 Ahlstrom, "The Golden Day of Democratic Evangelicalism," in Ahlstrom, *A Religious History of the American People* (New Haven: Yale University Press, 1979), 385–509; McLoughlin, introduction, to *Lectures on Revivals of Religion* by Charles Finney (Cambridge, Mass.: Belknap Press, 1960), vii.

19 Finney, *Memoirs* (New York: Fleming Revell, 1876), 9–11, 142.

20 *Lectures,* 53–54. The titles of the lectures on prayer are "Prevailing Prayer," "The Prayer of Faith," and "The Spirit of Prayer." See also Charles Hambrick-Stowe, *Charles Finney and the Spirit of American Evangelicalism* (Grand Rapids, Mich.: Eerdmans 1996), 157–158.

21 *Memoirs,* 36–37; Wright, *Charles Grandison Finney* (Boston: Houghton Mifflin, 1891), 274–279, quoted in *Charles G. Finney's Answers to Prayer,* edited by Louis Parkhurst (Minneapolis: Bethany House, 1983), 113–117.

22 The Revival of 1857–58 is discussed in Kathryn Long, *The Revival of 1857–58* (New York: Oxford University Press, 1997); Timothy L. Smith, *Revivalism and Social Reform* (New York: Abingdon Press, 1957), 63–79; J. Edwin Orr, *The Fervent Prayer* (Chicago: Moody Press, 1974), 1–33; William McLoughlin, *Modern Revivalism* (New York: Ronald Press, 1959), 162–165; and Lyrene.

23 *The Power of Prayer* (New York: Scribner, 1859), v, 289.

24 Ibid., 230–231.

25 Robert Hastings Nichols, "Samuel Irenaeus Prime," in *Dictionary of American Biography,* edited by Dumas Maline (New York: Charles Scribner's Sons, 1935), vol. 15, 228. The preface to a later volume claimed that *The Power of Prayer* "had a circulation almost unexampled among religious books of that day" and that sixty-five thousand copies were printed in London; *Prayer and Its Answer* (New York: Scribner's, 1882), 13–15.

26 "On Prayer," *Methodist* 2 (1819), 115; Tyler, *Prayer for Colleges* (New York: W. M. Dodd, 1855), 37–38; Clarke, *The Christian Doctrine of Prayer* (Boston: American Unitarian Association, 1854), xii.

27 *The Still Hour* (Boston: Gould and Lincoln, 1863), 14–15, 35–38.

28 Coe, *The Religion of a Mature Mind* (Chicago: Fleming Revell, 1902), 329; Blanchard, *Getting Things from God* (Wheaton, Ill.: Sword of the Lord, [1915]), 58; Frederick C. Spurr, "The Place of Prayer in Life," *Baptist* 5 (1924), 96.

29 Brown, *Life of Prayer* (New York: Scribner's, 1927), 18; Heiler, *Prayer* (London: Oxford University Press [1916]), 97; Jones, *The Inner Life* (New York: Macmillan, 1916), 112–113; McComb, "Some Modern Aspects of Prayer," *Living Age* 281 (1914), 160.

30 Henry Clay Trumbull, *Prayer: Its Nature and Scope* (Philadelphia: John D. Wattles, 1896), iii; Chamberlain, *The True Doctrine of Prayer* (New York: Baker and Taylor, 1906). Most rank-and-file Christians probably would have agreed with Grover Cleveland's oft-quoted remark that "the Bible is good enough for me, just the old book under which I was brought up"; quoted in Martin Marty, *Modern American Religion*, (Chicago: University of Chicago Press, 1986), vol. 1, 42.

31 Pierson, *Forward Movements of the Last Half Century* (New York: Funk and Wagnalls, 1905), 241; Jones, *The World Within* (New York: Macmillan, 1918), 19; Bounds, *Power through Prayer* (Chicago: Moody Press, [1912]), 124; Hale, "Why I Keep on Praying," *Baptist* 4 (1923), 840.

32 Jefferson, 97; Smith, "Providence, Prayer, and Physical Science," *Methodist Review* 45 (1897), 61.

33 Jellett, *The Efficacy of Prayer* (London: Macmillan, 1880), vi.

34 Marty, *Modern American Religion*, vol. 1. See, for example, Marty, 17–43; Cauthen, *American Religious Liberalism* (New York: Harper and Row, 1962); Hutchison, *The Modernist Impulse in American Protestantism* (Cambridge, Mass: Harvard University Press, 1976); and Sidney Ahlstrom, "The Golden Age of Liberal Theology," in *A Religious History of the American People* (New Haven: Yale University Press, 1972), 763–804.

35 Fosdick, "The New Religious Reformation," in *Adventurous Religion* (New York: Harper and Brothers, 1926), 233, 311; Morrison, "The Devotional Life of the Church," *Christian Century* 37 (January 8, 1920), 3; Morrison, "The New Reformation," *Christian Century* 40 (February 15, 1923), 198.

36 Niebuhr and Fosdick are quoted in Miller, *Harry Emerson Fosdick* (New York: Oxford University Press, 1985), 69–70. On the popularity of conservative evangelical devotional writers, see Virginia Brereton, *From Sin to Salvation* (Bloomington: Indiana University Press, 1991), 80–81.

37 In addition to numerous secondary works on turn-of-the-century American religion, some helpful background works specifically on prayer include the following: Friedrich Heiler, *Prayer: A Study in the History and Psychology of Religion*, Joseph Jungmanns, *Christian Prayer Through the Centuries*, Robert L. Simpson, *The Interpretation of Prayer in the Early Church*, Faye Kelly *Prayer in Sixteenth Century England*, and Perry LeFevre, *Understandings of Prayer*. On the American scene, the subject of prayer rarely appears in the secondary literature. In addition to Charles Hambrick-Stowe *The Practice of Piety*, James Turner, *Without God, Without Creed*, provides some good epistemological background to Protestant attitudes toward prayer and devotes a few pages to the so-called prayer-gauge debate in 1872. One recent book that deserves special mention is Robert Bruce Mullin *Miracles and the Modern Religious Imagination*. Mullin traces the decline in England and America of the traditional Protestant belief that miracles were limited to the biblical epoch. As a study of the

changing attitudes toward the supernatural, Mullin's book forms an important backdrop to my own project, and I occasionally draw on his insights in subsequent chapters. My project, however, is more narrowly focused than Mullin's; I am primarily interested in showing how one group of Americans, liberal Protestants, reinterpreted Christian prayer in response to the changing intellectual environment of the early twentieth century. For example, Mullin explains a new openness to faith healing and "mind cure" that emerged in the 1910s in Great Britain and America; in chapter 6, I show how liberal Protestants in America capitalized on this "new belief in prayer" in their explanations of petitionary prayer.

38 One work that treated prayer from a historical perspective was Lyrene, "The Role of Prayer in American Revival Movements, 1740–1860," which looked at some changes in the practice of revival prayer from Edwards to Charles Finney. Lyrene's focus was on revivals and revivalists—something peripheral to my subject—and his purpose was largely didactic, as such books often are.

One. A Final Act of Purification

1 Kingsley, "Why Should We Pray for Fair Weather?" quoted in Frank M. Turner, "Rainfall, Plagues, and the Prince of Wales: A Chapter in the Conflict of Religion and Science," *Journal of British Studies* 13 (1974), 51. The best background on the prayer-gauge debate is found here and in Turner's "John Tyndall and Victorian Scientific Naturalism," in *John Tyndall, Essays on a Natural Philosopher*, edited by W. H. Brock, (Dublin: Royal Dublin Society, 1981), 175–177.

2 Burchfield, "Biographical Sketch," in Brock, *John Tyndall.*

3 Tyndall, "Reflections on Prayer and Natural Law (1861)," in *Fragments of Science*, (New York: Collier, 1901), vol. 2, 5, 9–10. Conservation of Energy was still a hotly contested concept at this time. The older generation of scientists such as J. F. W. Herschel and Michael Faraday opposed it, and William Whewell's 1853 history of the inductive sciences made no reference to it; Henry Williams, *The Story of Nineteenth-Century Science* (New York: Harper, 1900), 214–221.)

4 Turner, "Rainfall, Plagues, and the Prince of Wales," 54–57, 59–60.

5 Means, ed., *The Prayer-Gauge Debate* (Boston: Congregational Publishing Society, 1876), 3. See Tyndall, "Providence in Physical Affairs," *Popular Science Monthly* 1 (September 1872), 638, and "Science and Religion," *Popular Science Monthly* 2 (November 1872), 79–82. For a typical example of comments on the prayer-gauge in American secular presses, see "Prayers and Pills," *Scribner's Monthly* 5 (November, 1872), 116–117.

6 Tyndall's American tour and Christian opposition are described in A. S. Eve and C. H. Creasy, *Life and Work of John Tyndall* (London: Macmillan, 1945), 168–171; Tyndall quoted in Eve and Creasy, 169. *New York Times*, December 22, 1972. See also reports on Tyndall in *New York Times*, December 18, 21, 25, 27, 30, and especially December 28, 1872. While praising Tyndall's scien-

tific lectures, the *New York Times* sided with the Presbyterians when it came to Tyndall's attack on prayer.

7 On Origen, see Eric George Jay, trans., *Origen's Treatise on Prayer* (London: S.P.C.K., 1954), 95–104. Davis, "The Prayer Test," *Baptist Quarterly* 7 (1873), 61. The earliest evidence of an awareness of objections to prayer based on the supposed inviolability of natural laws appears in the works of Samuel Clarke in the early eighteenth century; J. H. Jellett, *The Efficacy of Prayer* (London: Macmillan, 1880), xxxiii.

8 Chamberlain, *The True Doctrine of Prayer* (New York: Baker and Taylor, 1906), 139–141; King, "Difficulties Concerning Prayer," *Biblical World* 46 (1915), 131–134, 281–284, 348–352; Horton, "Does Prayer Change the Weather?" *Christian Century* 47 (September 10, 1930), 1085.

9 *Contemporary Review*, quoted in Means, 11–14. Ironically, interest in conducting such prayer experiments is becoming widespread. For example, a modern project quite similar to Thompson's proposal is currently underway at the University of New Mexico. The National Institute of Health has awarded psychiatry professor Scott Walker a grant of thirty thousand to head a project in which Protestants, Catholics, and Jews will pray for a pool of clients at a substance abuse clinic. See, among other sources, Joseph Pereira, "The Healing Power of Prayer Is Tested by Science," *Wall Street Journal*, December 20, 1995, and Gary Thomas, "Doctors Who Pray," *Christianity Today*, January 6, 1997, 20–30.

10 Editorial, *Spectator*, quoted in Means, (August 1872), 23, 25, 30–31.

11 McCosh had moved from Scotland to Princeton in 1868; he kept an ear to intellectual discussions in the United Kingdom.

12 McCosh, "On Prayer," *Contemporary Review* (August 1872), quoted in Means, 140, 138. McCosh's article, along with Tyndall's original essay, was republished for Americans in *Littell's Living Age* 27 (1872).

13 McCosh, "On Prayer," 143, 144.

14 Tyndall, "On Prayer as a Physical Force," *Contemporary Review* (October 1872), quoted in Means, 114–115, 111.

15 *Ibid.*, 112–114; Thompson, "On Prayer," *Contemporary Review* (October 1872), quoted in Means, 125.

16 Tyndall, of course, had done the same in "On Prayer as a Physical Force," but his earlier philosophical attack on prayer had indelibly stamped his test with the stigma—for Christians—of naturalism.

17 Galton, "Statistical Inquiries into the Efficacy of Prayer," *Fortnightly Review* (August 1872), cited in Means, 88–89; Thompson, "On Prayer," cited in Means's, 134.

18 Galton, 92, 94.

19 *Ibid.*, 100–101.

20 This threefold scheme, though my own construction, appears in a similar form in James B. Pratt, "An Empirical Study of Prayer," *American Journal of Religion, Psychology, and Education* 4 (1909), 53.

21 Many Christians would emphasize level one prayer, but in an "objective" sense, that is, that the personal benefit comes by direct response from a personal God.

Scientific naturalists would explain level one prayer in a strictly subjective sense, that the act of praying itself is what produces the benefit. This distinction, while irrelevant to this discussion, becomes important in later chapters.

22 Galton, 104.

23 "The Prayer Test," 62, 63, 65.

24 Quoted in Turner, "Rainfall," 57–58.

25 See William Knight, "The Function of Prayer in the Economy of the Universe," *Contemporary Review* (January 1873), quoted in Means, 229–246.

26 The "separate spheres" ideology does have antecedents in Christian history. The church father Tertullian seemed to intimate such an understanding of prayer when he wrote concerning Christian prayer: "It does not establish the angel of the dew in the midst of the fire, nor block the mouths of lions, nor transfer to the hungry the peasants' dinner. It turns away by delegated grace no perception of suffering, yet it arms with endurance those who do suffer and perceive and grieve"; *Tertullian's Tract on Prayer*, translated by Ernest Evans (London: S.P.C.K., 1953), quoted in Robert Simpson, *The Interpretation of Prayer in the Early Church* (Philadelphia: Westminster Press, 1965), 132.

27 Since the prayer-gauge was only proposed in late 1872, Hodge was primarily responding to Tyndall's remarks of the previous decade. An important difference emerged between mainstream Protestants in this period. Hodge, a "cessationist" in the Reformed tradition, defined miracles as special acts of God whose purpose was to confirm biblical revelation; thus, the age of miracles had ceased with the closing of the canon, and subsequent acts of God were "special providences" brought about through secondary causes. This distinction began to break down for some in the mid–nineteenth century, most notably Horace Bushnell, who defined the "supernatural" as "whatever it be, that is either not in the chain of natural cause and effect, or which acts on the chain of cause and effect nature, from without the chain," *Nature and the Supernatural* (New York: Scribner, 1859), 37. Therefore, all human and divine action was essentially "miracle," different only in degree. Hodge saw Bushnell's expansion of "miracle" to present phenomena as a dangerous trend in apologetics and severely criticized his book. For my purposes, however, what is important is that both sides in the dispute saw God's present action in the physical realm in answer to prayer as perfectly compatible with natural law. See Mullin, "Horace Bushnell and the Question of Miracles," *Church History* 58 (1989), 460–473, and *Miracles and the Modern Religious Imagination*, 66–77, on the threat to cessationism in nineteenth-century America.

28 Hodge, *Systematic Theology* (New York: Scribner's, 1872), vol. 3, 693, 696.

29 Prayer and the Prayer-Gauge (New York: Dodd and Mead, 1874), 10–28. This line of argumentation seems to have been rooted in *The Reign of Law*, by George Campbell, Duke of Argyll (New York: John B. Alden, 1866). Argyll was active in British politics but also involved himself in many of the theological and scientific debates of Victorian England, especially Darwinism; see Neal C. Gillespie, "The Duke of Argyll, Evolutionary Anthropology, and the Art of Scientific Controversy," *Isis* 68 (1977), 40–54. Argyll contributed to the prayer-gauge debate in Britain with a rebuttal to William Knight, "The Two Spheres:

Are They Two?" *Contemporary Review* (February, 1873), quoted in Means, 253–269. Another important antecedent to the analogy from human action was Bushnell's *Nature and the Supernatural* (1859), which I discuss hereafter.

30 Atkinson, "Tyndall on the Physical Value of Prayer," *Southern Presbyterian Review* 29 (January 1873), 73; Morris, *Natural Laws and Gospel Teachings* (New York: American Tract Society, 1887), 141; Kinsley, *Science and Prayer* (Meadville, Pa.: Flood and Vincent, 1893), 16.

31 See James Turner, *Without God, without Creed* (Baltimore: Johns Hopkins University Press, 1985), 39–40, for an example of "foreknowledge" reasoning in colonial America. Some twentieth-century observers claimed that this justification of prayer fell by the wayside. W. P. Paterson, overseer of a worldwide call for essays on prayer during World War I, asserted: "[S]atisfactory as this hypothesis seems on intellectual grounds, it is remarkable how little appeal it makes to the religious man of the present day.... One reason doubtless is that the general religious mind of our generation no longer finds itself at home in the predestinarian scheme of thought"; "Prayer and the Contemporary Mind," in *The Power of Prayer* (New York: Macmillan, 1920), 31.

32 McCosh, 142–143; Patton, *Prayer and Its Remarkable Answers* (Toronto: William Briggs, 1875), 131–133. The British writer Leonard Bacon demonstrated how the foreknowledge argument dispensed with the need for miracles or special providences. Concerning the Old Testament account of the walls of Jericho crashing down following the marching of the Israelites, Bacon noted that earthquakes were common in ancient Palestine. One such earthquake, he claimed, "had been timed in the prearrangements of creation as to spring forth at the eternally foreknown moment of that martial call of Joshua"; "Prayer, Miracle, and Natural Law," *Fraser's* (September 1873), 344–345.

33 On the significance of geology for nineteenth-century Christianity, see Charles Gillispie, *Genesis and Geology* (Cambridge, Mass.: Harvard University Press, 1951).

34 Accounts of Darwin are too numerous to list, but James Moore, *The Post-Darwinian Controversies* (Cambridge England: Cambridge University Press, 1978), is especially insightful. For accounts of the relationship between American Protestantism and nineteenth-century science, see James Turner, *Without God, without Creed*, and T. D. Bozeman, *Protestants in an Age of Science* (Chapel Hill: University of North Carolina Press, 1977). Charles Cashdollar, *The Transformation of Theology, 1830–1890* (Princeton: Princeton University Press, 1989), explores the rise of naturalistic assumptions in Western thought.

35 Turner, *Without God, without Creed*, 190, 180.

36 Tyndall, "On Prayer," 110.

37 Thompson, "On Prayer," 132–133.

38 Wells, "Law, Providence, and Prayer, *Bibliotheca Sacra* 30 (October 1873), 612.

39 *Spectator* (August 1872), quoted in Means, 177; Horton, in a symposium "Does Prayer Change the Weather?" *Christian Century* 47 (September 10, 1930), 1084.

40 Huxley, *Essay upon Some Controverted Questions* (London: Macmillan, 1892), 306.

41 Morris, 120–130.

42 For example, in the case of President Garfield, William Reddy claimed that God accomplished the *real* goal of the people's prayers—namely, the reunification of a divided country—through Garfield's death; *Prayer and Providence in Relation to the Death of President Garfield* (Syracuse, N.Y.: Masters and Stone, 1881), 14–15.

43 *The Still Hour* (Boston: Gould and Lincoln, 1863), 37–38.

44 Wells, 626; Tyndall, "On Prayer," 115.

45 Atkinson, 87; Turner, 150 (as my introduction suggested, however, one may well question how far doubts over Scripture penetrated rank-and-file Protestantism); Jellett, xxxv. Mullin describes the place of the miracles of Jesus for progressive Protestants in the late nineteenth century as "embarrassing heirlooms from an earlier age"; *Miracles and the Modern Religious Imagination*, 81.

46 Patton, 400, 34, 40, 43.

47 *Ibid.*, preface.

Two. Proving the Living God

1 Mueller, *The Life of Trust* (New York: Crowell, 1877), 419–422, vi.

2 On Wesley, see Henry Rack, *Reasonable Enthusiast: John Wesley and the Rise of Methodism* (London: Epworth Press, 1989), 540, and E. Brooks Holifield, *Health and Medicine in the Methodist Tradition* (New York: Crossroad, 1986), 36–37. On American Methodist enthusiasm, see John Wigger, "Taking Heaven by Storm" (Ph.D. diss., University of Notre Dame, 1994).

3 Wigger, "Taking Heaven." On cessationism, see chapter 1, 27. Of course, as orthodox responses to the prayer-gauge debate showed, one could believe in the most supernatural of occurrences even under a special providences paradigm.

4 Bushnell, *Nature and the Supernatural* (New York: Scribner, Armstrong, 1877), 453–454. See also Robert Bruce Mullin, "Horace Bushnell and the Question of Miracles," *Church History* 58 (1989), 460–473. Some of Bushnell's miraculous anecdotes were cited by William Patton in *Prayer and Its Remarkable Answers* (Toronto: William Briggs, 1875), 168–170.

5 McLoughlin, *Modern Revivalism* (New York: Ronald Press, 1959), 17–18; Louis G. Parkhurst, ed., *Charles G. Finney's Answers to Prayer* (Minneapolis: Bethany House, 1983), 114–115. Finney also claimed that he and some other Christians brought about the death through prayer of the prominent Unitarian Theodore Parker, who had been hampering revival efforts in Boston. They had prayed that Parker would either be converted or his evil influence might somehow be set aside. Parker became ill and died soon thereafter; Parkhurst, 111–112.

6 Bebbington, *Evangelicalism in Modern Britain* (London: Unwin Hyman, 1989), 80–94.

7 Donald Dayton, *Theological Roots of Pentecostalism* (Grand Rapids Mich.: Francis Asbury Press, 1987), 100–108.

8 J. C. Pollock, *The Keswick Story* (London: Hodder and Stoughton, 1964), 64–118; Bruce Shelley, "Sources of Pietistic Fundamentalism," *Fides et Historia* 5

(1973), 76; George Marsden, *Fundamentalism and American Culture* (New York: Oxford University Press), 72–80. Nuances and variations concerning the Keswick understanding of the baptism of the Holy Spirit are explained in John Fea, "Power from on High in an Age of Ecclesiastical Impotence: The 'Enduement of the Holy Spirit' in American Fundamentalist Thought, 1880–1936," *Fides et Historia* 26 (Summer 1994), 23–35.

9 Holifield, 29–38.

10 Dayton, 115–132; Holifield, 37–41; Raymond Cunningham, "From Holiness to Healing: The Faith Cure in America," in *Modern American Protestantism and Its World*, edited by Martin Marty (New York: Saur, 1993), vol. 14, 3–17. See also Mullin, *Miracles and the Modern Religious Imagination* (New Haven: Yale University Press, 1996), 91–93.

11 Gottschalk, *The Emergence of Christian Science in American Religious Life* (Berkeley: University of California Press, 1973), 289–290.

12 Blumhofer, *Restoring the Faith: The Assemblies of God, Pentecostalism, and American Culture* (Urbana: University of Illinois Press, 1993), 11–42; see also Vincent Synan, *The Holiness-Pentecostal Movement in the United States* (Grand Rapids, Mich.: Eerdmans, 1971), 18–31; Moody's experience is recounted in Synan, 218; Wacker, "The Holy Spirit and the Spirit of the Age in American Protestantism, 1880–1910," *Journal of American History* 72 (1985), 45–62. Of course, the orthodox did not see themselves as spiritually arid, nor have some of their historians. See, for instance, W. Andrew Hoffecker, *Piety and the Princeton Theologians* (Phillipsburg, N.J.: Presbyterian and Reformed Publishing, 1981). However, such perceived sterility was an important symbol to nineteenth-century religious innovators.

13 Moody, *Prevailing Prayer* (New York: Fleming Revell, 1885), 90, 115; Gordon, *The Ministry of Healing* (New York: Fleming Revell, 1882), 210; Biederwolf, *How Can God Answer Prayer?* (New York: Fleming Revell, 1910), 230.

14 Torrey, *How to Pray* (Chicago: Moody Press, 1900), 9; Blanchard, *Getting Things from God* (Wheaton, Ill.: Sword of the Lord, [1915]), 225.

15 Bounds, *The Possibilities of Prayer*, in *The Best of E. M. Bounds* (Grand Rapids, Mich.: Baker, [1913]), 204–205. The following serves as impressionistic evidence: in the index to Geraldine Taylor's devotional biography *Hudson Taylor in Early Years*, the "Prayer" listing simply states, "see 'Answers to Prayer' "; Philadelphia: China Inland Mission, 1911, 510.

16 A. T. Pierson, *Forward Movements of the Last Half Century* (New York: Funk and Wagnall, 1905), 93–95; Basil Miller, *George Mueller* (Minneapolis: Bethany House, 1941), 15–36.

17 This diary entry is quoted in *Answers to Prayer from George Mueller's Narratives*, edited by A. E. C. Brooks, (Chicago: Moody Press, 1903), 87, one of many reprints of Mueller's *The Life of Trust* that circulated in America. The claim of fifty-thousand answered prayers is cited in Miller, 47. Examples of divine healing in answer to prayer occur in *The Life of Trust*, 451–452, during a measles outbreak.

18 Quoted in Geraldine Taylor, *Hudson Taylor in Early Years*, 132, 478–479, 190. On faith missions, see Joel Carpenter and Wilbert R. Shenk, eds., *Earthen Ves-*

sels: American Evangelicals and Foreign Missions, 1880–1980 (Grand Rapids, Mich.: Eerdmans, 1990).

19 Quoted in Howard and Geraldine Taylor, *Hudson Taylor's Spiritual Secret* (Chicago: Moody Press, 1932), 227. David Bebbington, noting the confluence of faith-work and holiness teachings, has remarked, "just as human means must be laid aside in Christian mission, so human effort must be abandoned in the Christian life" (152).

20 Mueller accepted an invitation to visit America in 1877. In September, he spoke in a number of churches in New York City, including the Brooklyn Tabernacle and Plymouth Church, the largest churches in New York City. In all, Mueller spent ten months in America, speaking in churches, colleges, and seminaries from New England to California. His New York City host, E. P. Thwing, said that Mueller "has furnished the present age the most conspicuous illustration of the power and willingness of God to answer believing prayer"; *The Life of Trust*, 523–528. See also A. T. Pierson, *George Mueller of Bristol* (New York: Fleming Revell, 1899), 250–263.

21 Geraldine Taylor, *Hudson Taylor and the China Inland Mission* (Philadelphia: China Inland Mission, 1918), 437–453. On the Student Volunteer Movement, see Robert Wilder, *The Student Volunteer Movement* (New York: Student Volunteer Movement, 1935).

22 Pierson, *George Mueller of Bristol*; Geraldine Taylor, *Hudson Taylor in Early Years* and *Hudson Taylor and the China Inland Mission*. See also Geraldine Taylor, *The Story of the China Inland Mission* (London: Morgan and Scott, 1894); her condensed version of Taylor's life, *Hudson Taylor's Spiritual Secret*, became a mainstay of twentieth-century devotional literature.

23 The Goforths, in addition to being the most aptly named missionary couple in turn-of-the-century evangelicalism, were also one of the most fervent: Jonathan spent the money for Rosalind's engagement ring on evangelistic tracts; Alvyn Austin, *Saving China: Canadian Missionaries in the Middle Kingdom, 1888–1959* (Toronto: University of Toronto Press, 1986), 36. See also Rosalind Goforth, *Goforth of China* (Grand Rapids, Mich.: Zondervan, 1937).

24 Rosalind Goforth, *How I Know God Answers Prayer* (Chicago: Moody Press, 1921), 66–67.

25 *Ibid.*, 111, 103–104, 72. Similar "key-finding" instances were included in William Patton's answered prayer anthology (discussed in chapter 1) in a section entitled "The Smaller Events of Life"; *Prayer and Its Remarkable Answers*, 206–208.

26 Whittle, ed., *The Wonders of Prayer* (Chicago: Fleming Revell, 1885); Henry W. Adams, ed., *I Cried, He Answered* (Chicago: Bible Institute Colportage Association, 1918). Information on Whittle can be found in W. H. Daniels, ed., *Moody: His Words, Work, and Workers* (New York: Nelson and Phillips, 1877), 495–500.

27 Henry Frost, *Effective Praying* (Philadelphia: Sunday School Times, 1925), 67–68. On Cullis, see Mullin, *Miracles and the Modern Religious Imagination*, 91–92; Patton, 387–388. On the role of remarkable providences in the founding of

faith missions, see Joel Carpenter, introduction to *Missionary Innovation and Expansion* (New York: Garland, 1988).

28 Torrey, "What the Moody Bible Institute Has Stood for during the Twenty-Five Years of its History," *Christian Workers'* 16 (February 1916), 443. The incident concerning the six thousand dollars was also recounted in James Smith's *Our Faithful God: Answers to Prayer* (London: Marshall, 1914), a compilation of answered prayer by British evangelicals. On Moody's financial policy, see Gene Getz, *The Story of Moody Bible Institute* (Chicago: Moody Press, 1986), 52–61. It is a fitting testament to the importance of this highly supernatural ethic of prayer in radical evangelicalism that at two different points in his book on prayer, Wheaton College president Charles Blanchard felt the need to justify Wheaton's general policy of "Trust God, but tell His people"; *Getting Things from God*, 183–188, 234–236.

29 John Stam, quoted in Mrs. Howard Taylor, *The Triumph of John and Betty Stam* (Philadelphia: China Inland Mission, 1935), 22; Goforth, *How I know God Answers Prayer*, 111.

30 On the importance of answered prayer as a way for these evangelicals to increase their *own* faith in God and in themselves, see Rick Ostrander, "Proving the Living God: Answered Prayer as a Modern Fundamentalist Apologetic," *Fides et Historia* 28 (Fall 1996), 87–89.

31 By "apologetics" is meant "argumentation on behalf of the Christian faith"; T. H. Olbricht, "Apologetics," in *Dictionary of Christianity in America*, edited by Daniel Reid, (Downers Grove, Ill: Intervarsity, 1990), 71. This can take the form of logical arguments or, as in the case of answered prayer narratives, the assertion of evidence. In addition, such evidence may be intended for outright unbelievers or those within the church.

32 *The Christian's Secret of the Happy Life* (Boston: Christian Witness, [1875]), 191; Mason quoted in *The Power of Prayer*, edited by W. P. Paterson, (New York: Macmillan, 1920), 311; Bounds, *The Possibilities of Prayer*, 203.

33 *The Life of Trust*, 126–127. The minister's remark is contained in a letter to William Patton quoted in Patton, 397. Mueller did desire to help orphans, he said, "but still the first and primary object of the work was, and still is, that God might be magnified by the fact that the orphans under my care are provided with all they need, only by prayer and faith"; 128.

34 Although originally a moderate Old School Presbyterian, Prime came to identify himself with the Keswick holiness movement. His third volume of answered prayer, *Fifteen Years of Prayer* (New York: Scribner, Armstrong, 1872), closed with sections with such telltale titles as "Higher Christian Life," "Rest in Faith," "Higher Spiritual Life," and "Letting Go and Taking Hold."

35 *Fifteen Years of Prayer*, iii–iv. The popular magazine *Scribner's Monthly* gave Prime's book an approving review, contrasting it to "wise professors in their lecture-rooms" who "propose their arithmetical or statistical tests of the efficacy of prayer"; *Scribner's Monthly* 5 (November 1872), 135.

36 *Prayer and Its Answer* (New York: Scribner's, 1882), 18, 162. This "new evidentialist" approach represented a departure to some extent from the traditional

evidentialist apologetics that nineteenth-century Protestants like Prime had inherited. Christian apologetics in post-Enlightenment America had been founded on two pillars. Natural theology, namely the argument from design, established the existence of God, while "evidences" of Scriptural miracles and fulfilled prophecy established the veracity of Christianity. This approach, which peaked in the 1850s, began to crumble for many in the second half of the nineteenth century. Darwin's theory of evolution made the argument from design seem less convincing, and the rise of higher criticism made the testimony of Scripture problematic as well. However, traditional evidentialism did not completely disappear. The popular success of books by Josh McDowell employing traditional evidentialism—for example, *Evidence That Demands a Verdict* (San Bernardino, Calif.: Campus Crusade for Christ, 1972)—attests to the persistence of this tradition in modern evangelicalism. See also Robert Bruce Mullin's discussion of faith healing as a new form of evidentialism; *Miracles and the Modern Religious Imagination*, 97–99.

37 Taylor, *Hudson Taylor in Early Years*, 166–169.

38 Quoted in *Our Faithful God: Answers to Prayer*, edited by James H. Smith (London: Marshall, 1914), 217.

39 Quoted in *Touching Incidents and Remarkable Answers to Prayer*, edited by S. B. Shaw, (Chicago: S. B. Shaw, 1893), 231–232.

40 D. L. Moody interview with the *Chicago Tribune*, January 23, 1886, 3, quoted in Robert Flood and Jerry Jenkins, *Teaching the Word, Reaching the World: Moody Bible Institute, the First Hundred Years* (Chicago: Moody Press, 1985), 37. On Bible institutes, see Virginia Brereton, *Training God's Army: The American Bible School, 1880–1940* (Bloomington: Indiana University Press, 1990).

41 Edwards, "The Most High a Prayer-Hearing God," *Works of President Edwards*, (Worcester, Mass.: Isaiah Thomas, [1735]), vol. 8, 47, 51–55; Tomkins, *A Brief Testimony to the Great Duty of Prayer* (Philadelphia: Samuel Keimer, 1694); Scofield, *Bible History of Answered Prayer* (New York: Fleming Revell, 1899).

42 Tyler, *Prayer for Colleges* (New York: M. W. Dodd, 1855), 149–150; Accounts of answered prayers for spiritual conversions are sprinkled throughout Finney's *Memoirs*. See also Louis G. Parkhurst, ed., *Charles G. Finney's Answers to Prayer* (Minneapolis: Bethany House, 1983).

43 Pierson, *Forward Movements of the Last Half Century* (New York: Funk and Wagnalls, 1905), 70. This desire to display truly convincing answers to prayer helps explain the fundraising technique practiced by Mueller, Taylor, and their American imitators, which was considered extreme even by some fellow evangelicals. Wheaton College president Charles Blanchard, when using Mueller's method to raise funds for his school, explained that "though all good gifts are from Him, whether they are requested or not, the gift which is bestowed without any human intervention seems more obviously His work than that which comes in answer to any solicitation"; *Getting Things from God*, 182. When battling the prophets of Baal, how much more convincing to soak the altar with water first before asking God to set it ablaze.

44 *Remarkable Providences* (London: Reeves and Turner, [1683]), preface, 259.

45 Turner, *Without God, Without Creed* (Baltimore: Johns Hopkins, University Press), 133–135; Trumbull quoted in Henry W. Adams, ed., *I Cried, He Answered* (Chicago: Moody Colportage, 1918), 5; Bradt, 'introduction' to *Answered or Unanswered?* by Louisa Vaughan, (Philadelphia: Christian Life Literature Fund, [1917]).

46 It also had a historical antecedent in John Wesley. Biographer Henry Rack has labeled Wesley a "reasonable enthusiast: rational in form but enthusiast in substance." He was "thoroughly imbued with the contemporary fashion for empiricism and followed Locke in his approach to questions of knowledge." However, Wesley also retained a "strong sense of the supernatural intervention of God" long after the climate of opinion on such matters had changed; he simply "added Lockean empiricist arguments to justify them." George Whitefield and even other Methodists criticized him for this, but Wesley was undaunted. He believed in witches, "especially as a knock-down argument against skeptics denying supernatural intervention in the world." His journal contained accounts of divine activity in the weather, healings, and other supernatural phenomena. Writes Rack, "some of his friends regretted the inclusion of such material in the *Journal*, but Wesley defended them for apologetic reasons in a skeptical generation." Wesley thus combined two tendencies in his age: evangelical enthusiasm and Enlightenment empiricism; Rack, *Reasonable Enthusiast: John Wesley and the Rise of Methodism*, (London: Epworth Press, 1989), 384–388, 432.

47 Moore, *In Search of White Crows: Spiritualism, Parapsychology, and American Culture* (New York: Oxford University Press, 1977), vii. One can even cite a modern parallel: scientific creationism, which seeks to put forth scientific data to argue for a highly supernaturalistic interpretation of earth history; see Ronald Numbers, *The Creationists* (New York: Knopf, 1992).

48 Jastrow quoted in Karl Stolz, *The Psychology of Prayer* (New York: Abingdon, 1923), 154.

49 *Answers to Prayer*, 37.

50 Minister cited in Patton, 397; Campbell, *The Place of Prayer in the Christian Religion* (New York: Methodist Book Concern, 1915), 95–96; Campbell, *Prayer in its Present Day Aspects* (New York: Fleming Revell, 1916), 145.

51 Trumbull, *Prayer: Its Nature and Scope* (Philadelphia: John D. Wattles, 1896), 36–37; Patton, 400. Of course, like all writers on prayer, pietistic evangelicals offered reasons why in the sovereignty of God prayer was not always immediately answered in ways satisfactory to the pray-er. However, in general answered prayer advocates tended to place the burden of unanswered prayer on the individual—he or she did not ask in the right spirit, had not properly sought divine guidance, or was not surrendered completely to God. See, for example, William Biederwolf's chapter "Why Our Prayers Are Not Answered" in *How Can God Answer Prayer*, 229–253. For example, Rosalind Goforth believed that God allowed one of her children to die because at that point in her life she had not been *fully* surrendered; she had been willing to go to China but not to the most difficult and dangerous part of China; *How I Know God Answers Prayer*, 70–71.

52 Goforth, 87, 56, 52; biographical information in Austin, *Saving China*, 35–36.

53 *The Place of Prayer*, 97.

54 Since Gordon emphasized faith healing more than most holiness proponents, Garfield's death was especially pertinent to him.

55 *The Ministry of Healing*, 220–221.

56 *The Fundamentals, vol. 1* (New York: Garland, [1911]), 71.

57 *Ibid.*, 86.

58 To be sure, not all fundamentalists were descended from the late-nineteenth-century revivalistic subculture that emphasized answers to prayer. Fundamentalism was a coalition of various conservative groups rather than a unified movement, and the Princeton conservatives, to name one example, did not share this emphasis on answers to prayer. Benjamin Warfield, the leading conservative at Princeton Seminary, displayed a different tenor in respect to prayer. While not discouraging tangible answers to prayer, he focused on communion with God. "The heart of the matter lies in every case," Warfield maintained, "in the communion with God which the soul enjoys in prayer"; "Prayer as Practice," in Warfield, *Faith and Life* (Philadelphia: Banner of Truth Trust, 1974 [1916]), 438. In addition, Warfield's 1918 work *Counterfeit Miracles* criticized fellow conservatives such as Adoniram Gordon who practiced faith healing (New York: Scribner's, 1918), 159–192. However, for pietistic fundamentalists, as historian Bruce Shelley has called them, those fundamentalists descended from Keswick holiness and premillennialist networks, the ideology of answered prayer was tremendously important; Shelley, "Sources of Pietistic Fundamentalism," 68–78.

59 Getz, 192. On the formative role of Moody Bible Institute and other Bible schools in American fundamentalism, see Brereton, *Training God's Army*, 138–154.

60 This was a merger of Canadian Methodists, Congregationalists, and Presbyterians that resulted in the largest Protestant denomination in Canada.

61 D. B. Chesebrough, "Charles Albert Blanchard," in *Dictionary of Christianity in America*, edited by Daniel G. Reid (Downers Grove, Ill.: Intervarsity Press, 1990), 166–167.

62 *Fundamentalism and American Culture*, 4, 231. See also Marsden, *Fundamentalism*, 72–101; Shelley, "Sources of Pietistic Fundamentalism"; Brereton, *Training God's Army*; and Michael Hamilton, "The Fundamentalist Harvard: Wheaton College and the Continuing Vitality of American Evangelicalism, 1919–1945" (Ph.D. Diss., University of Notre Dame, 1995).

63 Torrey, "The Duty and Worth of Prayer," *Christian Workers'* 18 (September, 1917), 21. On the "prayer of faith," see Finney, *Lectures on Revivals of Religion* (Cambridge, Mass.: Belknap Press, 1960 [1835]), 72–88; and Torrey, *The Power of Prayer* (New York: Fleming Revell, 1924), 155–168. The fact that this fundamentalist doctrine of prayer differed little from that of Finney lends further credence to Marsden's contention that fundamentalism is best understood as "a sub-species of American revivalism rather than as an outgrowth of the movements espousing millenarianism or inerrancy. It characteristically emphasized doctrinal tendencies which were already strong in American cultural and religious traditions (224)."

64 Buswell, *Problems in the Prayer Life* (Chicago: Bible Institute Colportage Association, 1928), 74; Gray, "Modernism a Revolt against Christianity," *Moody Bible Institute Monthly* 25 (October 1924), 57. The prayer meeting figure is reported in Brereton, 120. Part of what gave fundamentalism its sense of urgency was the belief that theological liberalism undercut Christian piety. John Roach Straton, a prominent fundamentalist pastor in New York City, for example, claimed that "there has been a tragic decline in spirituality among American church members, which has been contemporaneous with the growth of rationalism within the ranks of religious leaders"; "How Rationalism in the Pulpit Makes Worldliness in the Pew," *Moody Bible Institute Monthly* (January, 1923), 195. For a similar argument, see Fred Hall, "Flattening the Spiritual Life," *Moody Bible Institute Monthly* (April 1925), 363–364.

Three. The Spiritual Unrest

1 Charles Blanchard, for example, in his introduction to *Getting Things from God*, admitted that he had little new to offer on the subject of prayer that had not been said by Moody, Bounds, and Torrey, and other writers before him. But, he said, "the fact that a number of persons have uttered their testimony is no reason why still others should not do the same"; (Wheaton, Ill.: Sword of the Lord, [1915]), 16.

2 *The Modernist Impulse* (Cambridge, Mass.: Harvard University Press, 1976), 2; On liberal Protestantism as part of the American establishment, see Hutchison, introduction to *Between the Times: The Travail of the Protestant Establishment in America, 1900–1960* (New York: Cambridge University, 1989). The situation of the liberal Protestant in early-twentieth-century American culture can be likened to that of a popular Harvard undergraduate plagued by a rustic cousin tagging along: trying to reform the embarrassing relative while at the same time protesting to his college peers that his family really was not like that. The liberals tried to reform their conservative counterparts in the church, a process based in seminaries, pastorates, and the liberal emphasis on Christian education. At the same time, they asserted to those in elite culture that conservative dogmas did not accurately reflect what Christianity was all about.

3 Fosdick, "Heckling the Church," *Atlantic* 108 (1911), 735; Butler, *Awash in a Sea of Faith* (Cambridge, Mass.: Harvard University Press, 1990), 293.

4 Hart, "Platitudes of Piety: Religion and the Modern Popular Novel," *American Quarterly* 6 (Spring 1954), 320. According to Roderick Nash, Wright had twelve bestsellers, while Hemingway did not make the top ten until 1940. In 1920, Wright's *Re-Creation of Brian Kent* sold a million copies, while F. Scott Fitzgerald's critically acclaimed *This Side of Paradise* found only fifty thousand buyers in the first few years after publication; *The Nervous Generation: American Thought, 1917–1930* (Chicago: Rand McNally, 1971), 1, 139.

5 *In His Steps* (Chicago: Moody Press, [1896]), 15.

6 Ibid., 25, 65, 146.

7 Sheldon, 104.

8 These quotes are from the front cover of *The Winning of Barbara Worth* (New York: A. L. Burt, 1911) Wright's bestseller of 1911.

9 See, for example, Hart, 314–315.

10 *That Printer of Udell's* (New York: A. L. Burt, 1902), 293, 299, 161.

11 Ibid., 62, 204.

12 Ibid., 221.

13 *The Calling of Dan Matthews* (New York: A. L. Burt, 1909), 72–73.

14 Ibid., 195, 295–296, 181, 117.

15 Ibid., 264, 313, 183.

16 Ibid., 275, 101, 338–340.

17 Ibid., 344.

18 Ibid., 352; back cover advertisements.

19 Stanley Kunitz, ed., *Twentieth Century Authors* (New York: Wilson, 1955), 282; Ralph Carey, "Bestselling Religion" (Ph.D. diss. Michigan State University, 1971), 190.

20 *The Inside of the Cup* (New York: Macmillan, 1914), 418, 345, 368, 508–509, 423.

21 Ibid., 267, 221, 383.

22 Everett Dean Martin, "Are We Facing a Revival of Religion?" *Harper's* 148 (April 1924), 680; *The Calling of Dan Matthews*, 103.

23 "Missionary Blood," *Harper's* 132 (1916), 929.

24 Ibid., 937.

25 *The Spiritual Unrest* (New York: Frederick A. Stokes, 1909), 47, preface.

26 Ibid., 251, 259, 256, 177.

27 Ibid., 231, 142, 3–4.

28 "New Loyalties for Old Consolations," *Forum* 52 (1914), 503–505.

29 M'Cready Sykes, "Shall We Send Our Children to Church?" *Atlantic* 140 (December 1927), 730–732; Katherine Gerould, "The Unsocial Christian," *Harper's* 158 (1929), 661.

30 Anonymous, "Ought I to Leave the Church?" *Harper's* 142 (February 1921), 345; Anonymous, "–But Why Preach?" *Harper's* 143 (June 1921), 81.

31 "The Failure of the Church," *Atlantic* 114 (1914), 731, 735, 729; "The Breakup of Protestantism," *Atlantic* 139 (1927), 303.

32 Quoted in *Christian Worker's* 13 (April 1913), 514.

33 "The Supreme Value of Christianity," *Christian Worker's* 17 (September 1916), 12; "The Optimist Nuisance," *Christian Worker's* 16 (September 1915), 10; Riley, "The Prestige of the Church," *Christian Worker's* 19 (April 1919), 541; Straton in Paul Carter, *Another Part of the Twenties* (New York: Columbia University Press, 1977), 51.

34 In Hutchison, *Modernist Impulse*, 258. Fosdick stated in retrospect, "multitudes of us would not have been Christians at all unless we could have escaped the bondage of the then reigning orthodoxy"; *The Living of These Days: An Autobiography* (New York: Harper, 1956), 66.

35 *Confessions of a Troubled Parson* (New York: Scribner's, 1928), 608.

36 Fosdick, *The Meaning of Faith* (New York: Association Press, 1917), 293; Willett, *The Daily Altar* (Chicago: Christian Century Press, 1918), 274.

37 *Leaves for Quiet Hours* (New York: A. C. Armstrong, 1904), 283–285. On the religious childhoods of liberal Protestants, see Hutchison, "Cultural Strain and Protestant Liberalism," *American Historical Review* 76 (1971), 386–411.

38 *An Outline of Christian Theology* (New York: Scribner's, 1896), 55, 482.

39 Fosdick, *The Manhood of the Master* (New York: Association Press, 1913), 151; Abbott, "The Nature of Prayer," *North American Review* 186 (1907), 339; Fosdick, *The Meaning of Prayer* (New York: Association Press, 1915), 22.

40 *The Forgotten Secret* (New York: Fleming Revell, 1906), 22–23.

41 *Manhood of the Master*, 79; Willett, 236; Jones, *The Inner Life* (New York: Macmillan, 1916), 64; Slattery, *Why Men Pray* (New York: Macmillan, 1918), 89–90.

42 "How to Pray and What to Pray for in the International Crisis," *Current Opinion* 57 (1914), 341–343; Jefferson, *Old Truths and New Facts* (New York: Fleming Revell, 1918), 81; Speer, "The War and the Religious Outlook," *Christian Century* 36 (July 17, 1919), 13.

43 W. P. Paterson, ed., *The Power of Prayer* (New York: Macmillan, 1920), v, 14. On McComb, see chapter 6.

44 *The Challenge of the Present Crisis* (New York: Association Press, 1917), 82.

45 *The World Within* (New York: Macmillan, 1918), v–ix; *The Inner Life*, ix.

46 Newton, "The Quiet Moment and the Busy Life," *Christian Century* 36 (June 26, 1919), 13; Gordon, *Religion and Miracle* (Boston: Houghton Mifflin, 1909), 180–181.

Four. Divine Immanence

1 Hodge, *Systematic Theology* (New York: Scribner's, 1872), vol. 3. 692–694; Kinsley, *Science and Prayer* (Meadville, Pa.: Flood and Vincent), 91.

2 Mullin, *Miracles and the Modern Religious Imagination* (New Haven: Yale University Press, 1996), 44.

3 Hutchison, *The Modernist Impulse* (Cambridge, Mass.: Harvard University Press, 1976), 11; King, "Reconstruction in Theology," reprinted in *Contemporary American Protestant Thought*, edited by William Miller (New York: Bobbs-Merrill, 1973 [1899]), 14. See Mullin, 78, 151–152.

4 Clarke, *An Outline of Christian Theology* (New York: Scribner's, [1896]), 130; Allen, *The Continuity of Christian Thought*, (Boston: Houghton Mifflin, 1884), in *American Protestant Thought: The Liberal Era*, edited by William Hutchison (New York: Harper and Row, 1968), 62, 57. Despite Allen's claims, belief in divine immanence was not unique to liberals. Charles Hodge, the antithesis of liberalism in the nineteenth century, described God in immanentist terms as "present in every blade of grass,... present also in every human soul, giving it understanding, endowing it with gifts, working in it both to will and to do.... As the birds in the air and the fish in the sea, so also are we always surrounded and sustained by God"; *Systematic Theology, vol. 1*, 383, 385. Christian orthodoxy, however, had counter-balanced divine immanence with the doctrine of human sin which separated unredeemed persons from fellowship with God. The real distinctiveness of the liberal position was an absence of this em-

phasis on human depravity which had traditionally moderated the idea of God's immanence in creation.

5 Sidney Ahlstrom has written, concerning the liberal theologians, that "probably none had a more numerous and devoted following than Borden Parker Bowne"; *Theology in America* (New York: Bobbs-Merrill, 1967), 72.

6 *Personalism* (Boston: Houghton Mifflin, 1908), in Hutchison, *The Liberal Era*, 83–87.

7 Bowne, *The Immanence of God* (Boston: Houghton Mifflin, 1905), preface, 3; Gordon, *Religion and Miracle* (Boston: Houghton Mifflin, 1909), 143–146.

8 Bowne, *Immanence*, 43, 27, 58.

9 Bowne, *Immanence*, 59, 76, 77, 116; Gordon, 153; Brown, "The Permanent Significance of Miracle for Religion," *Harvard Theological Review* 8 (1915), 307. For further discussion of Gordon, see Mullin, 171–173.

10 Bowne, *Immanence*, 153.

11 "Providence, Prayer, and Physical Science," *Methodist Review* 45 (1897), 62, 69.

12 "Praying for Things," *Methodist Review* 86 (1904), 286–288.

13 Bowne, *Immanence*, 48; Chamberlain, *The True Doctrine of Prayer* (New York: Baker and Taylor, 1906), 103. Even the fundamentalist Grant Stroh, professor at the Moody Bible Institute, justified petitionary prayer using divine immanence; "A Christian Defense of Prayer," *Moody Bible Institute Monthly* 31 (April, 1931), 395–397.

14 "How Shall We Think of God?" *Harpers* 152 (July 1926), reprinted in Fosdick, *Adventurous Religion and Other Essays* (New York: Harpers, 1926), 59–74. Brown, *The Life of Prayer in a World of Science* (New York: Scribner's, 1927), 90.

15 "Immanuel Kant." In *The Encyclopedia of Philosophy*, edited by Paul Edwards (New York: Macmillan, 1967), vol. 1, 305–323.

16 *The Meaning of Prayer* (New York: Association Press, 1915), 86; *The Meaning of Faith*, 68. Fosdick's 1913 devotional book *The Assurance of Immortality* illustrated well this different conception of revelation. "No one but a charlatan pretends to know the circumstances of the world to come," Fosdick claimed. "What lies across the sea, he cannot tell; his special expectations may all be mistaken; but his insight into the clear meanings of present facts may persuade him beyond doubt that the sea has another shore"; *The Assurance of Immortality* (London: James Clarke, 1913), 58. Fosdick assumed that no inside information on the circumstances of the afterlife (i.e., special revelation in the Bible) existed. One could infer, based on experience here on earth, that some sort of immortality existed, but one had no way of knowing any specifics about it. For liberal Protestants, God's transcendent side was like the far shore of the sea; it existed, but one could only know about that aspect of God—his immanence— that intersected with the world and with human consciousness.

17 Hutchison, *The Modernist Impulse*, 122–127.

18 The "oblong blur" reference is from *The Modernist Impulse*, 126.

19 Kant, *Religion Within the Limits of Reason Alone*, translated by Theodore Greene and Hoyt Hudson (New York: Harper and Row), 1960, quoted in Perry

LeFevre, *Understandings of Prayer* (Philadelphia: Westminster Press, 1981), 10–13; Heiler, *Prayer* (London: Oxford University Press, 1932), 89–93.

20 Schleiermacher, *The Christian Faith* (Edinburgh: T. and T. Clark, [1830]), 673; see also LeFevre, 14–16. The same attitude toward petitionary prayer was exhibited in the German idealists' American counterpart, Transcendentalism. Ralph Waldo Emerson, for instance, called prayer that seeks a particular object "viscious." "Prayer as a means to effect a private end, is meanness and theft. It supposes dualism and not unity in nature and consciousness"; "Self-Reliance," in *The American Intellectual Tradition*, edited by Charles Capper and David Hollinger, (New York: Oxford University Press, 1997 [1841]), vol. 1, 312.

21 Ritschl, *The Christian Doctrine of Justification and Reconciliation: The Positive Development of Doctrine*, translated by H. R. Mackintosh and A. B. Macaulay (Scribners, 1900), vol. 3, and *Three Essays*, translated by Philip Hefner (Fortress Press, 1972), quoted in LeFevre, 20–21; see also Alfred Garvie, *The Ritschlian Theology* (Edinburgh: T. and T. Clark, 1902), 354.

22 Allen, quoted in Hutchison, *American Protestant Thought: The Liberal Era*, 67; Coe, *The Religion of a Mature Mind* (Chicago: Fleming Revell, 1902), 333.

23 *Adventurous Religion* (New York: Harper, 1926), 124, 61–62, 229.

24 Coffin, *University Sermons* (New Haven: Yale University Press, 1914), 2, 16.

25 Coffin, 8; Brown, *The Life of Prayer in a World of Science*, 32, 5, 8.

26 This helps explain the meaning of Fosdick's cryptic statement in 1909: "Christianity is founded on a fact, and that fact is the character of Jesus" quoted in Robert M. Miller, *Harry Emerson Fosdick* (New York: Oxford University Press, 1985), 57.

27 *Finding the Comrade God* (New York: Association Press, 1918), 81–84, 90.

28 In Sinclair Lewis's *Elmer Gantry*, for example, the representative liberal pastor, Frank Shallard, considered leaving the church but hesitated because he found, said Lewis, "even as in childhood a magic in the stories of shepherds keeping watch by night, of the glorified mother beside the babe in the manger—he still had an unreasoning feeling Jesus was of more than human birth"; *Elmer Gantry* (New York: New American Library, 1927), 319. Historian Martin Marty has concluded much the same thing: "On this point most of the modernists, evidently drawing on their Sunday School memories as well as their faith and natural reverence more than on a disciplined tackling of problems, remained attached to Jesus"; *Modern American Religion* (Chicago: University of Chicago Press, 1986), vol. 1, 30.

29 Fosdick, *Christianity and Progress* (New York: Fleming Revell, 1922), 231; Abbott, *What Christianity Means to Me* (New York: Macmillan, 1922), 6–7.

30 Schleiermacher, *The Christian Faith*, 673; Thompson, "On Prayer," *Contemporary Review* (October 1872), reprinted in *The Prayer-Gauge Debate*, edited by John O. Means (Boston: Congregational Publishing Society, 1876), 122.

31 Edwards, "The Most High a Prayer-Hearing God," *Works of President Edwards*, (Worcester, Mass.: Isaiah Thomas, [1735]), vol. 8, 56; Buswell, *Problems in the Prayer Life* (Chicago: Bible Institute Colportage Association, 1928), 70; Goforth, *How I Know God Answers Prayer* (Chicago: Moody Press, 1921), 13–14. See also Mark Hopkins, *Prayer and the Prayer-Gauge* (New York: Dodd and Mead,

1874), 26. For a modern philosophical version of the same argument, see Michael J. Murray and Kurt Meyers, "Ask and It Will Be Given to You," *Religious Studies* 30 (1994), 311–330.

32 King, "Difficulties Concerning Prayer, 3," *Biblical World* 46 (1915), 351; Fiske, 5–6.

33 *Meaning of Prayer*, 28–29, 22–23.

34 Ibid., 56, 187.

35 Campbell, *Prayer in Its Present Day Aspects* (New York: Fleming Revell, 1916), 26, 46–47; Bowne, *Immanence*, 60. The historian Winthrop Hudson remarked that "the preachers of the New Theology found it difficult to conceive of a church which did not embrace humanity indiscriminately"; *The Great Tradition of the American Churches* (New York: Harper and Row, 1963), 194.

36 *The Best of E. M. Bounds* (Grand Rapids, Mich.: Baker Book House, [1913]), 227.

37 Fosdick, "Are Religious People Fooling Themselves?" *Harper's* 161 (June 1930), 63; Brown, "The Permanent Significance of Miracle for Religion," 320; Brown, *Why I Believe in Religion* (New York: Macmillan, 1924), 104–105.

38 Campbell, *The Place of Prayer in the Christian Religion* (New York: Methodist Book Concern, 1915), 292.

39 Fiske, 189.

40 Fosdick, "Beyond Reason," *Religious Education* 23 (1928), 471.

41 Clarke, *What Shall We Think of Christianity?* (New York: Scribner's, 1899), 44, 95.

42 Brown, "The Old and the New," 1910 address at Harvard University, in William Adams Brown, *A Teacher and His Times* (New York: Scribner's, 1940), 127; Gordon, 153; Fosdick, *Meaning of Faith*, 159, *Adventurous Religion*, 48.

43 Fosdick quoted in Allen, *Only Yesterday: An Informal History of the Nineteen-Twenties* (New York: Harper, 1957), 199; Gordon, 137–138; Brown, "The Permanent Significance of Miracle for Religion," 320.

44 *Christian Theology in Outline* (New York: Scribner's, 1906), 132–137.

45 Clarke, *What Shall We Think of Christianity*, 127.

46 *The Belief in God and Immortality* (Boston: Sherman, French, 1916), 225, 280–281.

47 Marsden, *Religion and American Culture* (San Diego: Harcourt Brace Jovanovich, 1990), 168–169. He also points out a third choice, one that fundamentalists chose—clinging to traditional Christianity but also fighting to maintain cultural dominance.

48 Gordon, 165.

49 Van Anda, *Prayer* (Cincinnati: Cranston and Stowe, 1891), 97; Editorial, *Watchman-Examiner* 4 (1914), 1451.

50 Buswell, 77; Warfield, *Faith and Life* (Philadelphia: Banner of Truth, [1916]), 434. The importance of the biblicist factor should not be underestimated. Karl Barth repudiated centuries of German theology when he asserted that "prayer is decisively petition." He did so using biblicist logic: "Prayer really has its basis in the order and command of God." *Church Dogmatics, Volume 3, Part 4*, translated by A. T. Mackay (Edinburgh: T. & T. Clark, 1961), 95, 97.

51 *Who Was Who in America (Chicago: Marquis Who's Who, 1981), vol. 1*, 208; R. R. Mathisen, "The Evangelical Alliance," in *Dictionary of Christianity in America*, edited by Douglas Reid (Downers Grove, Ill.: Intervarsity Press, 1990), 408–409.

52 Szasz, *The Divided Mind of Protestant America* (University, Ala.: University of Alabama Press, 1982), 42–67; McLoughlin, *Modern Revivalism* (New York: Ronald Press, 1959), 397.

53 *The True Doctrine of Prayer*, x, 104–105.

54 Ibid., 101, 40, 36, 93–96.

55 Ibid., 103.

56 Ibid., 96, 93, 1.

57 Ibid., 98, 25–26, 122–123.

58 See Grant Wacker, *Augustus H. Strong and the Dilemma of Historical Consciousness* (Macon, Ga.: Mercer University Press, 1985) and Mark Massa, *Charles Augustus Briggs and the Crisis of Historical Criticism* (Minneapolis: Fortress Press, 1990) for treatments of the impact of historicism on modern Christian thought. Simply put, conservative Protestants were "ahistorical" in that they believed that God had punctured the fabric of human history to give a message for all time in the Bible. Liberal Protestants were to various degrees "historicists" in that they saw Scripture, like everything else, as a product of historical and cultural processes. See Fosdick, *The Modern Use of the Bible* (New York: Macmillan, 1924), for the best statement of classic liberal views of Scripture.

59 One exception to this was the words of Jesus, which carried much weight for certain liberals. However, concerning prayer, liberals tended to cite the *example* of Jesus rather his words. For instance, Henry Churchill King asserted, concerning Christ's dependence on prayer: "The Christian man feels that one might well rest the entire argument for prayer upon this great single fact." King did not, as traditionalists did, cite the well-known words "ask and it shall be given to you"; rather, King remarked that "prayer evidently was his one great source of strength, of solace, and of courage"; "Difficulties Concerning Prayer," 284.

Five. A Sane Mysticism

1 Historian Richard Fox has remarked: "My suspicion is that liberal Protestants surrendered the miraculous to traditionalist evangelicals not all at once, but in stages"; "From Events and Institutions to Cultures and Experiences: Paradigm Shift in Twentieth Century American Religious History," Paper delivered at Wheaton College, Wheaton, Illinois, 1993, 19. Concerning prayer, Fox's surmise is correct.

2 Cauthen, *The Impact of American Religious Liberalism* (New York: Harper, 1963), 27–30; Smith et al., eds., *American Christianity* (New York: Scribner's, 1963), vol. 2, 255–308.

3 Hutchison, *The Modernist Impulse in American Protestantism* (Cambridge, Mass: Harvard University Press, 1976); Marty, *Modern American Religion* (Chicago:

University of Chicago, Press, 1986), vol. 1, 32. Nearly all the writers discussed in this chapter are cited or are mentioned by name in Smith, et al., chapter on Christocentric liberalism.

4 Smith et al., 295; Niebuhr quoted in Marty, *Modern American Religion* vol. 2, 53.

5 *The Andover Liberals* (New York: Octagon Books, 1970), 107, 102, 105, 111–113. Mullin, *Miracles and the Modern Religious Imagination* (New Haven: Yale University Press), 79.

6 Cadman, editorial, *Congregationalist,* December 9, 1905, 882, quoted in William McLoughlin, *Modern Revivalism* (New York: Ronald Press, 1959), 370; Patten, "Mysticism and Fundamentalism," *Christian Century* 40 (March 8, 1923), 298; Fosdick, *The Living of These Days* (New York: Harper, 1956), vii. All italics are added.

7 The situation was reversed from the fundamentalist perspective. The twentieth century, with its unbelief in orthodoxy, was, according to Charles Blanchard, an "age of insanity." The orthodox Christian was "the sane man, the honest man, the candid man, the intelligent man;" quoted in Marsden, *Fundamentalism and American Culture* (New York: Oxford University Press, 1980), 219).

8 "The Immanent God," *Christian Century* 39 (November 23, 1922), 1453.

9 Campbell, *The Place of Prayer in the Christian Religion* (New York: Methodist Book Concern, 1915), 276.

10 *Outlook* 83 (1906), 859; Davis, "Is Prayer Reasonable?" quoted in E. S. Smith, "Providence, Prayer, and Physical Science," *Methodist Review* 45 (1897), 62–63.

11 Coe, *The Religion of a Mature Mind* (Chicago: Fleming Revell, 1902), 339; Brown, *Christian Theology in Outline* (New York: Scribner's, 1906), 385–386.

12 *An Outline of Christian Theology* (New York: Scribner's, [1896]), 134. As noted in chapter 4, Brown, unlike Clarke, had studied in Germany and was Ritschl's main American expositor. Perhaps this fact played a role in their Brown and Clarke's divergent beliefs concerning petitionary prayer.

13 Dawson, *The Forgotten Secret* (New York: Fleming Revell, 1906), 9; King, "Difficulties Concerning Prayer," *Biblical World* 46 (1915), 133.

14 *The Meaning of Prayer* (New York: Association Press, 1915), 30–31.

15 Fosdick, 124; Jellett, *The Efficacy of Prayer* (London: Macmillan, 1880), ii.

16 Fiske, *Finding the Comrade God* (New York: Association Press, 1918), 33; King, 133; Fosdick, 109–110.

17 "The Relation of the Subconscious to Prayer," *American Journal of Religious Psychology and Education* 2 (1907), 165.

18 Ibid., 165–166.

19 Fosdick, *Meaning of Prayer* 109–110.

20 "Getting Full Credit for Intimacy with God," *Christian Century* 37 (January 15, 1920), 4; Brown, *Why I Believe in Religion* (New York: Macmillan, 1924), 90.

21 King, 351; Campbell, 90.

22 Whiton, "Fallacies Concerning Prayer," *Forum* 23 (1897), 356; Dawson, 45, 52. The distinctiveness of this "proof" of the efficacy of prayer lies in its relation to American Protestantism, not necessarily to Christian history as a whole. As

noted earlier (see chapter 1, n.26), the church father Tertullian seemed to believe that Christian prayer did not alter circumstances but only armed with endurance those who suffered.

23 Munger, "The Unconquerable Habit," *Outlook* 73 (1903), 401; Abbott, "Prayer," *Outlook* 83 (1906), 882.

24 Dawson, 38–40; 63. Liberals, like their conservative counterparts, were fond of using scientific terminology in their prayer writings. For instance, the Bible was, according to Fosdick, "the invaluable laboratory manual which records all phases of man's life with God and God's dealing with men" (xi).

25 Strong, 163.

26 Tyndall and Galton quoted in *The Prayer-Gauge Debate*, edited by John Means, (Boston: Congregational Publishing Society, 1876), 115, 105.

27 Fosdick, *Meaning of Prayer*, 161; Campbell, *Prayer in Its Present Day Aspects* (New York: Fleming Revell, 1916), 146, 56–57.

28 *The Still Hour* (Boston: Gould and Lincoln, 1863), 72–75.

29 Fosdick, *Meaning of Prayer*, 169; Dawson, 41; Kelly, "Praying for Things," *Methodist Review* 86 (1904), 290.

30 Fosdick, 165–166, 169. Here is a typical entry in Brainerd's diary, for instance: "I was in such anguish, and pleaded with such earnestness that when I rose from my knees I could scarcely walk straight. The sweat ran down from my face and body. I was wholly free from selfish ends in my supplications for the poor Indians"; quoted in *David Brainerd: The Man of Prayer*, edited by Oswald Smith (Grand Rapids, Mich.: Zondervan, 1941), 49.

31 Whiton, 360–362. The island analogy was explained by the Episcopalian Charles Slattery in *Why Men Pray* (New York: Macmillan, 1918), 16.

32 Fosdick, *Meaning of Prayer*, 69.

33 "Prayer and Its Answers," *Outlook* 100 (1912), 17; "Letters to Unknown Friends," *Outlook* 104 (1913), 324; "The Prayer of Love," *Outlook* 66 (1900), 392.

34 "Prayer and Its Answers," 18.

35 "Two Kinds of Prayer," *Outlook* 114 (1916), 411; "Letters to Unknown Friends," *Outlook* 99 (1911).

36 "Two Kinds of Prayer," 411; "Prayer and Its Answers," 17–18.

37 "Prayer and Law," *Outlook* 100 (1912), 488.

38 Ibid., 488–489; "Two Kinds of Prayer," 107.

39 Knox quoted in Robert M. Miller, *Harry Emerson Fosdick* (New York: Oxford University Press, 1985), 68, 70.

40 *Meaning of Prayer*, 95.

41 Abbott, "The Prayer of Love," 391; Fosdick, *Meaning of Prayer*, 84–85. Chapter 7 elaborates on this theme.

42 This magazine was essentially a forerunner to the *Reader's Digest*. See Theodore Peterson, *Magazines in the Twentieth Century* (Urbana: University of Illinois Press, 1956), 141–144.

43 "The Praying Football Hero," *Literary Digest* 85 (June 27, 1925), 32.

44 Ibid., 33.

45 Ibid., 32–33.

46 Warfield, *Faith and Life* (Philadelphia: Banner of Truth, [1916]), 152; Frost, *Effective Praying* (Philadelphia: Sunday School Times, 1925), 162.

47 Anonymous, "The Historic Baptist Emphasis on Prayer," *Baptist Fundamentals* (Philadelphia: Judson Press, 1920), 99, 101–102; Riley, "The Prestige of the Church," *Moody Bible Institute Monthly* 19 (April 1919), 539. Robert M. Miller notes a lack of conservative criticism of Fosdick's book in *Harry Emerson Fosdick*, 71.

48 Blanchard, *Getting Things from God* (Wheaton, Ill.: Sword of the Lord, [1915]), 59; McQuilken, foreword to *Answered or Unanswered?* Louisa Vaughan. (Philadelphia: Christian Life Literature Fund, 1917).

Six. The New Belief in Prayer

1 Cunningham, "The Emmanuel Movement: A Variety of American Religious Experience," in Martin Marty, *Modern American Protestantism and Its World*, edited by Martin Marty (New York: Saur, 1993), vol. 14, 37.

2 Brown, *Why I Believe in Religion* (New York: Macmillan, 1924), 108; Campbell, *The Place of Prayer in the Christian Religion* (New York: Methodist Book Concern, 1915), 281, 276; Ames, "Ernest Haeckel and the Passing of Naturalism," *Christian Century* 36 (September 18, 1919), 9–10.

3 "The New Belief in Prayer," *Century* 80 (1910), 787; "Some Modern Aspects of Prayer," *Living Age* 281 (1914), 160.

4 McComb's theological views are explained in Robert Bruce Mullin, "The Debate over Religion and Healing in the Episcopal Church, 1870–1930," *Anglican and Episcopal History* 60 (1991), 213–227; Ames, 10.

5 Jellett, *The Efficacy of Prayer* (London: Macmillan, 1880), 20.

6 Paterson, editor's introduction to *The Power of Prayer* (New York: Macmillan, 1920), 32; McComb, "Prayer: Its Meaning, Reality, and Power," in Paterson, 60.

7 *In Tune with the Infinite* (New York: Dodd, Mead, 1897), preface.

8 Ibid., 30–41, 52, 154.

9 Ibid., 94, 92, 213.

10 "The Evolution of Prayer," *North American Review* 196 (1912), 818–829.

11 "Is There Anything in Prayer?" *Atlantic Monthly* 128 (1921), 533–534.

12 Ibid., 534.

13 "Shall We Pray?" *Harper's* 150 (1925), 158–161.

14 Edward S. Martin, "Possibilities of Prayer," *North American Review* 157 (1895), 253–254. As a new field in its infancy, the power of mind and suggestion was granted tremendous potential. Northwestern University professor George Coe, typically not one to be gullible, gave credence to a story of a man who was tricked into believing he was bleeding to death so that his body went through all the appropriate symptoms and he died. He also recounted the testimony of his friend who visited the dentist to have a tooth extracted without laughing gas: "The operation was rendered almost painless by the writer vividly imagining pleasant ideas, and mentally repeating to himself, 'How delightful! how delightful!' " Coe himself repeated the same experiment and claimed the

same results; *The Spiritual Life* (New York: Eaton and Mains, 1900), 160–161, 163–164).

15 "Prayer," 41.

16 Meyer, *The Positive Thinkers* (New York: Pantheon, 1980), 315, 83; James, *The Varieties of Religious Experience* (New York: Longmans, Green 1902), 511–515.

17 James, 523, 463.

18 Ibid., 510, 501, 524. Mullin, *Miracles and the Modern Religious Imagination* (New Haven: Yale University Press, 1996), 191.

19 Biographical information from "Oliver Lodge," in *Dictionary of Scientific Biography*, edited by Charles C. Gillispie (New York: Scribner's, 1973), 443; On Lodge and Tyndall, see W. P. Jolly, *Sir Oliver Lodge* (London: Constable, 1974), 24, 35, 180.

20 Jolly, 56–58, 92, 143; Laurence Moore, *In Search of White Crows* (New York: Oxford, University Press, 1977), 142–168.

21 James quoted in Cushing Strout, "The Pluralistic Identity of William James: A Psycho-historical Reading of *The Varieties of Religious Experience*," in Marty, ed., *Modern American Protestantism and Its World, Vol. 14*, 21.

22 "Sir Oliver Lodge and Religion," *Christian Century* 37 (February 19, 1920), 13.

23 Ibid., 13–15.

24 Ibid., 13; Sherman, 828; Warfield, *Counterfeit Miracles* (New York: Scribner's, 1918), 164.

25 Maclachlan, 13–14.

26 Mullin, "The Debate over Religion and Healing," 214–219; Cunningham, "From Holiness to Healing: The Faith Cure in America 1872–1892," in Marty, *Modern American Protestantism and Its World*, vol. 14, 3–17.

27 Mullin, "The Debate over Religion and Healing," 221–223; see also Mullin, *Miracles and the Modern Religious Imagination*, 194–198. For a modern approximation of the Emmanuel Movement, see William Haynes, *A Physician's Witness to the Power of Shared Prayer* (Chicago: Loyola University, 1990).

28 "Prayer," 61, 59.

29 James, 463–464; McComb, "New Belief in Prayer," 789; "Prayer," 47, 59.

30 Dawson, *The Forgotten Secret* (New York: Fleming Revell, 1906), 19; Abbott, "A Medical Estimate of Prayer," *Outlook* 81 (1905), 110; "Letters to Unknown Friends," *Outlook* 103 (1913), 704.

31 *The Assurance of Immortality* (London: James Clarke, 1913), 90; *The Meaning of Faith* (New York: Association Press, 1917), 190; *The Meaning of Prayer* (New York: Association Press, 1915), 158.

32 This fact is not surprising, since Methodists had a long history of concern for physical health; see E. Brooks Holifield, *Health and Medicine in the Wesleyan Tradition* (New York: Crossroad, 1986).

33 *Prayer in Its Present Day Aspects* (New York: Fleming Revell, 1916), 106, 110; *The Place of Prayer in the Christian Religion*, 223.

34 Meyer, 217.

35 Ibid., 76.

36 "Prayer," 45, 62.

37 *Place of Prayer*, 223; *Prayer in Its Present Day Aspects*, 108.
38 McComb, "Prayer," 61; Gordon, *Religion and Miracle* (Boston: Houghton Mif-
     flin, 1909), 199–200; Abbott, "Praying and Waiting," *Outlook* 84 (1906), 69.
39 Fiske, *Finding the Comrade God* (New York: Association Press, 1918), 16, 164;
     Abbott, "Christ's Teaching Concerning Prayer," *Outlook* 62 (1899), 941–942.
40 *The Daily Altar* (Chicago: Christian Century Press, 1918), 12.
41 *The Future Leadership of the Church* (New York: YMCA, 1908), 137; *The Pas-
     tor and Modern Missions* (New York: Student Volunteer Movement, 1904), 194,
     202.
42 *A Discipline of Prayer* (New York: Association Press, 1916); Mott, preface to
     Fosdick, *The Meaning of Prayer*, vii.
43 *The Meaning of Prayer*, 187.
44 *Effective Praying* (Philadelphia: Sunday School Times, 1925), 84–86.
45 Some turn-of-the century psychologists asserted the existence of a "subliminal
     consciousness" that, in the words of Robert Bruce Mullin, "functioned like a
     vast psychical information superhighway interconnecting diverse souls" and that
     thus offered a scientific foundation for spiritual communication between souls;
     Miracles and the Modern Religious Imagination, 185.
46 Park, 533.
47 Paterson, 32; McComb, "Prayer," 56; Anonymous, "Learning to Pray," *Baptist*
     4 (1923), 1074.
48 "Prayer," 56.
49 "Letters to Unknown Friends," *Outlook* 103 (1913), 704.
50 *Place of Prayer*, 283–4; *Prayer in Its Present Day Aspects*, 92, 125.
51 *Prayer in Its Present Day Aspects*, 189–190; Trine, *In Tune With the Infinite*,
     176.

Seven. The Religion of a Mature Mind

1 Faye Kelly, *Prayer in Sixteenth Century England* (Gainesville: University of
    Florida Press, 1966), 29; Charles Hambrick-Stowe, *The Practice of Piety*
    (Chapel Hill: University of North Carolina Press, 1982), 156.
2 Hambrick-Stowe, 143–150; 156–186; Cotton, quoted in Hambrick-Stowe, 156.
3 Mather, "The Duty of Secret Prayer, Publicly Inculcated," (Boston: B. Green
    and J. Allen, 1703), 5, 23; Edwards, "Hypocrites Deficient in the Duty of
    Prayer," in *The Works of President Edwards* (New York: Leavitt, Trow and Co.,
    1849), vol. 4, 474–487; "The Most High a Prayer-Hearing God," in *The Works
    of President Edwards* (Worcester, Mass.: Isaiah Thomas, [1735]), vol. 8, 64–65;
    Niles, *Secret Prayer Explained and Inculcated* (Boston: Kneeland, 1773), 60.
4 Michael Hennell has observed of nineteenth-century England that "family
    prayers became almost the hallmark of Victorian Evangelicalism"; *The Study of
    Spirituality*, edited by "The Evangelical Revival in the church of England"
    Cheslyn Jones et al. (New York: Oxford University Press, 1986), 460.
5 Andover Association, *A Serious Call to Family Religion*, (Cambridge, Mass.:
    William Hilliard, 1802), 9; Moore, "An Essay on the Obligation of Family Wor-
    ship," *Methodist* 9 (1826), 294; Trumbull, "An Address on the Subjects of

Prayer and Family Religion," (Northampton, Mass.: William Butler, 1805), 21, 26.

6 Examples include Charles Wellbeloved, *Devotional Exercises* (Keene, N.H.: John Prentiss, 1810); James Bean, *Family Worship* (Philadelphia: S. Potter, 1819); Henry Thornton, *Family Prayers* (London, 1834); Anonymous, *Family Prayers* (Dublin: William Curry, 1835); and Henry A. Miles, ed., *The Altar at Home* (Boston, 1855). Written prayers from past eras from such figures as Matthew Henry and Philip Doddridge also circulated.

7 Bennett, *Religion of the Closet* (Andover: Flagg and Gould, 1818), 5, 7; Alexander, *Practical Truths* (New York: American Tract Society, 1852), 38.

8 "A Sermon on Secret Prayer," *Methodist* 11 (1828), 4, 6.

9 Finney, *Memoirs* (New York: Fleming Revell, 1876), 151–152; *Lectures on Revivals of Religion* (Cambridge, Mass.: Belknap Press, 1960 [1835]), 63; Clarke, *The Christian Doctrine of Prayer* (Boston: American Unitarian Association, 1854), 142, 161. Some examples of Finney's personal prayers can be found in *Memoirs*, 35, 142, 153.

10 *The Secret Prayer Life* (New York: International Committee of Young Men's Christian Association, 1904), 8; *The Morning Watch* (International Committee of Young Men's Christian Association, 1893), 6–7.

11 Meyer, *The Protestant Search for Political Realism, 1919–1941* (Berkeley: University of California, 1960), 116; Lewis, *Babbitt* (New York: Harcourt, Brace, 1922). On the emergence of the middle class, see Robert Wiebe, *The Search for Order, 1877–1920* (New York: Hill and Wang, 1967).

12 Robert and Helen Lynd, *Middletown: A Study in Contemporary American Culture* (New York: Harcourt, Brace, 1929), 337; Biederwolf, *How Can God Answer Prayer?* (New York: Fleming Revell, 1910), 26; Torrey, *The Power of Prayer and the Prayer of Power* (New York: Fleming Revell, 1924), 16; Horr, "Family Worship," *Biblical World* 27 (1906), 107; Brown, *The Life of Prayer in a World of Science* (New York: Scribner's, 1927), 5.

13 Hambrick-Stowe, 136.

14 Trumbull, 2; Tyler, *Prayer for Colleges* (New York: M. W. Dodd, 1855), 55–56; Pierson, "Supernatural Answers to Prayer," (Indianapolis: Second Presbyterian Church, 1883), 186.

15 Getting Things from God (Wheaton, Ill.: Sword of the Lord, 1915), 57.

16 Bounds, *Power through Prayer* (Grand Rapids, Mich.: Zondervan, [1912]), 117, 121, 48; Murray, *The Prayer Life* (Chicago: Moody Press, [1912]), 98; Torrey, "The Duty and Worth of Prayer," *Christian Worker's* 18 (September, 1917), 21. Murray decried the sorry state of spirituality among modern Christians because among many "there is no time to spend *one hour* with God"; *The Prayer Life*, 16. Murray, a South African minister, was a frequent speaker at American Bible conferences and Bible institutes; his numerous books have sold widely among American conservative evangelicals.

17 Gordon, *Quiet Talks on How to Pray* (Chicago: Fleming Revell, c. 1910), 12; Mueller, *Answers to Prayer from George Mueller's Narratives*, edited by A. E. C. Brooks (Salem, Ohio: Schmul, [1903]), 87–91; Torrey, *How to Pray* (Chicago: Moody Press, [1900]), 90, 54. Evangelicals also recommended a time of eve-

ning prayer for reflection and confession, but this did not preclude extensive morning devotions. See, for example, Torrey, *How to Succeed in the Christian Life* (Chicago: Moody Press, 1906), 76–79, and Graham Scroggie, *Method in Prayer* (New York: Hodder and Stoughton, 1916), 21.

18 Bounds, 48–61; Gordon, 50; Biederwolf, 32; Torrey, *Power of Prayer*, 22.

19 Torrey, *Power of Prayer*, 18; Gordon, 17; Murray, *Prayer Life*, 94–95; Bounds, selections from *The Necessity of Prayer*, in *The Best of E. M. Bounds* (Grand Rapids, Mich.: Baker Book House, [1929]), 12.

20 Torrey, *How to Pray*, 112; Gordon, *Quiet Talks on Prayer* (New York: Fleming Revell, 1904), 166; Howard and Geraldine Taylor, *Hudson Taylor's Spiritual Secret* (Chicago: Moody Press, 1932), 227, 236; Goforth quoted in Edwin and Lillian Harvey, *How They Prayed* (Hampton, Tenn.: Harvey and Tait, 1987), vol. 3, 65; Horton quoted in Douglas Frank, *Less Than Conquerors: How Evangelicals Entered the Twentieth Century* (Grand Rapids, Mich.: Eerdmans, 1986), 122.

21 For the rationale behind this intense devotional ethic, see Rick Ostrander, "The Battery and the Windmill: Two Models of Protestant Devotionalism in Early Twentieth-Century America," *Church History* 65 (March, 1996), 51–53.

22 "The Daily Altar Movement," *Christian Century* 36 (1919), 5.

23 Willett and Morrison, *The Daily Altar* (Chicago: Christian Century Press, 1918), foreword; Newton, "The Quiet Moment and the Busy Life" *Christian Century* 36 (June 26, 1919), 12–14, and "The Strength of Quietness," *Christian Century* 36 (November 13, 1919), 10–11.

24 "Letters to Unknown Friends," *Outlook* 104 (1913), 323–324.

25 All times for these devotionals were arrived at by a leisurely run-through, reading out loud to avoid skimming.

26 The two most influential books of the Keswick writer Andrew Murray, *Abide in Christ* and *With Christ in the School of Prayer*, were also written in this standard daily devotional format of short daily readings. Yet Murray was adamant that his words not be substituted for a more lengthy time of daily devotions: "It is not enough to read God's Word, or meditations as here offered, and when we think we have hold of the thoughts and have asked God for His blessing, to go out in the hope that the blessing will abide. No, it needs day by day time with Jesus and with God. . . . Take time each day, ere you read, and while you read, and after you read, to put yourself into living contact with the living Jesus"; *Abide in Christ* (Fort Washington, Pa.: Christian Literature Crusade, 1883), 7.

27 Brown, *The Quiet Hour* (New York: Association Press, 1926); Campbell, *The Place of Prayer in the Christian Religion* (New York: Methodist Book Concern, 1915), 257.

28 Fosdick, *The Meaning of Prayer* (New York: Association Press, 1915), 84, 85, 169–170; Brown, *The Life of Prayer in a World of Science*, 53–54, 173–174.

29 Brown, *Life of Prayer*, 51–54; Horr, "Family Worship," 110.

30 Symington, *Religious Liberals and Conservatives: A Comparison* (New York: Columbia University Teacher's College, 1935), 62–63; Shailer Mathews, "Evangelizing the Inevitable," *Christian Century* 34 (January 25, 1917), 13–14; Fosdick, *Meaning of Prayer*, 22; Willett and Morrison, foreword; Morrison, editorial, *Christian Century* 37 (1920), 3; Campbell, 257.

31 Brown, *Life of Prayer*, 14; Fiske, *Finding the Comrade God: The Essentials of a Soldierly Faith* (New York: Association Press, 1918), 168.

32 Bowne, *The Immanence of God* (Boston: Houghton, Mifflin, 1905), 3, 127, 126, 145, 149; Campbell, 201.

33 *The Place of Prayer*, 15, 246, 91–92.

34 *The Quiet Hour*, 48.

35 Fiske, 168; Brown, *Life of Prayer*, 176–178. Implicit in this, of course, was a "historicist" understanding of Scripture, in contrast to the "ahistoricism" of traditionalists (see chapter 4).

36 *The Daily Altar*, 224, 19; *Life of Prayer*, 174.

37 One should also avoid carrying the analogies too far. The windmill is completely dependent on the initiative of the wind for its power, but one could hardly argue that liberals displayed a Calvinistic sense of dependence on divine initiative in the spiritual life.

38 Moody, *Thoughts for the Quiet Hour* (Chicago: Moody Press, c. 1900), foreword.

39 Coe, *The Religion of a Mature Mind* (Chicago: Fleming Revell, 1902).

Eight. Modernism and Prayer in the Twenties

1 *The Meaning of Prayer* (New York: Association Press, 1915), 109–110.

2 *Adventurous Religion* (New York: Harper, 1926), 87, 80, 144.

3 Ibid., 87, 236, 89–90. Richard J. Coleman, in *Issues of Theological Warfare: Evangelicals and Liberals* (Grand Rapids, Mich.: Eerdmans, 1972), correctly classified Fosdick's *Meaning of Prayer* as expressive of the evangelical position and then marveled at the shift that has since occurred in liberalism. "In contrast to Fosdick, a liberal of yesterday," he wrote, "the liberal of today has serious questions about the power of prayer to change an external situation (148)." It would appear that Fosdick himself changed his position on prayer in the 1920s. In addition, a comparison of Fosdick's two works on prayer leads one to question Robert M. Miller's claim that in no further works "does he go much beyond the thoughts expressed in the earlier volume"; *Harry Emerson Fosdick* (New York: Oxford University Press, 1985), 238.

4 Atkins, *Religion in Our Times* (New York: Round Table Press, 1932), 86. See chapter 5 for a discussion of Cauthen's distinction between evangelical and modernistic liberals.

5 Marty, *Modern American Religion* (Chicago: University of Chicago Press, 1991), vol. 2, 213.

6 Morrison, "Fundamentalism and Modernism: Two Religions," *Christian Century* 41 (January 3, 1924), 5–6. Moody Bible Institute President James Gray, among other conservatives, cited Morrison's remarks in "Modernism a Revolt against Christianity," *Moody Bible Institute Monthly* 25 (October 1924), 55.

7 Wills, *Under God: Religion and American Politics* (New York: Simon and Schuster, 1990), 97–107. See also Richard Fox, "From Events and Institutions to Cultures and Experiences: Paradigm Shift in Twentieth Century American Religious History," given at Wheaton College, Wheaton, Illinois, 1993, 19.

8 Mullin, *Miracles and the Modern Religious Imagination* (New Haven: Yale Uni-

versity Press, 1996), 222–223. See also William Hutchison, *The Modernist Impulse* (Cambridge, Mass.: Harvard University Press, 1976), 208–225. Psychical research managed to maintain a tenuous existence in academia through a parapsychology laboratory that existed at Duke University from 1928 to 1965, Laurence Moore, *In Search of White Crows* (New York: Oxford, 1977), 187–203.

9 On the fate of the Emmanuel Movement, see Raymond Cunningham, "The Emmanuel Movement: A Variety of American Religious Experience," in *Modern American Protestantism and Its World*, edited by Martin Marty, (New York: Saur, 1993), vol. 14, 50–51; Dilworth Lupton, "Does Prayer through the weather?" *Christian Century* 47 (1930), 1086; Moore, 221.

10 Cerullo, *The Secularization of the Soul* (Philadelphia: Institute for the Study of Human Issues, 1982), 167; Stolz, *The Psychology of Prayer* (New York: Abingdon Press, 1923), 137–138.

11 Macintosh, *The Reasonableness of Christianity* (New York: Scribner's, 1925), 98.

12 "The Value of Prayer," in *Why I Believe in Religion* (New York: Macmillan, 1924), 89, 84, 86 (italics added).

13 "The Validity of Prayer in Modern Religious Experience," *Religious Education* 20 (1925), 31–36.

14 *The Life of Prayer in a World of Science* (New York: Scribner's, 1927), 18, 13.

15 E. Brooks Holifield, *A History of Pastoral Care in America* (Nashville, Tenn.: Abingdon Press, 1983), 210–231; Sidney Ahlstrom, *A Religious History of the American People* (New Haven: Yale University Press, 1972), 904–905.

16 Brown, 48, 69.

17 Ibid., 48, 3, 4, 132.

18 Ibid., 144.

19 *Methods of Private Religious Living* (New York: Macmillan, 1929), 18–19, 22–23.

20 Ibid., 20; Trine, *In Tune With the Infinite* (New York: Dodd, Mead, 1897), 131; Cabot, "The Conversion of a Sinner," *Atlantic* 132 (1923), 147–158.

21 Wieman, 22–33.

22 See Mark Noll, *A History of Christianity in the United States and Canada* (Grand Rapids, Mich.: Eerdmans, 1992), 375–376.

23 Mathews, "Putting Religion to the Test," interview by Neil M. Clark, *American Magazine* 109 (June 1930), 50–51. One indicator of the changed climate concerning prayer in the 1920s is Wheaton College president J. Oliver Buswell's defense of prayer in 1928. Whereas earlier conservatives mainly defended God's ability and propensity to answer prayer (as evidenced by William Biederwolf's title *How Can God Answer Prayer?* in 1910), Buswell saw it as one of his main tasks to defend the idea that there was a personal God at all who heard prayer; *Problems in the Prayer Life* (Chicago: Moody Colportage, 1928), 89–113.

24 In *Dictionary of Christianity in America*, edited by Douglas Reid (Downers Grove, Ill.: Intervarsity Press, 1990), 253. Silva's statement should more accurately designate the *Christian Century* as the voice of *liberal* mainline Protestants, since liberalism and mainline Protestantism were not necessarily synonymous. See also Martin Marty, *Modern American Religion*, vol. 1, *The Irony of It All* (Chicago: University of Chicago Press), 164.

25 This description of religious humanism is based on Donald Meyer, "Secular Transcendence: The American Religious Humanists," in Martin Marty, *Modern American Protestantism and Its World, vol. 14*, 223–241. The "friend behind the phenomena" quotation is in Meyer, 230.

26 Meyer, 226.

27 Holmes, "A Humanistic Interpretation of Prayer," *Christian Century* 46 (October 16, 1929), 1275–1277.

28 "Did Dr. Holmes Leave Something Out?" *Christian Century* 46 (October 30, 1929), 1343–1348.

29 Holmes, "Dr. Holmes Puts Something In," *Christian Century* 46 (November 13, 1929), 1405.

30 "A Humanistic Prayer Meeting," *Christian Century* 46 (November 27, 1929), 1464.

31 "Did Dr. Holmes Leave Something Out?" 1348.

32 Correspondence, *Christian Century* 46 (November 6, 1929), 1381.

33 Morrison, "Let Us Pray!" *Christian Century* 47 (January 15, 1930), 70–72.

34 Holmes, "A Humanistic Interpretation of Prayer," 1275; Morrison, 71.

35 Morrison, 71.

36 Ibid., 72.

37 "Does Prayer Change the Weather?" *Christian Century* 47 (September 10, 1930), 1084.

38 Ibid., 1085; "Praying for Rain," *Moody Bible Institute Monthly* 31 (April 1931), 398.

39 "Does Prayer Change the Weather?" 1084–1086.

40 Ibid., 1084; Hudson, *The Great Tradition of the American Churches* (New York: Harper and Row, 1963), 220.

41 "Does Prayer Change the Weather?" 1085–1086; correspondent quoted in Robert M. Miller, *Harry Emerson Fosdick* (New York: Oxford University Press, 1985), 238–239.

42 Lake, "Prayer," and Clark, "The Soul's Sincere Desire," *Atlantic Monthly* 134 (1924), 163–167; 167–172; Brown, "After Fundamentalism—What?" *North American Review* 223 (1926), 408; Editor's Easy Chair, *Atlantic Monthly* 135 (1925), 429.

43 "Will Prayer Bring Rain?" *Literary Digest* 106 (1930), 18–19.

44 Correspondence, *Christian Century* 47 (September 24, 1930), 1156–1157.

45 James B. Pratt, for instance, remarked concerning Leuba's study, "I have called it a 'revelation,' for the author is not here giving us his guess, but recording certain facts which he gleaned by means of one of the most careful and truly scientific questionnaire investigations ever conducted"; "The Psychological Study of Religion," *American Journal of Theology* 21 (1917) 631.

46 Fosdick, *The Living of These Days: An Autobiography* (New York: Harper, 1956), 164–165; Hofstadter, *Anti-Intellectualism in American Life* (New York: Knopf, 1963), 123.

47 "Southern Prayers," *Christian Century* 47 (September 3, 1930), 1060–1062.

Select Bibliography

Primary Works

Books

Abbott, Lyman. *What Christianity Means to Me*. New York: Macmillan, 1922.

Adams, Henry W., ed. *I Cried, He Answered*. Chicago: Bible Institute Colportage Association, 1918.

Alexander, Archibald. *Practical Truths*. New York: American Tract Society, 1852.

Allen, A. V. G. *The Continuity of Christian Thought*. Boston: Houghton Mifflin, 1884.

Alleine, Richard A. *A Companion for Prayer*. Boston: S. Kneeland, 1750.

Ames, Edward Scribner. *The Psychology of Religious Experience*. Boston: Houghton Mifflin, 1910.

Andover Association. *A Serious Call to Family Religion*. Cambridge, Mass.: William Hilliard, 1802.

Andover Review editors. *Progressive Orthodoxy*. Boston: Houghton, Mifflin, 1892.

Anonymous. *Family Prayers*. Dublin: William Curry, 1835.

Baker, Ray Stannard. *The Spiritual Unrest*. New York: Frederick A. Stokes, 1909.

Barton, Bruce. *The Man Nobody Knows*. New York: Bobbs-Merrill 1924.

Barth, Karl. *Church Dogmatics, Volume 3, Part 4*, translated by A. T. Mackay. Edinburgh: T. & T. Clark, 1961.

Bean, James. *Family Worship*. Philadelphia: S. Potter, 1819.

Beaven, Thomas. *On Prayer*. Philadelphia: B. and T. Kite, 1815.

Bennett, James. *Religion of the Closet*. Andover, Mass.: Flagg and Gould, 1818.

Bickersteth, Edward. *A Treatise on Prayer*. Philadelphia: Thomas Kite, 1829.

Biederwolf, William Edward. *How Can God Answer Prayer?* New York: Fleming Revell, 1910.

Blanchard, Charles. *Getting Things from God: A Study of the Prayer Life*. Wheaton, Ill.: Sword of the Lord, [1915].

Boardman, William E. *The Higher Christian Life*. New York: Garland, 1984 [1858].

Boston Society for the Moral and Religious Improvement of Seamen. *The Duty and Reasonableness of Prayer*. Boston: John Eliot, 1814.

Bounds, E. M. *The Best of E. M. Bounds*. Grand Rapids, Mich.: Baker Book House, 1981 [1913].

———. *Power through Prayer*. Chicago: Moody Press, [1912].

Bowne, Borden P. *The Immanence of God*. Boston: Houghton, Mifflin, and 1905.

———. *Personalism*. Boston: Houghton Mifflin, 1908.

Brown, Charles Reynolds. *Why I Believe in Religion*. New York: Macmillan, 1924.

Brown, William Adams. *Christian Theology in Outline*. New York: Charles Scribner's, 1906.

————. *God at Work: A Study of the Supernatural.* New York: Charles Scribner's, 1933.

————. *Is Christianity Practicable?* New York: Scribner's, 1916.

————. *The Life of Prayer in a World of Science.* New York: Scribner's, 1927.

————. *The Quiet Hour.* New York: Association Press, 1926.

————. *A Teacher and His Times.* New York: Scribner's, 1940.

Brownel, Baker, ed. *Religious Life.* Vol. 2. *Man and His World.* New York: D. Van Nostrand, 1929.

Bushnell, Horace. *Nature and the Supernatural.* New York: Scribner, 1859.

Buswell, J. Oliver. *Problems in the Prayer Life.* Chicago: Bible Institute Colportage Association, 1928.

Campbell, George Douglas. *The Reign of Law.* New York: John B. Alden, [1866].

Campbell, James M. *The Place of Prayer in the Christian Religion.* New York: Methodist Book Concern, 1915.

————. *Prayer in Its Present Day Aspects.* New York: Fleming Revell, 1916.

Chamberlain, Leander. *The True Doctrine of Prayer.* New York: Baker and Taylor, 1906.

Chambers, Oswald. *My Utmost for His Highest.* New York: Dodd, Mead, 1935.

Churchill, Winston. *The Inside of the Cup.* New York: Macmillan, 1914.

Clarke, James Freeman. *The Christian Doctrine of Prayer.* Boston: American Unitarian Association, 1854.

Clarke, William Newton. *An Outline of Christian Theology.* New York: Scribner's, 1914 [1896].

————. *What Shall We Think of Christianity?* New York:Scribner's, 1899.

Closet and Altar. Boston: W. L. Greene, 1899.

Coe, George A. *The Religion of a Mature Mind.* Chicago: Fleming Revell, 1902.

————. *The Spiritual Life.* New York: Eaton and Mains, 1900.

Coffin, Henry Sloane. *University Sermons.* New Haven: Yale University Press, 1914.

Conwell, Russell H. *Acres of Diamonds.* New York: Harper, c.1915.

Cowman, Mrs. Charles. *Streams in the Desert.* Grand Rapids, Mich.: Zondervan, [1925].

Dawson, William James. *The Forgotten Secret.* New York: Fleming Revell, 1906.

Dayton, Donald W., ed. *Late Nineteenth Century Revivalist Teachings on the Holy Spirit.* New York: Garland, 1985.

The Discipline of Prayer. New York: Association Press, 1916.

Douglas, Lloyd C. *Magnificent Obsession.* Chicago: Willett, Clark, 1929.

Drummond, Henry. *Natural Law in the Spiritual World.* New York: John B. Alden, 1887.

Elliot, Elizabeth. *Through Gates of Splendor.* Wheaton, Ill.: Living Books, 1981.

Finney, Charles G. *Lectures on Revivals of Religion.* Cambridge, Mass: Belknap Press, 1960 [1835].

————. *Memoirs.* New York: Fleming Revell, 1876.

————. *The Promise of the Spirit.* Minneapolis: Bethany House, 1980.

Fiske, Charles. *The Confessions of a Troubled Parson.* New York: Scribner's, 1928.

Fiske, G. Walter. *Finding the Comrade God: The Essentials of a Soldierly Faith.* New York: Association Press, 1918.

Fosdick, Harry Emerson. *Adventurous Religion and Other Essays*. New York: Harper, 1926.

———. *The Assurance of Immortality*. London: James Clarke, 1913.

———. *The Challenge of the Present Crisis*. New York: Association Press, 1917.

———. *Christianity and Progress*. New York: Fleming Revell, 1922.

———. *The Living of These Days: An Autobiography*. New York: Harper, 1956.

———. *The Manhood of the Master*. New York: Association Press, 1913.

———. *The Meaning of Faith*. New York: Association Press, 1917.

———. *The Meaning of Prayer*. New York: Association Press, 1915.

———. *The Meaning of Service*. New York: Association Press, 1920.

———. *The Modern Use of the Bible*. New York: Macmillan, 1924.

———. *The Second Mile*. New York: Young Man's Christian Association, 1908.

———. *Twelve Tests of Character*. New York: Association Press, 1923.

Frazer, Sir James George. *The Golden Bough: A Study in Magic and Religion*. New York: Macmillan, 1922.

Frost, Henry. *Effective Praying*. Philadelphia: Sunday School Times, 1925.

———. *Men Who Prayed*. Philadelphia: Sunday School Times, 1914.

Gilkey, Charles W. *Present-Day Dilemmas in Religion*. Nashville: Cokesbury Press, 1928.

Gladden, Washington. *The Lord's Prayer*. Boston: Houghton, Mifflin, 1886.

Goforth, Rosalind. *How I Know God Answers Prayer*. Chicago: Moody Press, 1921.

Gordon, Adoniram J. *The Ministry of Healing*. New York: Fleming Revell, 1882.

Gordon, George A. *Religion and Miracle*. Boston: Houghton Mifflin, 1909.

Gordon, Samuel D. *Quiet Talks on How to Pray*. Chicago: Fleming Revell, c.1910.

———. *Quiet Talks on Prayer*. Chicago: Fleming Revell, 1904.

———. *The Treasury of Quiet Talks*. Chicago: Fleming Revell, 1951.

Grenfell, Wilfred T. *Religion in Everyday Life*. Chicago: American Library Association, 1926.

Hallimond, John G. *The Miracle of Answered Prayer*. New York: Christian Herald Bible House, 1916.

Harnack, Adolf von. *What is Christianity?* New York: Putnam's, 1904.

Haynes, William F. *A Physician's Witness to the Power of Shared Prayer*. Chicago: Loyola University Press, 1990.

Henry, Matthew. *A Method for Prayer*. New York: R. Carter 1851.

Hocking, William E. *The Meaning of God in Human Experience*. New Haven: Yale University Press, 1912.

Hodge, Charles. *Systematic Theology*. 3 vols. New York: Scribner's, 1872.

Hopkins, Mark. *Prayer and the Prayer-Gauge*. New York: Dodd and Mead, 1874.

Horton, Walter Marshall. *Christian Theology: An Ecumenical Approach*. New York: Harper and Row, 1955.

Huxley, Thomas H. *Essays upon Some Controverted Questions*. London: Macmillan 1882.

Hyde, William DeWitt. *The Gospel of Good Will*. New York: Macmillan, 1916.

Inge, W. R. *Personal Religion and the Life of Devotion*. London: Longmans, Green, 1924.

James, William. *The Varieties of Religious Experience.* New York: Longmans, Green, 1902.

Jefferson, Charles E. *Old Truths and New Facts.* New York: Fleming Revell, 1918.

Jellett, J. H. *The Efficacy of Prayer.* London: Macmillan, 1880.

Jones, E. Stanley. *The Christ of the Indian Road.* New York: Abingdon Press, 1925.

Jones, Rufus M. *The Inner Life.* New York: Macmillan, 1916.

———. *The World Within.* New York: Macmillan, 1918.

King, Henry Churchill. *Religion as Life.* New York: Macmillan, 1913.

Kinsley, William W. *Science and Prayer.* Meadville, Pa.: Flood and Vincent, 1893.

Knox, George William. *The Direct and Fundamental Proofs of the Christian Religion.* New York: Scribner's, 1903.

Law, William. *A Serious Call to a Devout and Holy Life.* Philadelphia: Westminster Press, 1955 [1728].

———. *The Spirit of Prayer.* Providence, R. I.: John Miller, 1823.

Leuba, James H. *The Belief in God and Immortality: A Psychological, Anthropological and Statistical Study.* Boston: Sherman, French, 1916.

Lewis, Sinclair. *Arrowsmith.* New York: Harcourt, Brace, 1925.

———. *Babbitt.* New York: Harcourt Brace Jovanovich, 1922.

———. *Elmer Gantry.* New York: The New American Library, 1970 [1927].

———. *Main Street.* New York: Harcourt, Brace, 1920.

Lippmann, Walter. *A Preface to Morals.* New York: Macmillan, 1929.

MacDuff, J. R. *Thoughts for the Quiet Hour.* New York: American Tract Society, 1894.

Machen, J. Gresham. *Christianity and Liberalism.* Grand, Rapids, Mich.: Eerdmans, 1983 [1923].

Macintosh, Douglas Clyde. *The Reasonableness of Christianity.* New York: Scribner's, 1925.

Marsden, George M., ed. *The Fundamentals: A Testimony to the Truth. 4 vols..* New York: Garland, 1988 [1910–1915].

Mather, Increase. *Remarkable Providences Illustrative of the Earlier Days of American Colonization.* London: Reeves and Turner, 1890 [1683].

Matheson, George. *Leaves for Quiet Hours.* New York: A. C. Armstrong, 1904.

Mathews, Shailer. *The Faith of Modernism.* New York: AMS Press, 1969 [1924].

McDowell, Josh. *Evidence That Demands a Verdict.* San Bernardino, Cal.: Campus Crusade for Christ, 1972.

Means, John O., ed. *The Prayer-Gauge Debate.* Boston: Congregational Publishing Society, 1876.

Miles, Henry A., ed. *The Altar at Home: Prayers for the Family and the Closet.* Boston: American Unitarian Association, 1855.

Moody, Dwight Lyman. *Prevailing Prayer.* New York: Fleming Revell, 1885.

More, Hannah. *Reflections on Prayer.* Boston: Wells and Lilly, 1819.

Morris, Herbert W. *Natural Laws and Gospel Teachings.* New York: American Tract Society, 1887.

Mott, John R. *The Future Leadership of the Church.* New York: Young Men's Christian Association, 1908.

———. *The Morning Watch.* New York: The International Committee of Young Men's Christian Associations, 1893.

————. *The Pastor and Modern Missions*. New York: Student Volunteer Movement for Foreign Missions, 1904.

————. *The Secret Prayer Life*. New York: The International Committee of Young Men's Christian Associations, 1904.

Mueller, George. *Answers to Prayer from George Mueller's Narratives*. Edited by A. E. C. Brooks. Chicago: Moody Press [1903].

————. *Answers to Prayer from George Mueller's Narratives* (revised version). Edited by A. E. C. Brooks. Salem, Ohio: Schmul, 1903.

Mueller, George. *The Life of Trust*. New York: Thomas Y. Crowell, 1877 [1873].

Murray, Andrew. *Abide in Christ*. Fort Washington, Pa.: Christian Literature Crusade, 1972 [1883].

————. *The Prayer Life*. Chicago: Moody Press, [1912].

————. *With Christ in the School of Prayer*. Lakeland: Marshall Pickering, 1987 [1885].

Nicoll, W. Robertson, ed. *A Book of Family Worship*. New York: Dodd, Mead, 1900.

Niles, Nathaniel. *Secret Prayer Explained and Inculcated*. Boston: Kneeland, 1773.

Parkhurst, Louis Gifford, ed. *Charles G. Finney's Answers to Prayer*. Minneapolis: Bethany House, 1983.

Paterson, W. P., ed. *The Power of Prayer*. New York: Macmillan, 1920.

Patton, William W. *Prayer and Its Remarkable Answers*. Toronto: William Briggs, 1875.

Paul, William. *A Treatise on Prayer*. West Springfield, Mass.: Edward Gray, 1797.

Phelps, Austin. *The Still Hour, or, Communion with God*. Boston: Gould and Lincoln, 1863.

Pierson, Arthur T. *Forward Movements of the Last Half Century*. New York: Funk and Wagnalls, 1905.

————. *George Mueller of Bristol*. New York: Fleming Revell, 1899.

Porter, Eleanor. *Pollyanna*. New York: Scholastic, [1913].

Pratt, James B. *The Religious Consciousness*. New York: Macmillan, 1926.

Prime, *Fifteen Years of Prayer in the Fulton Street Meeting*. New York: Scribner, Armstrong, 1872.

————. *The Power of Prayer*. New York: Scribner, 1864.

————. *Prayer and Its Answer*. New York: Scribner's, 1882.

Rauschenbusch, Walter. *Prayers of the Social Awakening*. Boston: Pilgrim Press, 1910.

Reddy, William. *Prayer and Providence in Relation to the Death of President Garfield*. Syracuse, N.Y.: Masters and Stone, 1881.

Schleiermacher, Friedrich. *The Christian Faith*. Edited by H. R. Mackintosh. Edinburgh: T. and T. Clark, 1928 [1830].

Scofield, William Campbell. *The Bible History of Answered Prayer*. New York: Fleming Revell, 1899.

Scroggie, Graham. *Method in Prayer*. New York: Hodder and Stoughton, 1916.

Shaw, S. B., ed. *Touching Incidents and Remarkable Answers to Prayer*. Chicago: S. B. Shaw, 1895.

Sheldon, Charles M. *In His Steps*. Chicago: Moody Press, 1956 [1896].

Simmons, Charles E. *The Bible Doctrine of Prayer*. New York: Fleming Revell, 1892.

Simpson, A. B. *The Life of Prayer.* New York: Christian Alliance, 1890.

Slattery, Charles Lewis. *Why Men Pray.* New York: Macmillan, 1918.

Smith, Gerald Birney. *Principles of Christian Living.* Chicago: University of Chicago Press, 1924.

Smith, Hannah Whitall. *The Christian's Secret of a Happy Life.* Boston: Christian Witness, 1885.

Smith, Henry Boynton. *System of Christian Theology.* New York: A. C. Armstrong, 1890.

Smith, James H. *Our Faithful God: Answers to Prayer.* London: Marshall, 1914.

Smith, Oswald, ed., *David Brainerd: The Man of Prayer.* Grand Rapids, Mich.: Zondervan, 1941.

Spalding, Josiah. *The Duty and Importance of Calling upon God.* Northampton, Mass.: William Butler, 1800.

Speer, Robert Elliott. *The Marks of a Man, or The Essentials of Christian Character.* Cincinnati, Ohio: Jennings and Graham, 1907.

Spurgeon, Charles H. *Effective Prayer.* London: Evangelical Press, c.1860.

Stolz, Karl R. *The Psychology of Prayer.* New York: Abingdon Press, 1923.

Strong, Augustus H. *Systematic Theology: A Compendium.* Philadelphia: Judson Press, N.J.: 1907.

Strong, Sidney, ed. *We Believe in Prayer: Affirmations by One Hundred Men and Women of Many Lands.* New York: Coward-McCann, 1930.

Taylor, Geraldine Guinness. *Borden of Yale.* Chicago: Moody Press, 1926.

———. *Hudson Taylor and the China Inland Mission.* Philadelphia: China Inland Mission, 1918.

———. *Hudson Taylor in Early Years.* Philadelphia: China Inland Mission, 1911.

———. *The Story of the China Inland Mission.* London: Morgan and Scott, 1894.

Taylor, Howard and Geraldine. *Hudson Taylor's Spiritual Secret.* Chicago: Moody Press, 1932.

Thornton, Henry. *Family Prayers.* Dublin: William Curry, 1835.

Tileston, Mary. *Prayers Ancient and Modern.* Boston: Little, Brown, 1925.

Tomkins, John. *A Brief Testimony to the Great Duty of Prayer.* Philadelphia: Samuel Keimer, 1694.

Torrey, Reuben A. *How to Pray.* Chicago: Moody Press, [1900].

———. *How to Succeed in the Christian Life.* Chicago: Moody Press, [1906].

———. *The Power of Prayer and the Prayer of Power.* New York: Fleming Revell, 1924.

Trine, Ralph Waldo. *In Tune with the Infinite.* New York: Dodd, Mead, 1897.

Trumbull, Henry Clay. *Illustrative Answers to Prayer.* New York: Fleming Revell, 1900.

———. *Prayer: Its Nature and Scope.* Philadelphia: John D. Wattles, 1896.

Tyler, W. S. *Prayer for Colleges.* New York: M. W. Dodd, 1855.

Tyndall, John. *Fragments of Science.* vol. 2. New York: Collier, [c. 1880].

Underhill, Evelyn. *The Life of the Spirit and the Life of Today.* New York: E. P. Dutton, 1922.

Van Anda, C. A. *Prayer: Its Nature, Conditions, and Effects.* Cincinnati, Ohio: Cranston and Stowe, 1891.

Vanderlaan, Eldred C., ed. *Fundamentalism Versus Modernism.* New York: H. W. Wilson, 1925.

Vaughan, Louisa. *Answered or Unanswered?* Philadelphia: Christian Life Literature Fund, [1917].

Vincent, Boyd. *God and Prayer: A Discussion of the Reasonableness of Prayer.* New York: James Pott, 1897.

Wallace, Lew. *Ben-Hur.* New York: Harper, 1880.

Warfield, Benjamin B. *Counterfeit Miracles.* New York: Scribner's, 1918.

———. *Faith and Life.* Philadelphia: Banner of Truth Trust, 1974 [1916].

Watt, Gordon B. *Effectual Fervent Prayer.* Los Angeles: Biola Book Room, 1927.

Watts, Isaac. *A Guide to Prayer.* Trenton, N.J.: Daniel Fenton, 1739.

Wellbeloved, Charles. *Devotional Exercises.* Keene, N.H.: John Prentiss, 1810.

Whittle, D. W., ed. *The Wonders of Prayer.* Chicago: Fleming Revell, 1885.

Whyte, Alexander. *Lord, Teach Us to Pray.* New York: Harper, c. 1906.

Wieman, Henry Nelson. *The Issues of Life.* New York: Abingdon Press, 1930.

———. *Methods of Private Religious Living.* New York: Macmillan, 1929.

Wilder, Thornton. *The Bridge of San Luis Rey.* New York: Avon Books, 1976 [1927].

Willett, Herbert, and Charles C. Morrison. *The Daily Altar.* Chicago: Christian Century Press, 1918.

Williams, Solomon. *The Power and Efficacy of the Prayers of the People of God.* Boston: S. Kneeland and T. Green, 1742.

Wright, Harold Bell. *The Calling of Dan Matthews.* New York: A. L. Burt, 1909.

———. *That Printer of Udell's.* New York: A. L. Burt, 1902.

———. *The Winning of Barbara Worth.* New York: A. L. Burt, 1911.

Articles, Sermons, Tracts

Abbott, Lyman. "Can We Pray to Our Own Instincts?" *Outlook* 85 (1907), 303–304.

———. "Christ's Teaching Concerning Prayer." *Outlook* 62 (1899), 939–943.

———. "Does God Answer Prayer?" *Outlook* 114 (1916), 411.

———. "A History of Prayer." *Outlook* 61 (1899), 456–460.

———. "Is Prayer a Form of Selfishness?" *Outlook* 100 (1912), 803–805.

———. "Learning to Pray." *Baptist* 4 (1923), 1073–1074.

———. "Letters to Unknown Friends." *Outlook* 99 (1911); *Outlook* 103 (1913), 703–705; *Outlook* 104 (1913), 323–324.

———. "A Medical Estimate of Prayer." *Outlook* 81 (September 1905), 110.

———. "The Nature of Prayer." *North American Review* 186 (1907), 337–339.

———. "Prayer." *Outlook* 83 (1906), 882–883.

———. "Prayer and Its Answers." *Outlook* 100 (1912), 17–18.

———. "Prayer and Law." *Outlook* 100 (1912), 488–489.

———. "The Prayer of Love." *Outlook* 66 (1900), 391–392.

———. "Praying and Waiting." *Outlook* 84 (1906), 69–70.

———. "Saying Prayers." *Outlook* 111 (1915), 855–856.

———. "Two Kinds of Prayer." *Outlook* 114 (1916), 106–107.

Allen, J. Henry. "Altars of the Ages." *Moody Bible Institute Monthly* 28 (June 1928), 458.

Ames, Edward Scribner. "Ernest Haeckel and the Passing of Naturalism." *Christian Century* 36 (1919), 9–10.

———. "A Letter to God." *Christian Century* 37 (October 14, 1920), 11–14.

———. "Prayer." In *University of Chicago Sermons*, edited by Theodore Soares. Chicago: University of Chicago Press, 1915, 165–178.

Anonymous. "A Boy's Ideas on Religion." *Atlantic Monthly* 133 (1924), 632–634.

"Anonymous." "The Art of Prayer." *Outlook* 83 (1906), 857–859.

Anonymous. "–But Why Preach?" *Harper's* 143 (1921), 81–85.

Anonymous. "The Modernist's Quest for God." *Atlantic Monthly* 137 (1920), 228–233.

Anonymous. "Ought I to Leave the Church?" *Harper's* 142 (1921), 343–349.

Anonymous. "The Tyranny of the Congregation." *Harper's* 133 (1916), 501–508.

Atkinson, W. R. "Tyndall on the Physical Value of Prayer." *Southern Presbyterian Review* 29 (1873).

Bacon, Benjamin. "Does It Pay the Modern Man to Pray?" *Current Literature* 39 (1905), 401–402.

Bacon, Leonard. "Prayer, Miracle, and Natural Law." *Fraser's Magazine* (September 1873).

Barry, William F. "A Defence of Prayer." *Nineteenth Century and Beyond* 38 (1895), 348–360.

Bell, Bernard Iddings. "Social Service and the Churches." *Atlantic Monthly* 115 (1915), 161–164.

Bell, James W. "Praying for Rain." *Moody Bible Institute Monthly* 31 (April 1931), 398.

Bigham, John. "The Meaning of Prayer." *Methodist Review* 79 (1897), 356–364.

Brain, Belle M. "Prayer in the Missionary Meeting." *Missionary Review of the World* 26 (1903), 350–356.

Brown, Rollo Walter. "The Creative Spirit and the Church." *Harper's* 150 (1924), 42–49.

Brown, William Adams. "After Fundamentalism–What?" *North American Review* 223 (1926), 406–419.

———. "The Permanent Significance of Miracle for Religion." *Harvard Theological Review* 8 (1915), 298–322.

Buswell, J. Oliver. "Praying and Serving." *Moody Bible Institute Monthly* 28 (February 1928), 275–276.

"But What Became of the Prayers?" *Independent* 53 (1901), 2250.

Cabot, Philip. "The Conversion of a Sinner." *Atlantic* 132 (1923), 147–158.

Calkins, Ernest Elmo. "The Natural History of a Soul." *Atlantic Monthly* 136 (1925), 625–633.

"A Call to Prayer." *Baptist* 6 (1925), 111.

Clark, Glenn. "The Lost Art of Jesus." *Atlantic Monthly* 135 (1925), 316–325.

———. "The Soul's Sincere Desire." *Atlantic Monthly* 134 (1924), 167–172.

Coe, George A. "The Social Value of Prayer and Worship." *World Tomorrow* 15 (1932), 175–177.

Congdon, James E. "Prayer Was Made for Rain, and It Fell." *Moody Bible Institute Monthly* 34 (July 1934), 499.

Craig, Samuel G. "The Christian Way of Life and the Supernatural." *Princeton Theological Review* 20 (1922), 15–40.

Daggett, Mabel Potter. "Are There Modern Miracles?" *Ladies Home Journal* 40 (June 1923), 20, 165–166.

"The Dangerous Decline of the Church." *Literary Digest* 106 (July 5, 1930), 20–21.

Davis, Elmer. "God without Religion." *Harper's* 160 (1930), 397–409.

Davis, Noah. "The Prayer Test." *Baptist Quarterly* 7 (1873).

"Death of President Garfield." *Harper's* 63 (1881), 624–625, 784–785, 949.

"The Death of the President." *Atlantic Monthly* 88 (1901), 432b–432c.

Deck, Northcote. "Prayer in the Mission Field." *Missionary Review of the World* 40 (1917), 179–181.

Decker, Sarah N. "A Strange Prayer Strangely Answered." *Moody Bible Institute Monthly* 25 (July 1925), 501–502.

"Devotional Life." *Bulletin of the Moody Bible Institute.* Chicago, 1921.

"Did Dr. Holmes Leave Something Out?" *Christian Century* 46 (1929), 1343–1349, 1381.

"Divine Guidance Illustrated in Personal Experience." *Christian Worker's* 14 (1914), 451–453.

"Divine Guidance in God's Service." *Moody Bible Institute Monthly* 25 (January 1915), 212.

"Does Prayer Change the Weather?" *Christian Century* 47 (1930), 1084–1086, 1156–1157.

Doughty, W. E. "Prayer Indispensable to World-Winners." *Methodist Review* 96 (1914), 451–466.

Duncan, Norman. "Higgins—A Man's Christian." *Harper's* 119 (1909), 165–179.

Eastman, Fred. "Shall I Remain in the Church?" *Harper's* 150 (1925), 385–393.

Edwards, Jonathan. "Hypocrites Deficient in the Practice of Prayer." *The Works of President Edwards.* Vol. 4 New York: Leavitt, Trow, 1849, 474–487.

———. "The Most High a Prayer-Hearing God." *The Works of President Edwards.* Vol. 3. Worcester, Mass.: Isaiah Thomas, 1809 [1735], 44–65.

Emerson, Ralph Waldo. "Self-Reliance." In *The American Intellectual Tradition,* edited by Charles Capper and David Hollinger. Vol. 1. New York: Oxford University Press, 1997 [1841], 302–316.

"Episcopal Endorsement of Faith-Healing." *Literary Digest* 75 (October 28, 1922), 30–31.

Ewers, John R. "A Study of Prayer." *Christian Century* 39 (1922), 1026.

"The Exposed Fleece." Chicago: Moody Bible Institute Colportage Association, c.1929.

"Failure of Prayers for Peace or Victory." *Literary Digest* 49 (November 28, 1914), 1068–1069.

Field, Elliot. "The Wish That Prays." *Biblical World* 47 (1916), 291–297.

Finley, John H. "Faith in Prayer." *Forum* 66 (1921), 116–118.

Fiske, Charles. "The Church's Loss of Prestige." *Harper's* 153 (1926), 600–608.

Fosdick, Harry Emerson. "Beyond Reason." *Religious Education* 23 (1928), 471.

———. "Are Religious People Fooling Themselves?" *Harper's* 161 (1930), 59–70.

———. "Heckling the Church." *Atlantic* 121 (1911), 735–742.

———. "Religion without God?" *Harper's* 160 (1929), 50–60.

———. "A Sense of God's Reality." *Christian Century* 36 (November 6, 1919), 12–14.

———. "What Is Christianity?" *Harper's* 158 (1929), 551–561.

———. "What Is Religion?" *Harper's* 158 (1929), 424–434.

Gerould, Katherine Fullerton. "The Unsocial Christian." *Harper's* 158 (1929), 661–667.

"Getting Full Credit for Intimacy with God." *Christian Century* 37 (January 15, 1920), 4.

Gilchrist, Beth Bradford. "The Miracle." *Harper's* 141 (1920), 217–225.

"God and Provincialism." *Forum* 52 (1914), 786–788.

Godbey, J. E. "Prayer and the Law of Spiritual Life." *Methodist Quarterly Review* 67 (1919), 60–67.

"The God of a Scientist." *Literary Digest* 85 (June 27, 1925), 31–32.

"God's Intercessors." *Missionary Review of the World* 24 (1901), 218.

Goodchild, R. J. "Can We Believe the Miracles?" *Moody Bible Institute Monthly* 23 (September 1922), 17–19.

Gordon, Samuel D. "Prayer and the 'Uttermost Parts.'" *Missionary Review of the World* 39 (1916), 820–824.

Gray, James M. "Is Any among You Afflicted? Let Him Pray." Chicago: Moody Bible Institute, c.1920.

———. "Modernism a Revolt against Christianity." *Moody Bible Institute Monthly* 25 (October 1924), 55–57.

Hale, Harris G. "Why I Keep on Praying." *Baptist* 4 (1923), 840–841.

Hall, Fred. "Flattening the Spiritual Life." *Moody Bible Institute Monthly* 25 (April 1925), 363–364.

"A Harvest in Answer to Prayer." *Literary Digest* 75 (December 30, 1922), 30.

"Historic Baptist Emphasis on Prayer." *In Baptist Fundamentals.* Philadelphia: Judson Press, 1920, 97–105.

Hitchcock, J. M. "Charles G. Finney's Intercessory Prayer." *Christian Worker's* 11 (1911), 358–360.

Hodge, Caspar W. "What Is a Miracle?" *Princeton Theological Review* 14 (1916), 202–244.

Holmes, John Haynes. "Dr. Holmes Puts Something In." *Christian Century* 46 (1929), 1403–1406.

———. "A Humanistic Interpretation of Prayer." *Christian Century* 46 (1929), 1275–1277.

Horr, George E. "Family Worship." *Biblical World* 27 (1906), 104–111.

Horton, Robert Forman. "Effective Prayer for Missions." *Missionary Review of the World* 48 (1925), 363–364.

Horton, Walter. "Does Prayer Change the Weather?" *Christian Century* 47 (September 10, 1930), 1085

"How to Pray and What to Pray for in the International Crisis." *Current Opinion* 57 (1914), 341–343.

"A Humanistic Prayer Meeting." *Christian Century* 46 (1929), 1464–1466.

Hungerford, Edward. "Prayers Subjective and Objective." *Andover Review* 14 (1890).

"The Instinct of Prayer." *Living Age* 242 (1904), 380–383.

Johnson, Samuel. "A Demonstration of the Reasonableness, Usefulness, and Great Duty of Prayer." New York: Weyman, 1760.

Jones, Rufus M. "What I Believe—About Prayer." In *Ventures in Belief*, edited by Henry P. Van Dusen. New York: Scribner's 1930, 161–180.

Kelly, William V. "Praying for Things." *Methodist Review* 86 (1904), 286–291.

Kenna, James Brett. "The Minister as Business Executive." *Harper's* 157 (1928), 38–44.

King, Henry Churchill. "Difficulties Concerning Prayer." *Biblical World* 46 (1915), 131–134, 281–284, 348–352.

Krumbine, Miles H. "What Has Happened to Prayer?" *Christian Century* 48 (1931), 741–743.

Lake, Kirsopp. "Prayer." *Atlantic Monthly* 134 (1924), 163–167.

"Learning to Pray." *Baptist* 4 (1923), 1073–1074.

Lewis, Edward. "The Failure of the Church." *Atlantic Monthly* 114 (1914), 729–737.

Lum, Hermann A. "Organized Prayer as a Missionary Agency." *Missionary Review of the World* 48 (1925), 845–847.

Maclachlan, H. D. C. "Sir Oliver Lodge and Religion." *Christian Century* 37 (1920), 13–15.

Martin, Edward S. "Immortality as a World-Cure." *Harper's* 152 (1926), 787–790.

———. "An Optimist? Why Not?" *Harper's* 119 (1909), 364–369.

———. "Possibilities of Prayer." *North American Review* 157 (1893), 252–254.

———. "Theological Discussions." *Harper's* 147 (1923), 421–424.

Martin, Everett Dean. "Are We Facing a Revival of Religion?" *Harper's* 148 (1924), 677–687.

Mather, Cotton. "Family-Religion, Excited and Assisted." Newport, R. I. Widow Franklin, 1707.

———. "Family Religion Urged." Boston: D. Henchman, 1747.

———. "The Duty of Secret Prayer." Boston: B. Green and J. Allen, 1703.

Mathews, Shailer. "Evangelizing the Inevitable." *Christian Century* 34 (January 25, 1917), 13–14.

———. "Putting Religion to the Test." Interview by Neil M. Clark. *American Magazine* 109 (June 1930), 50–51, 88–90.

Matthews, W. R. "Can We Still Believe in the Holy Spirit?" *Christian Century* 40 (1923), 265–267.

McComb, Samuel. "The New Belief in Prayer." *Century* 80 (1910), 787–790.

———. "Prayer: Its Meaning, Reality, and Power." In *The Power of Prayer*, edited by W. P. Paterson. New York: Macmillan, 1920, 41–70.

———. "Some Modern Aspects of Prayer." *Living Age* 281 (1914), 160–166.

McLaren, William E. "Prayer and Law." *American Church Review* 27 (1874), 354–366.

Meeser, Spenser B. "Rekindling Religious Enthusiasm." *Christian Century* 38 (July 28, 1921), 9–12.

Meyer, Louis. "Evidences of Answered Prayer." *Missionary Review of the World* 47 (1924), 248–250.

———. "Prayer in the Present Crisis." *Missionary Review of the World* 40 (1917), 411–412.

———. "The Prayer Life of Native Christians." *Missionary Review of the World* 34 (1911), 439–442.

Montgomery, Helen Barrett. "In Answer to Prayer." *Baptist* 7 (1926).

———. "Therefore, Pray." *Baptist* 4 (1923), 46–47.

Moore, Jacob. "An Essay on the Obligation of Family Worship." *Methodist* 9 (1826), 294.

Morrison, Charles Clayton. "A Daily Altar Movement." *Christian Century* 36 (1919), 5–6.

———. "The Devotional Life of the Church." *Christian Century* 37 (January 8, 1920), 3–4.

———. "Editorial." *Christian Century* 37 (1920), 3.

———. "Fundamentalism and Modernism: Two Religions." *Christian Century* 41 (January 3, 1924), 5–6.

———. "Let Us Pray!" *Christian Century* 47 (1930), 70–72.

———. "Lord, Teach Us to Pray." *Christian Century* 39 (1922), 900.

———. "The New Reformation." *Christian Century* 40 (1923), 198–199.

Morrison, Hugh T. "Prayer at Church." *Christian Century* 48 (1931), 1175–1176.

Mudge, James. "Prayer." *Methodist Review* 75 (1893), 707–720.

Munger, Theodore T. "The Unconquerable Habit." *Outlook* 73 (1903), 401–402.

Newton, Joseph Fort. "The Quiet Moment and the Busy Life." *Christian Century* 36 (June 26, 1919), 12–14.

———. "The Strength of Quietness." *Christian Century* 36 (November 13, 1919), 10–11.

Nixon, Justin W. "The Evangelicals' Dilemma." *Atlantic Monthly* 136 (1925), 368–374.

"On Prayer." *Methodist* 2 (1819), 115.

"The Optimist Nuisance." *Christian Worker's* 16 (September, 1915), 9–10.

Ostrom, Henry. "Prayer Hour Talks." *Christian Worker's* 19 (April 1919), 568–570.

"Our Neglect of Prayer for Victory." *Literary Digest* 57 (June 8, 1918), 31–32.

Overstreet, H. A. "New Loyalties for Old Consolations." *Forum* 52 (1914), 499–512.

Packard, Hezekiah. "Two Discourses on Prayer." Wiscasset, Me.: Babson and Rust, 1804.

Park, J. Edgar. "Is There Anything in Prayer?" *Atlantic Monthly* 128 (1921), 532–535.

Parrish, Herbert. "The Break-up of Protestantism." *Atlantic Monthly* 139 (1927), 297–305.

Parsons, Edward S. "Prayer in a Universe of Law." *New Englander* 55 (1891), 362–366.

Patten, Arthur B. "The Immanent God." *Christian Century* 39 (1922), 1452–1454.

———. "Mysticism and Fundamentalism." *Christian Century* 40 (1923), 297–299.

———. "Mysticism and the Bible." *Christian Century* 40 (1923), 494–497.

Pearson, Norman. "True and False Notions of Prayer." *Nineteenth Century* 37 (1895), 813–818.

Phelps, William Lyon. "Prayer and Miracles." *Ladies Home Journal* 41 (February 1924), 9, 75–78.

Pier, Florida. "The Great Little Man." *Harper's* 126 (1913), 854–862.

Pierson, Arthur T. "Divine Efficacy of Prayer." In *The Fundamentals*. Vol. 9. Chicago: Testimony, c.1914, 66–83.

———. "A Half-Century of Prayer, with Signs Following." *Missionary Review of the World* 33 (1910), 7–14.

———. "Pray without Ceasing." *Missionary Review of the World* 30 (1907), 887–889.

———. "The Privilege and Power of Prayer." *Missionary Review of the World* 16 (1903), 1–3.

———. "The Proof of the Living God." In *The Fundamentals*. Vol. 1. Chicago: Testimony, c. 1912, 70–86.

———. "Supernatural Answers to Prayer." Indianapolis: Second Presbyterian Church, 1883.

Pope, Howard W. "Daily Bible Reading." *Christian Worker's* 16 (1915), 278.

Porter, Edward C. "Finding the Key to Prayer That Prevails." *Moody Bible Institute Monthly* 28 (June 1928), 455–457.

Pratt, James B. "An Empirical Study of Prayer." *American Journal of Religion, Psychology, and Education* 4 (1909), 48–67.

———. "The Psychological Study of Religion." *American Journal of Theology* 21 (1917), 631.

"Prayer as a World Power." *Methodist Review* 107 (1924), 617–627.

"Prayers and Pills." *Scribners Monthly* 5 (November 1872), 116–117.

"A Praying Football Hero." *Literary Digest* 85 (June 27, 1925), 32–33.

"The Praying Football Team." *Literary Digest* 67 (December 11, 1920), 39.

Riley, William B. "The Prestige of the Church." *Christian Worker's* 19 (April 1919), 539–541.

Robinson, Joseph. "On the Duty of Morning and Evening Devotion." Baltimore: Book-Society of the Protestant Episcopal Church, 1811.

Ross, G. A. Johnston. "Thanksgiving: A Reply to Professor Lake." *Atlantic* 135 (1925), 201–203.

"Science and Religion." *Popular Science Monthly* 2 (November 1872), 79–82.

"A Sermon on Secret Prayer." *Methodist* 11 (1828), 4, 6.

Sheldon, Charles M. "Prayer Meeting at Eleven A.M." *Christian Century* 47 (1930), 241–242.

Shepherd, William G. "The Church of Today and Tomorrow." *Harper's* 141 (1920), 363–374.

Sherman, Ellen Burns. "The Evolution of Prayer." *North American Review* 196 (1912), 818–829.

Smith, E. S. "Providence, Prayer, and Physical Science." *Methodist Review* 45 (1897), 61–74.

Smith, J. Ritchie. "Prayer." *Princeton Theological Review* 17 (1919), 87–97.

Speer, Robert. "The War and The Religious Outlook." *Christian Century* 36 (July 17, 1919), 30–31.

Spurr, Frederick C. "The Place of Prayer in Life." *Baptist* 5 (1924), 96, 620, 644, 668.

"The State and Prayers for Rain." *Literary Digest* 87 (October 10, 1925), 32.

Stidman, John Randolph. "Prayer." *Baptist* 3 (1922), 1305.

Straton, John Roach. "How Rationalism in the Pulpit Makes Worldliness in the Pew." *Moody Bible Institute Monthly* (January 1923), 193–197.

Strickland, Francis L. "Prayer and Psychology." *Christian Century* 47 (1930), 523–525.

Stroh, Grant. "A Christian Defense of Prayer." *Moody Bible Institute Monthly* 31 (April 1931), 395–397.

Strong, Anna Louise. "The Relation of the Subconscious to Prayer." *American Journal of Religious Psychology and Education* 2 (1907), 160–167.

"The Supernatural Element in Prayer." *Missionary Review of the World* 30 (1907), 617–618.

"The Supreme Value of Christianity." *Christian Worker's* 17 (September 1916), 11–12.

Sykes, McCready. "Shall We Send Our Children to Church?" *Atlantic Monthly* 140 (1927), 730–736.

Thompson, John Beauchamp. "Southern Prayers." *Christian Century* 47 (1930), 1060–1062.

Tittle, Ernest F. "The Devotional Life." *Baptist* 6 (1925), 1056.

Tompkins, Juliet. "Missionary Blood." *Harper's* 132 (1916), 929–937.

Torrey, Reuben A. "The Duty and Worth of Prayer." *Christian Worker's* 18 (September 1917), 21–23.

———. "The Holy Spirit Sending Men Forth to Definite Lines of Work." *Christian Worker's* 11 (1910), 89–94.

———. "The Place of Prayer in Evangelism." In *The Fundamentals*. Vol. 12. Chicago: Testimony c. 1915, 97–107.

———. "What the Moody Bible Institute Has Stood for during the Twenty-Five Years of Its History and What It Still Stands for Today." *Christian Worker's* 16 (February 1916), 438–449.

Trotter, Melvin. "The Mission of the Soul-Winner." *Christian Worker's* 18 (September 1917), 19–20.

Trout, David M. "The Validity of Prayer in Modern Religious Experience." *Religious Education* 20 (1925), 31–36.

Trumbull, Benjamin. "An Address on the Subjects of Prayer and Family Religion." Northampton, Mass.: William Butler, 1805.

Tuttle, A.H. "The Art of Prevailing Prayer." *Methodist Review* 94 (1912), 370–375.

Tyndall, John. "Providence in Physical Affairs." *Popular Science Monthly* (November 1872), 79–82.

Van Lissel, Carrie E. "Homer Hamontree Became a Gospel Soloist by Prayer." *Moody Bible Institute Monthly* 27 (December 1926), 172.

"A Village Prays." *Moody Bible Institute Monthly* 23 (March 1923), 282.

Warfield, Benjamin B. "Prayer as a Means of Grace" and "Prayer as a Practice." In *Faith and Life*. Carlisle Penn.: Banner of Truth Trust, 1974 [1916], 146–153, 428–439.

Wayland, H. L. "Prayer as an Offensive Weapon." *Outlook* 53 (1896), 662.

Wells, J. E. "Law, Providence, and Prayer." *Bibliotheca Sacra* 30 (1873), 593–627.

Whiton, James M. "Fallacies Concerning Prayer." *Forum* 23 (1897), 351–362.

"Will Prayer Bring Rain?" *Literary Digest* 106 (September 27, 1930), 18–19.

Willcox, Louise Collier. "Shall We Pray?" *Harper's* 150 (January 1925), 158–161.

Secondary Works

Books

Ahlstrom, Sidney E. *A Religious History of the American People.* New Haven: Yale University Press, 1972.

———, ed. *Theology in America: The Major Protestant Voices from Puritanism to New-Orthodoxy.* New York: Bobbs-Merrill, 1967.

Allen, Frederick Lewis. *Only Yesterday: An Informal History of the Nineteen-Twenties.* New York: Harper and Row, 1957.

Atkins, Gauis Glenn. *Religion in Our Times.* New York: Round Table Press, 1932.

Austin, Alvin. *Saving China: Canadian Missionaries in the Middle Kingdom, 1888–1959.* Toronto: University of Toronto Press, 1986.

Averill, Lloyd J. *American Theology in the Liberal Tradition.* Philadelphia: Westminster Press, 1967.

Barth, Karl. *Protestant Thought: From Rousseau to Ritschl.* New York: Harper and Row, 1959.

Beale, David. *In Pursuit of Purity: American Fundamentalism Since 1850.* Greenville, S.C.: Unusual Publications, 1986.

Bebbington, David W. *Evangelicalism in Modern Britain.* London: Unwin Hyman, 1989.

Bledstein, Burton J. *The Culture of Professionalism.* New York: Norton, 1976.

Blumhofer, Edith W. *Restoring the Faith: The Assemblies of God, Pentecostalism, and American Culture.* Urbana: University of Illinois Press, 1993.

Bozeman, T. Dwight. *Protestants in an Age of Science: The Baconian Ideal and Antebellum Religious Thought.* Chapel Hill: University of North Carolina, 1977.

Brereton, Virginia Lieson. *From Sin to Salvation.* Bloomington: Indiana University Press, 1991.

———. *Training God's Army: The American Bible School, 1880–1940.* Bloomington: Indiana University Press, 1990.

Brown, Ira V. *Lyman Abbott: Christian Evolutionist.* Cambridge, Mass.: Harvard University Press, 1953.

Butler, Jon. *Awash in a Sea of Faith: Christianizing the American People.* Cambridge, Mass.: Harvard University Press, 1990.

Caplow, Theodore. *All Faithful People: Change and Continuity and Middletown's Religion.* Minneapolis: University of Minnesota Press, 1983.

Carpenter, Joel A., and Wilbert R. Shenk. *Earthen Vessels: American Evangelicals and Foreign Missions, 1880–1980.* Grand Rapids, Mich.: Eerdmans, 1990.

Carpenter, Joel A. ed. *Missionary Innovation and Expansion.* New York: Garland, 1988.

————. *Sacrificial Lives: Young Martyrs and Fundamentalist Idealism*. New York: Garland, 1988.

Carter, Paul A. *Another Part of the Twenties*. New York: Columbia University Press, 1977.

————. *The Decline and Revival of the Social Gospel*. Ithaca, N.Y.: Cornell University Press, 1956.

————. *The Spiritual Crisis of the Gilded Age*. DeKalb: Northern Illinois University Press, 1971.

Cashdollar, Charles D. *The Transformation of Theology, 1830–1890: Positivism and Protestant Thought in Britain and America*. Princeton: Princeton University Press, 1989.

Cauthen, Kenneth. *The Impact of American Religious Liberalism*. New York: Harper and Row, 1962.

Cerullo, John J. *The Secularization of the Soul. Psychical Research in Modern Britain*. Philadelphia: Institute for the Study of Human Issues, 1982.

Cole, Stewart. *The History of Fundamentalism*. Hamden, Conn.: Archon Books, 1963 [1931].

Coleman, Richard J. *Issues of Theological Warfare: Evangelicals and Liberals*. Grand Rapids, Mich.: Eerdmans, 1972.

Chadwick, Owen. *The Victorian Church*. London: Adam and Charles Black, 1970.

Commager, Henry S. *The American Mind*. New Haven: Yale University Press, 1950.

Curti, Merle. *The Growth of American Thought*. New York: Harper and Row, 1964.

Curtis, Susan. *A Consuming Faith: The Social Gospel and Modern American Culture*. Baltimore: Johns Hopkins University Press, 1991.

Daniels, W. H., ed. *Moody: His Words, Work, and Workers*. New York: Nelson and Phillips, 1877.

Dayton, Donald W. *Theological Roots of Pentecostalism*. Grand Rapids, Mich.: Francis Asbury Press, 1987.

Douglas, J. D., and Philip W. Comfort, eds. *Who's Who in Christian History*. Wheaton, Ill.: Tyndale House, 1992.

Douglas, Mary, and Steven Tipton, eds. *Religion in America: Spiritual Life in a Secular Age*. Boston: Beacon Press, 1982.

Dupre, Louis and Donald E. Saliers, eds. *Christian Spirituality: Post-Reformation and Modern*. New York: Crossroad, 1989.

Edward, Paul. *The Encyclopedia of Philosophy*. New York: MacMillan, 1967.

Eve, A. S., and C. H. Creasy. *Life and Work of John Tyndall*. London: Macmillan 1945.

Ferre, John P. *A Social Gospel for Millions: The Religious Bestsellers of Charles Sheldon, Charles Gordon, and Harold Bell Wright*. Bowling Green, Ohio: Bowling Green State University Press, 1988.

Flood, Robert, and Jerry Jenkins. *Teaching the Word, Reaching the World: Moody Bible Institute, The First Hundred Years*. Chicago: Moody Press, 1985.

Fox, Richard W., and T. J. Jackson Lears, eds. *The Power of Culture: Critical Essays in American History*. Chicago: University of Chicago Press, 1993.

Frank, Douglas. *Less Than Conquerors: How Evangelicals Entered the Twentieth Century*. Grand Rapids, Mich.: Eerdmans, 1986.

Furay, Conal. *The Grass-Roots Mind in America: The American Sense of Absolutes.* New York: Franklin Watts, 1977.

Furniss, Norman F. *The Fundamentalist Controversy, 1918–1931.* New Haven: Yale University Press, 1954.

Garvie, Alfred E. *The Ritschlian Theology.* Edinburgh: T. and T. Clark, 1902.

Gatewood, Robert. *Controversy in the Twenties: Fundamentalists, Modernists, and Evangelicals.* Nashville, Tenn.: Vanderbilt University Press, 1969.

Getz, Gene A. *MBI: The Story of Moody Bible Institute.* Chicago: Moody Press, 1986.

Gillispie, Charles C., ed. *Dictionary of Scientific Biography.* New York: Scribner's, 1973.

———. *Genesis and Geology.* Cambridge, Mass.: Harvard University Press, 1951.

Goforth, Rosalind. *Goforth of China.* Grand Rapids, Mich.: Zondervan, 1937.

Gordon, James M. *Evangelical Spirituality from the Wesleys to John Stott.* London: S.P.C.K., 1991.

Gottschalk, Stephen. *The Emergence of Christian Science in American Religious Life.* Berkeley: University of California Press, 1973.

Hackett, Alice Payne. *Fifty Years of Best Sellers, 1895–1945.* New York: Bowker, 1945.

Hambrick-Stowe, Charles E. *Charles Finney and the Spirit of American Evangelicalism.* Grand Rapids, Mich.: Eerdmans, 1996.

———. *The Practice of Piety: Puritan Devotional Disciplines in Seventeenth-Century New England.* Chapel Hill: University of North Carolina Press, 1982.

Harvey, Edwin and Lillian. *How They Prayed.* Vol. 3. *Missionaries and Revival.* Hampton, Tenn.: Harvey and Tait, 1987.

Hassey, Janette. *No Time For Silence: Evangelical Women in Public Ministry around the Turn of the Century.* Grand Rapids, Mich: Academia Books, 1986.

Heiler, Friedrich. *Prayer: A Study in the History and Psychology of Religion.* London: Oxford University Press, 1932.

Hill, Patricia. *The World Their Household: The American Women's Foreign Missions Movement and Cultural Transformation, 1870–1920.* Ann Arbor: University of Michigan Press, 1985.

Hoffecker, W. Andrew. *Piety and the Princeton Theologians.* Phillipsburg, N.J.: Presbyterian and Reformed Publishing, 1981.

Hofstadter, Richard. *Anti-Intellectualism in American Life.* New York: Knopf, 1963.

Holifield, E. Brooks. *Health and Medicine in the Methodist Tradition.* New York: Crossroad, 1986.

———. *A History of Pastoral Care in America.* Nashville, Tenn.: Abingdon Press, 1983.

Holmes, Urban T. *A History of Christian Spirituality.* New York: Seabury Press, 1980.

Hopkins, C. Howard. *John R. Mott.* Grand Rapids, Mich.: Eerdmans, 1979.

Hordern, William. *A Layman's Guide to Protestant Theology.* New York: Macmillan, 1968.

Horton, Walter. *Christian Theology: An Ecumenical Approach.* London: Lutterworth Press, 1956.

Hudson, Winthrop. *The Great Tradition of the American Churches.* New York: Harper and Row, 1963.

Hutchison, William R., ed. *American Protestant Thought: The Liberal Era*. New York: Harper and Row, 1968.

———. *Between the Times: The Travail of the Protestant Establishment in America, 1900–1960*. New York: Cambridge University Press, 1989.

———. *The Modernist Impulse in American Protestantism*. Cambridge, Mass.: Harvard University Press, 1976.

Jay, Eric George, trans. *Origen's Treatise on Prayer*. London: S.P.C.K., 1954.

Jolly, W. P. *Sir Oliver Lodge*. London: Constable, 1974.

Jones, Cheslyn, Geoffrey Wainwright, and Edward Yarnold, eds. *The Study of Spirituality*. New York: Oxford University Press, 1986.

Jungmann, Joseph A. *Christian Prayer Through the Centuries*. Translated by John Coyne. New York: Paulist Press, 1978.

Kelley, Dean. *Why Conservative Churches Are Growing*. San Francisco: Harper and Row, 1972.

Kelly, Faye L. *Prayer in Sixteenth Century England*. Gainesville: University of Florida Press, 1966.

Kunitz, Stanley, ed. *Twentieth Century Authors*. New York: Wilson, 1955.

Lears, T. J. Jackson. *No Place of Grace: Antimodernism and the Transformation of American Culture, 1880–1920*. New York: Pantheon Books, 1981.

LeFevre, Perry. *Understandings of Prayer*. Philadelphia: Westminster Press, 1981.

Leuchtenberg, William. *The Perils of Prosperity, 1914–1932*. Chicago: University of Chicago Press, 1958.

Lippmann, Walter. *American Inquisitors: A Commentary on Dayton and Chicago*. New York: MacMillan, 1928.

———. *A Preface to Morals*. New York: Macmillan, 1929.

Loetscher, Lefferts E. *The Broadening Church: A Study of Theological Issues in the Presbyterian Church since 1869*. Philadelphia: Westminster Press, 1954.

Long, Kathryn T. *The Revival of 1857–58*. New York: Oxford University Press, 1997.

Longfield, Bradley. *The Presbyterian Controversy*. New York: Oxford University Press, 1991.

Lovelace, Richard F. *The American Pietism of Cotton Mather: Origins of American Evangelicalism*. Grand Rapids, Mich.: Christian University Press, 1979.

———. *Dynamics of Spiritual Life*. Downers Grove, Ill.: Intervarsity Press, 1979.

Lynd, Robert S., and Helen Merrell. *Middletown: A Study in Contemporary American Culture*. New York: Harcourt, Brace, 1929.

Marsden, George. *Fundamentalism and American Culture*. New York: Oxford University Press, 1980.

———. *Religion and American Culture*. San Diego, Calif.: Harcourt Brace Jovanovich, 1990.

———. *The Soul of the American University*. New York: Oxford University Press, 1994.

Marty, Martin. *Modern American Religion*. Vol. 1. *The Irony of It All*. Chicago: University of Chicago Press, 1986.

———. *Modern American Religion*. Vol. 2. *The Noise of Conflict, 1919–1941*. Chicago: University of Chicago Press, 1986.

————, ed. *Modern American Protestantism and Its World*. Vol. 14. *Varieties of Religious Expression*. New York: Saur, 1993.

Massa, Mark. *Charles Augustus Briggs and the Crisis of Historical Criticism*. Minneapolis: Fortress Press, 1924.

May, Henry F. *The End of American Innocence, 1912–1917*. Chicago: Quadrangle, 1964.

May, Henry F. *The Enlightenment in America*. New York: Oxford University Press, 1976.

McLoughlin, William G. *Modern Revivalism: Charles Grandison Finney to Billy Graham*. New York: Ronald Press, 1959.

Meyer, Donald. *The Positive Thinkers: Religion as Pop Psychology from Mary Baker Eddy to Oral Roberts*. New York: Pantheon Books, 1980.

————. *The Protestant Search for Political Realism, 1919–1941*. Berkeley: University of California Press, 1960.

Michaelson, Robert S., and Wade Clark Roof, eds. *Liberal Protestantism: Realities and Possibilities*. New York: Pilgrim Press, 1986.

Miller, Basil. *George Mueller: Man of Faith and Miracles*. Minneapolis: Bethany House, 1941.

Miller, Robert M. *Harry Emerson Fosdick: Preacher, Pastor, Prophet*. New York: Oxford University Press, 1985.

Miller, William Robert, ed. *Contemporary American Protestant Thought, 1900–1970*. New York: Bobbs-Merrill, 1973.

Morgan, H. Wayne. *William McKinley and His America*. Syracuse, N.Y.: Syracuse University Press, 1963.

Moore, James R. *The Post-Darwinian Controversies*. Cambridge, England: Cambridge University Press, 1979.

Moore, R. Laurence. *In Search of White Crows: Spiritualism, Parapsychology, and American Culture*. New York: Oxford University Press, 1977.

Mullin, Robert Bruce. *Miracles and the Modern Religious Imagination*. New Haven: Yale University Press, 1996.

Nash, Roderick. *The Nervous Generation: American Thought, 1917–1930*. Chicago: Rand McNally, 1971.

Niebuhr, H. Richard, Wilhelm Pauck, and Francis Miller. *The Church against the World*. Chicago: Willett, Clark, 1935.

Noll, Mark A., ed. *Amazing Grace: Evangelicalism in Australia, Britain, Canada, and the United States*. Grand Rapids, Mich.: Baker Books, 1993.

————. *A History of Christianity in the United States and Canada*. Grand Rapids, Mich.: Eerdmans, 1992.

Numbers, Ronald. *The Creationists*. New York: Knopf, 1992.

Orr, J. Edwin. *The Fervent Prayer: The Worldwide Impact of the Great Awakening of 1858*. Chicago: Moody Press, 1974.

————. *The Flaming Tongue: Evangelical Awakenings, 1900 to the Present*. Chicago: Moody Press, 1975.

Peskin, Allan. *Garfield*. Youngstown, Ohio: Kent State University Press, 1978.

Peterson, Theodore. *Magazines in the Twentieth Century*. Urbana: University of Illinois Press, 1956.

Pollock, J. C. *The Keswick Story*. London: Hodder and Stoughton, 1964.

Rack, Henry D. *Reasonable Enthusiast: John Wesley and the Rise of Methodism.* London: Epworth Press, 1989.

————. *Twentieth Century Spirituality*. London: Epworth Press, 1969.

Raser, Harold E. *Phoebe Palmer: Her Life and Thought*. Lewiston, P.: Edwin Mellen Press, 1987.

Reid, Daniel G., ed. *Dictionary of Christianity in America*. Downers Grove, Ill.: Intervarsity Press, 1990.

Roberts, Jon. *Darwinism and the Divine in America*. Madison: University of Wisconsin Press, 1988.

Rudolph, L. C. *Francis Asbury*. Nashville, Tenn.: Abingdon Press, 1966.

Russell, C. Allyn. *Voices of American Fundamentalism: Seven Biographical Studies.* Philadelphia: Westminster Press, 1976.

Sandeen, Ernest R. *The Roots of Fundamentalism*. Chicago: University of Chicago Press, 1970.

Saum, Lewis O. *The Popular Mood of America, 1860–1890*. Lincoln: University of Nebraska Press, 1990.

Schneider, Louis and Sanford Dornbusch. *Popular Religion: Inspirational Books in America*. Chicago: University of Chicago Press, 1958.

Simpson, Robert L. *The Interpretation of Prayer in the Early Church*. Philadelphia: Westminster Press, 1965.

Smith, H. Shelton, Robert T. Handy, and Lefferts A. Loetscher. *American Christianity: An Historical Interpretation*. Vol. 2. New York: Scribner's, 1963.

Smith, Timothy L. *Revivalism and Social Reform in Mid-Nineteenth Century America.* New York: Abingdon Press, 1957.

Stark, Rodney, and Charles Glock. *American Piety: The Nature of Religious Commitment*. Berkeley: University of California Press, 1968.

Symington, Thomas A. *Religious Liberals and Conservatives: A Comparison*. New York: Teacher's College, Columbia University, 1935.

Synan, Vinson. *The Holiness-Pentecostal Movement in the United States*. Grand Rapids, Mich.: Eerdmans, 1971.

Szasz, Ferenc Morton. *The Divided Mind of Protestant America, 1880–1930*. University, Ala.: University of Alabama Press, 1982.

Thayer, William M. *From Log Cabin to White House: The Life of James A. Garfield.* New York: Hurst, 1881.

Trollinger, William V. *God's Empire: William Bell Riley and Midwestern Fundamentalism*. Madison: University of Wisconsin Press, 1990.

Turner, James. *Without God, without Creed: The Origins of Unbelief in America*. Baltimore: Johns Hopkins University Press, 1985.

Wacker, Grant. *Augustus H. Strong and the Dilemma of Historical Consciousness.* Macon, Ga.: Mercer University Press, 1985.

Weber, Timothy P. *Living in the Shadow of the Second Coming: American Premillennialism, 1875–1925*. New York: Oxford University Press, 1979.

White, Charles Edward. *The Beauty of Holiness: Phoebe Palmer as Theologian, Revivalist, Feminist, and Humanitarian*. Grand Rapids, Mich.: Francis Asbury Press, 1986.

Wiebe, Robert. *The Search for Order: 1877–1920.* New York: Hill and Wang, 1967.

Wilder, Robert. *The Student Volunteer Movement.* New York: Student Volunteer Movement, 193.

Williams, Daniel Day. *The Andover Liberals: A Study in American Theology.* New York: Octagon Books, 1970.

Williams, Henry Smith. *The Story of Nineteenth Century Science.* New York: Harper, 1900.

Wills, Garry. *Under God: Religion and American Politics.* New York: Simon and Schuster, 1990.

Witten, Marsha G. *All Is Forgiven: The Secular Message in American Protestantism.* Princeton: Princeton University Press, 1993.

Articles, Dissertations, Chapters

Bonney, Katharine A. "Harry Emerson Fosdick's Doctrine of Man." Ph.D. diss., Boston University, 1958.

Burchfield, Joe D. "John Tyndall—A Biographical Sketch." In *John Tyndall, Essays on a Natural Philosopher,* edited by W. H. Brock. Dublin: Royal Dublin Society, 1981.

Carey, Ralph Allison. "Bestselling Religion: A History of Popular Religious Thought in America as Reflected in Religious Best Sellers, 1850–1960." Ph.D. diss., Michigan State University, 1971.

Carpenter, Joel A. "Fundamentalist Institutions and the Rise of Evangelical Protestantism, 1929–1942." *Church History* 49 (March 1980), 62–75.

———. Introduction to *Missionary Innovation and Expansion.* New York: Garland, 1988.

———. "The Renewal of American Fundamentalism, 1930–1945." Ph.D. diss., Johns Hopkins University, 1984.

Carter, Paul. "The Fundamentalist Defense of the Faith." In *Change and Continuity in Twentieth Century America: The Twenties,* edited by John Braeman. Columbus: Ohio State University Press, 1968.

Cunningham, Raymond J. "The Emmanuel Movement: A Variety of American Religious Experience." In *Modern American Protestantism and Its World.* Vol. 14. *Varieties of Religious Expression,* edited by Martin Marty. New York: Saur, 1993, 36–51.

———. "From Holiness to Healing: The Faith Cure in America, 1872–1892." In *Modern American Protestantism and Its World,* edited by Martin Marty. *Vol. 14. Varieties of Religious Expression.* New York: Saur, 1993, 3–17.

Encyclopedia Americana. "Parapsychology," "Spiritualism," and "Telepathy." Danbury, Conn.: Grolier, 1991.

Fea, John. "Power from on High in an Age of Ecclesiastical Impotence: The 'Enduement of the Holy Spirit' in American Fundamentalist Thought, 1880–1936." *Fides et Historia* 26 (Summer 1994), 23–35.

Fox, Richard W. "The Culture of Liberal Protestant Progressivism, 1875–1925." *Journal of Interdisciplinary History* (Winter 1993), 639–660.

————. "From Events and Institutions to Cultures and Experiences: Paradigm Shift in Twentieth Century American Religious History." Given at Wheaton College, Wheaton, Illinois, 1993.

Gillespie, Neal C. "The Duke of Argyll, Evolutionary Theology, and the Art of Scientific Controversy." *Isis* 68 (1977), 40–54.

Hamilton, Michael S. "The Fundamentalist Harvard: Wheaton College and the Continuing Vitality of American Evangelicalism, 1919–1945." Ph.D. diss., University of Notre Dame, 1995.

Handy, Robert T. "The American Religious Depression, 1925–1935." *Church History* 29 (March 1960), 1–29.

————. "Fundamentalism and Modernism in Perspective." *Religion in Life* 24 (1955): 381–394.

Harper, J. Steven. "The Devotional Life of John Wesley, 1703–1738." Ph.d. diss., Duke University, 1981.

Hart, James D. "Platitudes of Piety: Religion and the Modern Popular Novel." *American Quarterly* 6 (Spring 1954), 311–323.

Hatch, Nathan O. "*Sola Scriptura* and *Novus Ordo Seclorum*." In *The Bible in America*, edited by Hatch and Mark A. Noll. New York: Oxford University Press, 1982, 59–78.

Hutchison, William R. "Cultural Strain and Protestant Liberalism." *American Historical Review* 76 (1971), 386–411.

Lyrene, Edward Charles, Jr. "The Role of Prayer in American Revival Movements, 1740–1860." Ph.D. diss., Southern Baptist Theological Seminary, 1985.

Meyer, Donald. "Secular Transcendence: The American Religious Humanists." In *Modern American Protestantism and Its World*, edited by Martin Marty. Vol. 14. *Varieties of Religious Expression*. New York: Saur, 1993, 223–241.

Mullin, Robert Bruce. "The Debate over Religion and Healing in the Episcopal Church, 1870–1930." *Anglican and Episcopal History* 60 (1991), 213–234.

————. "Horace Bushnell and the Question of Miracles." *Church History* 58 (1989), 460–473.

Murray, Michael J., and Kurt Meyers. "Ask and It will be Given to you." *Religious Studies* 30 (1994), 311–330.

Nichols, Robert Hastings. "Samuel Irenaeus Prime." In *Dictionary of American Biography*, edited by Dumas Malone. New York: Charles Scribner's Sons, 1935. Vol. 15, 228.

Ostrander, Rick. "The Battery and the Windmill: Two Models of Protestant Devotionalism in Early Twentieth Century America." *Church History* 65 (March 1996), 42–61.

————. "Proving the Living God: Answered Prayer as a Modern Fundamentalist Apologetic." *Fides et Historia* 28 (Fall 1996), 69–89.

Pereira, Joseph. "The Healing Power of Prayer is Tested by Science." *Wall Street Journal* (December 20, 1995).

Shelley, Bruce. "Sources of Pietistic Fundamentalism." *Fides et Historia* 5 (1973), 68–78.

Svelmoe, William. " 'Evil Spirits Have Come In': Fundamentalists Respond to the Pentecostals, 1900–1928." Unpublished manuscript, 1992.

Thomas, Gary. "Doctors Who Pray." *Christianity Today* (January 6, 1997), 20–30.

Turner, Frank M. "John Tyndall and Victorian Scientific Naturalism." In *John Tyndall, Essays on a Natural Philosopher*, edited by W. H. Brock. Dublin: Royal Dublin Society, 1981.

————. "Rainfall, Plagues, and the Prince of Wales: A Chapter in the Conflict of Religion and Science." *Journal of British Studies* 13 (1974), 51.

Wacker, Grant. "The Holy Spirit and the Spirit of the Age in American Protestantism, 1880–1910." *Journal of American History* 72 (June 1985), 45–62.

Wigger, John H. "Taking Heaven by Storm: Methodism and the Popularization of American Christianity, 1770–1820." Ph.D. diss., University of Notre Dame, 1994.

Wills, Garry. "The Superman Trial." In *Under God: Religion and American Politics*. New York: Simon and Schuster, 1990.

Index